CRIMINAL LONDON

CRIMINAL LONDON

A Sightseer's Guide to the Capital of Crime

Kris and Nina Hollington

First published in Great Britain
2013 by Aurum Press Ltd
1st and 2nd Floor
74-75 White Lion Street
London N1 9PF
www.aurumpress.co.uk

Alamy: 29, 135, 151, 155, 169, 181, 206, 208 (both), 214 (top), 233, 241, 317, 329
Getty Images: 46, 74, 78, 86, 88 (bottom), 89 (bottom), 91 (bottom), 167 (both),
168, 170 (both), 182, 202 (bottom), 221, 223, 326, 330
Heritage Images: 274
Mary Evans: 37
Mirrorpix: 249
Press Association Images: 41
Rex Features: 100, 148, 266

Maps: © OpenStreetMap © Crown copyright and database right 2010-12
www.openstreetmap.org

Every effort has been made to trace the copyright holders of material quoted in
this book. If application is made in writing to the publisher, any omissions will
be included in future editions.

A catalogue record for this book is available from the British Library.

ISBN 978 1 84513 778 6

10 9 8 7 6 5 4 3 2 1
2017 2016 2015 2014 2013

Design by Transmission
Typeset in FS Clerkenwell
Printed in China

CONTENTS

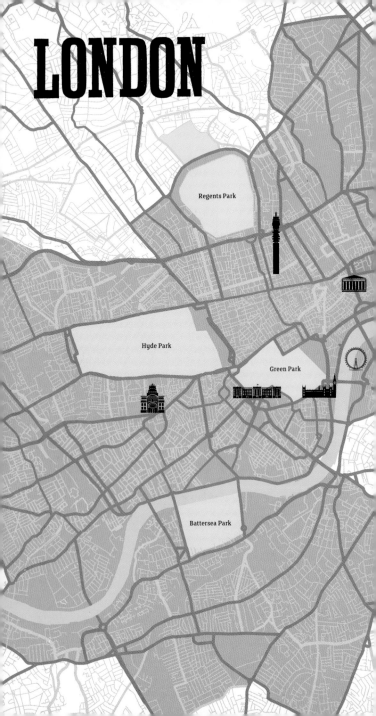

LONDON

Regents Park

Hyde Park

Green Park

Battersea Park

Monument Index

V&A Museum
Buckingham Palace
Houses of Parliament
London Eye
Tate Modern
Tower Bridge
Tower of London
St Paul's Cathedral
British Museum
BT Tower

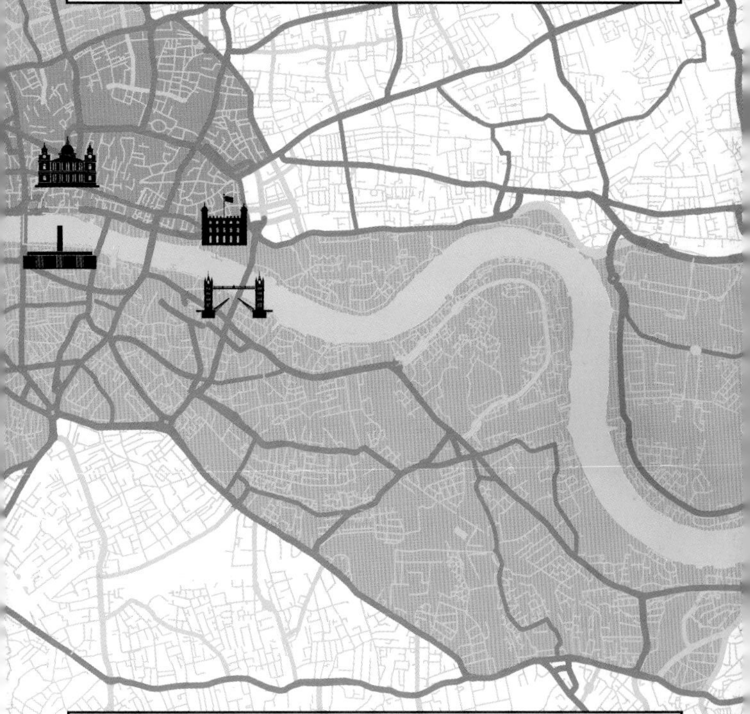

London Index

INTROD

All criminal life is here.

Stay in London long enough and you'll end up stumbling across it or, if you're unlucky, crime will find you – like the wife of Patrick Mahon in 1924, whose doubts about her husband's fidelity led her to a left-luggage office. Unfortunately, as well as discovering that her husband had a mistress, Mrs Mahon also found out that he'd murdered and dismembered her.

Of course, some people decide to become criminals out of choice, like 'Brilliant' Chang, responsible for the creation of the phrase 'den of vice', thanks to his post-World War I Soho and Limehouse drug hangouts. Then there's the Knight, Kray and Richardson brothers of the 1950s and 60s, where crime runs in the family – often a lethal combination.

Many spend their lives fighting crime or become agents of justice – like Albert Pierrepoint and John Ellis, two of London's last executioners, who hanged dozens of young men and women between them, from serial killers to seductresses – and in at least one instance an innocent man. Pierrepoint and Ellis were never as busy as the 17th-century executioners working in the time of 'Hanging' Judge Jeffreys however, who sentenced 300 men to death in just one session.

Others became crime-fighting pioneers, such as the author Henry Fielding, founder of the Bow Street Runners in 1749, 20th-century pathologist Sir Bernard Spilsbury, creator of the 'murder bag', and Constables Arthur Cross and Fred Tibbs, who developed the art of forensic photography during and after World War II.

Criminals can be pioneers too, of course, such as mobster Billy 'boss of the underworld' Hill, founder in 1952 of the 'project' – the carefully planned heist – and the men who laundered the millions generated by the stolen bullion from Brink's-Mat throughout the 1980s.

Occasionally, a remarkable character even makes the switch from criminal to agent of justice, such as Daniel Harvey, the first Commissioner of the City

Police (appointed in 1839) who, just a few years earlier, did time in King's Bench prison for libelling George IV.

Crime has played a huge role in London's development and it is quite remarkable to see how, when you start looking, just how many reminders and artefacts remain, from the 700-year-old seat of justice at the Guildhall to the aforementioned City Commissioner's first residence and former police station. Then there's the noose that still hangs at the back of a Wapping pub, the world's smallest police station in Trafalgar Square, the last remaining section of Newgate's prison wall hidden behind the Old Bailey, the execution bell stored in a City church and the ancient prison cells hidden in not one but two separate pub basements. The list, as this book proves, is long.

So within these pages lies *Criminal London*, an underexplored history of this great and ancient city. The guiding principle for *Criminal London* was that it should be a sightseer's guide, so our detective's magnifier has been placed over central London. Locations were chosen for their accessibility, importance and proximity to one another, so that this book may be used as a walking guide. At the same time, several other relevant London crime sites (or sights) are often mentioned within the text that accompanies each pictured location.

Those who explore London using this book will come across many surprising but logical connections and coincidences (a personal favourite is the hangman who witnessed a murder while in his local pub and then ended up executing the perpetrator a few months later), and while familiar names are included (the Kray twins and the Richardson brothers, for example, are essential), many lesser-known stories also feature, along with a good dose of more modern crime.

I've attempted to be as rigorous as Sherlock Holmes when it comes to accuracy but the odd error might have slipped in. If you see anything that needs to be amended in future editions, then do please email me at kris@criminallondon. co.uk. And finally, do take care. London's underworld, a world most of us rarely get to see, is as active as ever.

SOUTH

1. South of the River

◎ Globe Theatre

⚲ Bankside, SE1

☎ 020 7928 9444

🅦 www.shakespearesglobe.com

🕐 9am-5pm

£ A number of tours and price options are available. Adult prices for the exhibition and tour start from £12.50. See website for details.

⊖ London Bridge Tube *(Mainline, Northern and Jubilee Lines)*

In the words of London writer Benedict le Vay: 'Southwark was where all the things the city could not tolerate but could not live without were sent.' The northern city dumped its dirt and rubbish on the south bank of the Thames. It became a home to the 'stink' industries, which had been forced out of the main city. The tanneries were in Bermondsey; Lambeth housed vinegar makers, dye manufacturers and makers of soap and tallow. Gravediggers worked in Lambeth, excavating bodies for 'candles of the fat, bonemeal and dog's meat'.

It was also home to whores, highwaymen and wild bears, bulls, cocks and mastiffs that fought in front of screaming crowds in Bear Gardens behind the current location of the Globe Theatre. The first recorded instance of bear baiting was in 1546 at Bankside and also took place at Tothill Fields, Hockley-in-the-Hole (see page 141), Saffron Hill (see page 137) and Islington until it was finally outlawed in 1835.

The diarist John Evelyn (1620–1706) wrote: 'I went with some friends to the bear-garden … there was cock-fighting, dog-fighting, bear and bull-baiting … One of the bulls tossed a dog into a lady's lap, as she sat in one of the boxes at a considerable height from the arena. Two poor dogs were killed, and so all ended with an ape on horseback, and I most weary of the rude and dirty pastime.'

Also south of the river were some of the liveliest and most dangerous pubs in the world, where many drunken arguments took place each night, leaving the sawdust soggy with blood.

If they were in the mood, passers-by could lob rotten food or a dead cat at the unfortunates held in the pillories near the Clink, or if you were feeling more cultured, you could head to the Globe Theatre and perhaps catch the hot new production of the prolific playwright William Shakespeare.

By the 17th century there were seven prisons south of the river. Despite these fearful places, where 20 people could be left suffocating overnight in a six-foot-square pit, South Londoners remained the most criminally active and provided the city's authorities with more riot and disorder than they could handle.

2. God's Banker Meets His Maker

◉ Blackfriars Bridge

⊖ Southwark Tube *(Jubilee Line)* or Blackfriars Tube *(District & Circle Line)*

On 15 June 1982, the 62-year-old head of Banco Ambrosiano, Roberto Calvi, nicknamed 'God's banker' because of his close ties to the Vatican, was found hanging from Blackfriars Bridge with a length of orange rope woven into a lover's knot around his neck. He was weighed down by bricks and found with about £15,000 in cash in different currencies in his pockets. He had been missing for nine days. In the wake of his death, the Ambrosiano bank collapsed.

Calvi became chairman of Banco Ambrosiano, then Italy's largest private bank, in 1975 and built up a vast financial empire, but in 1978 a report by the Bank of Italy on Ambrosiano concluded that several billion lire – some of which was Mafia drugs money – had been illegally exported.

In May 1981, Calvi was arrested, found guilty, and sentenced to four years' imprisonment, but released pending an appeal. During his short spell in jail he attempted suicide. Shortly after his release from prison, Calvi fled Italy on a private jet to London. The day before he was found dead, his secretary committed suicide in Milan by jumping off the fourth floor of the bank's headquarters.

The Vatican was linked to Calvi via Archbishop Paul Marcinkus, the Pope's bodyguard. Marcinkus was a governor of the Vatican and head of the Vatican Bank, which owned a share of Ambrosiano. He was also a director of Ambrosiano Overseas.

Calvi also had intimate knowledge of regular payments made by large Italian companies to political parties and it was widely suspected that to save himself from a prison sentence he had threatened to reveal all about the bank's shadier dealings, incriminating a great many investors.

On 23 July 1982 an inquest jury returned a verdict of suicide. This was overturned in 1983 when a second inquest delivered an open verdict. In October 2002 forensic experts appointed by Italian judges concluded that the banker had been murdered.

They said his neck showed no evidence of the injuries usually associated with death by hanging and his hands had never touched the stones found in the pockets of his clothes.

American Archbishop Paul Marcinkus was sought for questioning but was granted immunity as a Vatican employee. He retired in 1990 and died in 2006.

In October 2005 five people went on trial for Calvi's murder in Rome, including his former bodyguard and a convicted Cosa Nostra treasurer. They were all acquitted in June 2007.

3. Smugglers' Den

◎ Anchor Inn

⌂ Park Street, Southwark, SE1

☏ 020 7407 1577

🕐 Mon-Wed 11am-11pm, Thurs-Sat 11am-12am, Sun 12-11pm

⊖ London Bridge Tube *(Mainline, Northern and Jubilee Lines)*

The current building, the Anchor, dates back to the 18th century and comes complete with minstrel's gallery, old oak beams and cubby holes where escapees from the Clink could hide or where smugglers might stash their contraband, desperate to avoid the duties due at Custom House (see page 97).

This may be the very pub from where the diarist Samuel Pepys (1633–1703) watched the Great Fire of London in 1666. He wrote that he took refuge in 'a little alehouse on Bankside ... and there watched the fire grow'.

The Anchor is the sole survivor of the riverside inns that existed here in Shakespeare's time, and may have been visited by the playwright himself, whose Globe Theatre was just three or four minutes' walk away. Indeed, the Anchor was often full of actors, although by the 18th century it was a hangout for river-pirates and smugglers. When a huge oak beam was removed during early 19th-century renovations, the workmen found a collection of intricately designed hiding places for contraband.

Smugglers were opportunists who fed a huge demand for cheap luxury goods. Although smuggling was punishable by death, the policing of the UK's ports was so bad it was considered to be worth the risk. According to some 18th-century estimates, 75 per cent of all the tea in England had been smuggled into the country.

In the 21st century smuggling is still rife, although now it's the tonnes of illegal drugs that are brought into the capital every year. Some are brought in by mules through London's airports – normally packets of pure cocaine swallowed to be retrieved after arrival (although ingenious methods have also included plaster casts protecting 'broken limbs' and designer shoes made of cocaine paste) – while other consignments arrive on lorries and occasionally ships from the Continent.

A spectacular operation took place in London in November 1992 when the Special Boat Service assisted the Met Police's firearms team, SO19, in making a bust. *Fox Trot Five*, a 300-tonne vessel, travelled up the Thames after arriving from Colombia and moored by a South London warehouse. When the SBS and SO19 raided the ship and warehouse they found 1.1 tonnes of cocaine (worth £200m).

4. In the Clink

◎ **Clink Street Prison**

⌂ 1 Clink Street, SE1

☎ 020 7403 0900

ⓦ www.clink.co.uk

🕐 July-Sept, Mon-Sun 10am-9pm; Oct-June, Mon-Fri 10am-6pm, Sat and Sun 10am-7.30pm

💷 Adults £7, Children under 16 £5.50

⊖ London Bridge Tube *(Mainline, Northern and Jubilee Lines)*

This small prison, which the museum says dates back to the 1100s, was used for people who disturbed the peace on the Bankside and in the nearby brothels. A ducking stool on the bank outside the Clink was used for punishing scolds, erring ale sellers, and bakers who sold underweight or bad bread. Often the offenders were also made to sit outside their own front door in a commode-like armchair, for their humiliation.

In 1530 Henry VIII legalised boiling in oil for women who had murdered their husbands. They were usually strapped to a pole before being dropped into the oil, although the jailer could decide to put them into cold oil and boil them slowly.

The prison was often flooded and, to avoid drowning, inmates would fight for the safety of the top bunk. Those who could not afford to buy their own food were forced to hunt for rats to survive.

The jailers, who were poorly paid, accepted payments from wealthier inmates for lighter leg-irons, candles, fuel, bedding and alcohol (at twice the going rate). In one case, a jailer allowed an imprisoned Madam to run a brothel from her cell in return for a cut of the action.

When Mary I came to the throne in 1553 the Clink was used to incarcerate Protestants. Food was withheld, they were kept in stocks and pillories, and the prisoners who didn't starve to death or drown were executed later.

The Clink fell into disuse in the first part of the 18th century. In 1732 there were only two registered inmates. In 1745 the building was considered too decayed to use any more, but by 1776 the prison was taking in debtors. Four years later it was burned down during the Gordon Riots and was not rebuilt.

No. 1 Clink Street is now the Clink Prison Museum, a modern reconstruction in a Victorian warehouse basement on the original site, complete with cells and instruments of torture, including such delightful items as a whipping post, a torture chair and a foot crusher.

5. London's First Pimps

◎ **Winchester Palace**

⌂ **Clink Street, SE1**

⊖ **London Bridge Tube** *(Mainline, Northern and Jubilee Lines)*

A 14th-century rose-window and a section of wall are all that remains of the Palace of Winchester, which stood on this site for over 500 years. It had a long river frontage and a 70-acre park, which lay outside the bounds of the City of London and over which the bishops held the Liberty of the Clink (in other words, what they said was pretty much law).

Built in 1109 for William Giffard, Bishop of Winchester, from the 14th century to 1550 the bishops held high office and many important visitors stayed here, including, in 1424, James I of Scotland and Joan Beaufort, who held their wedding reception here after getting married in nearby Southwark Cathedral (see page 23). In 1642 it became a prison for Royalists during the English Civil War; it was destroyed by fire in 1814.

Perhaps the most colourful fact about the Bishops of Winchester was that they were – to an extent – pimps. They regulated and oversaw local brothels and prostitutes, known as 'Winchester Geese', who lived and worked in Southwark under the bishops' regulation. Prostitution was completely banned north of the river, so the ferrymen were kept busy paddling lusty northerners across the Thames. The brothels (18 at their peak), known as Stewes, lined the banks of the river, just next to the bear gardens. The term 'bitten by a Winchester goose' was a commonly used 16th-century phrase to describe syphilis.

The Geese provided a good income for the bishops, through fines and rents. They operated by 11 commandments, including:

No woman to be kept against her will that would leave her sin.

No man to be drawn or enticed to any stew-house.

No Stew holder to receive any woman of religion, or any man's wife.

No single woman to take money to lie with any man, but she lie with him all night till the morrow.

Breaking these rules led to a fine and a spell in the Clink (see page 19). Although the bishops licensed whores, they weren't prepared to let them into heaven. They were forbidden from church so long as they continued their sinful lives. They were also forbidden a Christian burial if they were still 'living in sin' at the time of their death. A plot of ground called the Single Women's Churchyard (see page 31) was put aside for these prostitutes, a safe distance from the parish church.

The bishops lost their privilege over the Geese thanks to Henry VIII in 1546 but nonetheless continued to operate brothels for some time afterwards (until about 1640).

6. Seeking Sanctuary

◎ Southwark Cathedral

⌂ Montague Close, SE1

☎ 020 7367 6700

🌐 www.cathedral.southwark.anglican.org

🕐 10am-5pm

💲 Free but guided tours cost £4 per adult, £3.50 concessions and £2 for children under 11

⊖ London Bridge Tube *(Mainline, Northern and Jubilee Lines)*

The oldest building in Southwark and the oldest Gothic church in London, Southwark Cathedral is mentioned in the Domesday Book. It's not certain, but it's believed there has been a church on this site since 606 and a recent excavation here uncovered the statue of a Roman hunter god.

Inside the cathedral, a carved stone memorial depicts Chaucer, John Bunyan and Shakespeare, all of whom may have attended services here. Shakespeare's younger brother – Edmund – was buried here on 31 December 1607. Thomas Becket, later murdered by four of King Henry II's knights, preached at Southwark Cathedral in the 12th century and made his final journey to Canterbury from here.

Southwark stands at what was the only southern entrance to the City of London for many centuries. Contained within the Liberty of the Clink (see Winchester Palace, page 20) and outside of the jurisdiction of the City, it was a place of sanctuary – a sacred place in which fugitives were immune to arrest (a status recognised in English law from the 4th to the 17th century). There's even a Sanctuary Street nearby, in Little Dorrit Park, just off Borough High Street. In the time of Elizabeth I, the cathedral was owned by Catholics and, in the run-up to war with Spain, secret masses were held there and it provided a safehouse for Catholic priests.

By the 1620s, Montague Close, the street surrounding the cathedral, had become a debtors' sanctuary, where people unable to pay their bills fled the City to live here in tiny, crowded cottages. People also hid here during the English Civil War, but as the war progressed press gangs began to ignore the Liberty of the Clink as their search for recruits became more desperate.

Although the cathedral preached law and order, many genuine wrong-doers claimed sanctuary from the City, making up most of the population of the surrounding area and establishing the lawless culture of Bankside with its bear baiting, prostitution, gambling and theatre.

The law of sanctuary came to an end in 1697 but today the concept remains important to Southwark Cathedral and speeches and debates about the modern issue of asylum take place here.

7. The Railway Killers

◎ London Bridge Station Tunnel

◒ Weston Street

⊜ London Bridge Tube *(Mainline, Northern and Jubilee Lines)*

The two men carried a 'rape kit' of balaclavas, knives and tape. A toss of a coin decided who would rape first. They attacked dozens of women throughout the 1980s, and were called the Railway Rapists by the press because they struck near train stations, railway lines and on trains across London, picking lonely vulnerable points that isolated their targets.

The first rape occurred in 1982 near Hampstead Heath station. Eighteen more followed in the next year and more throughout 1984. On 29 December 1985, a 19-year-old woman was dragged off a train at Hackney Wick station in East London and repeatedly raped. She was then strangled with a piece of string. The murderers were re-named the Railway Killers. On 17 April the following year, a 15-year-old girl was raped and murdered in West Horsley. The next month, a female TV presenter was murdered after she got off a train at Brookmans Park, Hertfordshire.

To help with the spiralling investigation, the police brought in psychologist Dr David Canter from the University of Surrey. This was the first use of 'psychological offender profiling'.

One of the main clues was the crime map – the locations of the rapes, successful and attempted (including Weston Street), suggested that the attackers must have researched the areas before they struck. By concentrating on possible suspects at the centre of the map, and using Dr Canter's profile, detectives decided that John Duffy, a martial arts instructor – previously convicted of raping his wife – was the prime suspect.

Rope found in his parents' house linked Duffy to the second murder victim. Duffy was arrested while following a woman through a secluded park. In February 1988 he was convicted of two murders and four rapes and sentenced to a minimum tariff of 30 years.

While in prison, Duffy revealed what the police already knew – that he had not operated alone. It took another decade before he finally revealed his accomplice's identity: David Mulcahy, a friend since school, in Haverstock Hill, near Hampstead in North London.

Both men had worked at Westminster City Council, where Mulcahy was a plumber and Duffy a carpenter. Mulcahy, taller and better-looking, was the leader. He dominated the diminutive, ginger-haired Duffy, whose face was pockmarked by acne.

When Mulcahy – a married father of four – appeared at the Old Bailey in 2000, Duffy appeared as witness for the prosecution, the first time a highest-category prisoner had ever given evidence against an accomplice.

Convicted of the three murders and numerous rapes, neither man is expected to be released from prison alive.

8. Stand and Deliver

◎ George Inn

⌂ 77 Borough High Street, SE1

☎ 020 7407 2056

ⓦ www.nationaltrust.org.uk/george-inn

🕐 Mon-Sat 11am-11pm, Sun 12pm-10.30pm

⊖ London Bridge Tube *(Mainline, Northern and Jubilee Lines)*

London's only remaining galleried public house first appears in historical records in 1542 and probably existed long before that. The present Grade I listed building dates from 1676. Owned by the National Trust, it features in Charles Dickens' *Little Dorrit* and today Shakespeare's plays are sometimes performed in the courtyard.

The ground floor is divided into a number of connected bars. The Old Bar used to be a waiting room for passengers on coaches. The Middle Bar was the coffee room. The bedrooms, now a restaurant, were upstairs in the galleried part of the building.

It is one of only two coaching inns to survive in Greater London. In the 18th century, people would travel by coach to towns and villages in the South of England, via the Dover Road. It was a dangerous journey – highwaymen were waiting on most roads and would send men to stake out the George Inn in the hope of spotting wealthy and vulnerable targets.

The rich often travelled with armed servants as guards, and some carriages carried pistols and swords. Often passengers would take their own guns. The most common type of pocket pistol, the 'Queen Anne', was available throughout most of the 18th century. Its main disadvantage was the exposed lock and trigger, which frequently caught in the lining of the pocket. A few had spring bayonets fitted to them, so they could be used as a weapon even after firing.

Particularly cautious travellers cut their bank notes in half and sent one half by a separate mail-coach. Several carriers even paid protection money to a highwayman to ensure safe passage.

Once the highwayman's spy had found a target, he would dash to the Dog and Duck pub (on the site of Bedlam, Lambeth, where the Imperial War Museum is today, see page 47) to inform his masters. They would then race ahead and lie in wait on Shooter's Hill – which owes its name to these ambushes – just past Woolwich on the Great Dover Road.

The penalty for robbery with violence was hanging. Famous highwaymen who ended their lives on Tyburn's (see page 271) and Newgate's (see page 125) nooses included French gentleman thief Claude Du Vall (1643–70), who notoriously danced with a lady victim, James MacLaine (1724–50), another gentleman, who once robbed Horace Walpole in Hyde Park and received 3,000 visitors while imprisoned in Newgate, and John Rann, aka Sixteen-string Jack (1750–74), who dressed, shall we say, gaily and danced a jig and bantered with the hangman before his execution.

9. Don't Show Me the Money

◎ **Bureaux de Change**

⌂ **Borough High Street, SE1 (and London-wide)**

⊖ **Borough Tube** *(Northern Line)* **and London Bridge Tube**
(Mainline, Northern and Jubilee Lines)

Anyone selling drugs, from the guy who sells grams on the street, through his supplier to the people bringing in multi-tonne shipments, generates huge amounts of cash – dirty, crumpled, drug-tainted cash that needs to be cleaned and hidden from the authorities if the gangsters are ever going to enjoy spending it.

In the mid-1990s rumours began to circulate that a dodgy bureau de change in Borough High Street was being used to launder millions of pounds of drugs money – it turned out to be tens of millions. And as other independent bureaux doing the same thing were uncovered, the grand total rocketed to about £2 billion each year. One particular bureau managed to launder £70m. Unsurprisingly, the owner, 'Sami' El-Kurd, was always running out of money and frequently had to request large amounts from local banks and travel agents as well as several Arab banks.

When he was arrested, El-Kurd was found to have £1.2m deposited in 51 bank accounts across Europe, a £50,000 collection of jewellery, £750,000 in two safety-deposit boxes and a 'float' of £250,000 in his bureau's safe.

He was cleared of knowingly laundering drug-trafficking proceeds, but convicted of money laundering nonetheless. El-Kurd said he had no idea where the money had come from, but ignorance was no longer bliss. He was handed a £1m fine and a 14-year prison sentence in 1999.

Problem solved, you might think, but dodgy bureaux de change still thrive in London despite this crackdown and new regulations. SOCA, the Serious Organised Crime Agency (see page 67), still identifies bureaux de change as high-risk areas open to abuse by money launderers. Of course, the clientele of these bureaux isn't limited to drug dealers. Terrorist organisations also avail themselves of the launderers' services. Although the amounts spent by terrorists on their ops are small (the 7/7 attacks in London only cost about £8,000 to set up), financing the day-to-day running of a terrorist network is extremely expensive: SOCA estimated that al-Qaeda spent about £30m on running costs between 2000 and 2001. They raised a great deal of those funds through illegal drug and diamond dealing, the proceeds of which were washed by money-changers across the world.

Cross Bones Graveyard

In medieval times this was an unconsecrated graveyard for prostitutes or 'Winchester Geese'. By the 18th century it had become a paupers' burial ground, which closed in 1853. Here, local people have created a memorial shrine.

The Outcast Dead
R.I.P

10. RIP Winchester Geese

◎ Cross Bones Graveyard
⌂ Redcross Way, SE1
Ⓦ www.crossbones.org.uk
⊕ Events throughout the year (see below and website for details)
⊖ Borough Tube *(Northern Line)*

One of London's oddest and most morbidly charming sights is located on this quiet back street. Surrounded by weathered London Underground hoardings is a rusty gate covered in ivy, ribbons, feathers, flowers and jewellery. On it is a small bronze plaque with the words: 'The Outcast Dead R.I.P.'.

Once known as the Single Women's Churchyard, Cross Bones was an unconsecrated graveyard for the Winchester Geese (see Winchester Palace, page 20), operating for some centuries until 1546.

It is thought to have since been used as a plague pit, and by the middle of the 19th century the area was full of slums overflowing with cholera. Cross Bones was shut in 1853 when it was stated to be 'completely overcharged with dead' and that 'further burials' would be 'inconsistent with a due regard for the public health and public decency'.

The graveyard was left for almost a century. Then, in the 1990s, before London Underground started work on an electricity sub-station for the Jubilee Line Extension, which would cover some of the site, Museum of London archaeologists removed 148 skeletons, buried between 1800 and 1853.

The recovered skeletons represented 'less than 1 per cent of the total number of burials that were made at this site'. The archaeologists found that the graveyard was overcrowded, with bodies piled on top of one another. Tests showed people buried here had smallpox, tuberculosis, Paget's disease and osteoarthritis, and that over one third of the buried women had been pregnant or had recently given birth before they died.

Since 1998, a ritual has been observed every Halloween night, with hundreds of people gathering for a candlelit procession to the gates, to honour the 'outcast dead' with songs and offerings.

More recently, since 2004 the Friends of Cross Bones have held a vigil at the gates at 7pm on the 23rd day of each month – hence the regular supply of fresh flowers, ribbons and ornaments.

11. Dickens' Debtors' Prison

◎ **Marshalsea Prison**
⬆ **South of Angel Place, SE1**
⊕ **Borough Tube** *(Northern Line)*

The original Marshalsea was situated north of Mermaid Court, less than 100m from here, and dated back to at least the 14th century. In the late 18th century it was moved here, just north of St George's Church.

In later periods it was a debtors' prison and also held Admiralty prisoners, smugglers, those charged with excise offences, as well as men charged with 'unnatural acts', and sailors awaiting court-martial.

In February 1824, Charles Dickens' father, John Dickens, was imprisoned for debt. John, who was a clerk, owed a baker over £40 (you could be imprisoned for owing less than £20).

In *Little Dorrit* (1856), Dickens describes Marshalsea as 'an oblong pile of barrack buildings, partitioned into squalid houses standing back to back, so that there were no back rooms: environed by a narrow paved yard, hemmed in by high walls duly spiked at the top'. Rooms were small, less than ten feet square, and had to be shared, sometimes by up to four people.

Whole families lived there; the debtor, usually head of the household, was not able to leave the prison, but his wife and children were able to move freely in and out, except at night-time when they were locked in together.

There were, naturally, many rules. The debtors' committee, run by prisoners (at one time John Dickens was its chairperson) governed the prison and imposed fines for theft, noise, littering, singing rude songs, swearing fighting, smoking in the beer room between 8am and 10am or 12pm and 2pm (beer could be purchased for five pence a pot and prisoners could drink as much as they liked), urinating in the yard and for criticizing the committee. Prostitutes were tolerated.

Dickens was only 12 years old when his father was imprisoned here. It was one of his worst memories, something that haunted the writer for the rest of his life. He was at least spared having to live with the rest of his family in prison and was put into lodgings at nearby Lant Street (a blue plaque marks the spot). He went to work in a boot-blacking factory, on the site of present-day Hungerford Bridge (see page 56) until the day his father inherited £450 and was able to pay his debts.

Imprisonment for debt was outlawed in 1869 (excluding cases that involved fraud or deliberate non-payment). The Marshalsea was closed by an Act of Parliament in 1842 and the lands sold off. The inmates were moved to the nearby King's Bench Prison. The southern wall, now preserved, is all that remains of Marshalsea.

12. London's Most Notorious Murder

◉ **Southwark Coroner's Court**
⬆ Tennis Street, SE1
⊖ Borough Tube *(Northern Line)*

At the end of the eastern extent of the Marshalsea prison wall, in Tennis Street, is Southwark Coroner's Court; a Coroner's Court has been on this site since 1550. A coroner is a doctor or lawyer responsible for investigating violent and unnatural deaths – or deaths of an unknown cause.

On 22 April 1993 black teenager Stephen Lawrence was stabbed to death in an unprovoked attack by a gang of white youths as he waited at a bus stop in Eltham, Southeast London, with his friend Duwayne Brooks.

The 18-year-old, who had ambitions of becoming an architect, ran 130 yards with a punctured lung and paralysed arm before collapsing and bleeding to death from an arterial wound.

The police bungled the murder investigation and by the time of the inquest, which was held here in February 1997, no one had been prosecuted for the crime. The police's own inquiry largely exonerated the officers for their alleged failings while an independent public inquiry concluded that the police had failed Stephen and his family in part because the Metropolitan Police Service was 'institutionally racist', in that its structures and processes inevitably resulted in racist outcomes.

It was hoped that the inquest might succeed where the police had not but it quickly descended into mockery when the five men suspected of the attack refused to answer any questions relating to the teenager's death. The five included Neil Acourt, 21, Luke Knight, 19, and Gary Dobson, 21, who had all been formally acquitted of murdering Stephen at the Old Bailey the previous year, and Jamie Acourt, 19, and David Norris, 20, who never stood trial.

Due to their silence, the inquest became a grim farce. At one point, counsel for the Lawrence family, Michael Mansfield QC, lost his temper after he asked Norris: 'Are you called David Norris?'

To laughter, Norris replied: 'I am claiming privilege on that question.'

The inquest's jurors concluded that Stephen was unlawfully killed 'in a completely unprovoked racist attack by five white youths'. This went far beyond the normally bland verdicts of 'unlawful' or 'accidental' death or, in cases of doubt, an 'open' verdict. Their decision reflected the strong feelings generated by the Lawrence murder.

In the UK, murder cases are never closed and a team of detectives continued trying to gather enough evidence to identify and prosecute Stephen's killers. Almost 15 years after the inquest, Stephen's clothes were re-examined using newly developed forensic techniques and this time scientists found a tiny bloodstain on Gary Dobson's jacket from which they were able to extract DNA that appeared to match Stephen's. Also, a single 2mm hair they found on Norris's jeans was said to belong to the teenager.

In January 2012, an Old Bailey jury found Gary Dobson and David Norris guilty of murder. Dobson, who was by then 36, will serve a minimum of 15 years and two months, and David Norris 14 years and three months. Both men contiune to press their innocence. The hunt for the rest of those involved in Stephen's death continues.

13. Executions with a View

◎ Horsemonger Lane Gaol
⌂ Newington Gardens, Harper Road, SE1
⊖ Borough Tube *(Northern Line)* and Elephant and Castle
  (Northern and Bakerloo Lines)

Built between 1791 and 1799, this 300-capacity model prison operated until 1878, and was demolished in 1880–81. Executions were carried out on the rooftop of the guardhouse, with 131 men and four women hanged here between 1800 and 1877.

In 1812, the poet Leigh Hunt and his brother John, printer and editor of *The Examiner*, were convicted of libel. They'd published an article in which Hunt described the Prince Regent (the future George IV) as 'a fat Adonis of fifty'. They were sentenced to two years' imprisonment and given a £500 fine. Leigh was sent here, where the poets Shelley and Lord Byron came to visit him (see the Star and Garter, page 275). Together, they would go on to found and publish the left-wing journal, *The Liberal*. To get around England's tough libel laws, they published the journal in Italy — a method that has been repeated up to the present day, as the UK's libel laws incur some of the highest legal costs and fines in the world, restricting freedom of speech and favouring the wealthy. The Libel Reform Campaign is currently battling to get them changed.

Another campaigner, in this instance against public execution, was Charles Dickens, who in November 1849 wrote a letter to *The Times* after witnessing the hangings of Maria and Frederick Manning at Horsemonger Lane Gaol. The Mannings had killed a friend for his money and buried him under his kitchen floor and theirs was the first husband-and-wife execution for more than 150 years. The papers billed it as the 'Hanging of the Century'. Thirty thousand people surrounded the guardhouse on the morning of the execution. Dickens had found an upstairs room close to the prison where he had a clear view.

He wrote:

I believe that a sight so inconceivably awful as the wickedness and levity of the immense crowd collected at that execution this morning could be imagined by no man, and could be presented in no heathen land under the sun. The horrors of the gibbet and of the crime which brought the wretched murderers to it faded in my mind before the atrocious bearing, looks, and language of the assembled spectators ... When the day dawned, thieves, low prostitutes, ruffians, and vagabonds of every kind, flocked on to the ground, with every variety of offensive and foul behaviour ... When the sun rose brightly — as it did — it gilded thousands upon thousands of upturned faces, so inexpressibly odious in their brutal mirth or callousness, that a man had cause to feel ashamed of the shape he wore, and to shrink from himself, as fashioned in the image of the Devil.

There has been a judicial building on the site since 1794. Currently it is home to the Inner London Sessions House Crown Court, known as the Inner London Crown Court.

14. Shot in the Butts

◉ King's Bench Prison
⬆ St Mary Newington Churchyard, Newington Butts, SE1
⊖ Elephant and Castle Tube *(Northern and Bakerloo Lines)*

A short distance from Horsemonger Lane Gaol is the site of King's Bench prison (now the Scovell Housing Estate). Opened in 1758, King's Bench had 224 cells and an open courtyard surrounded by a high wall.

The most chaotic of London's prisons, an 1828 writer described it as 'the most desirable place of incarceration in London'. Wealthy prisoners could buy a limited freedom known as the 'Liberty of the Rules' – they were allowed to roam the three square miles surrounding the prison, including pubs. While poorer prisoners had to make do with a begging box at the gate, the wealthy had their own cook. Tailors, barbers, hatters, piano makers, chandlers and oyster sellers set up shop in the courtyard and 120 gallons of gin were sold to the prison each week.

Radical, free-speech campaigner and all-round libertine John Wilkes was imprisoned here in 1768 for libel after he wrote an article for the *North Briton*, severely criticising King George III – and after writing a pornographic poem. He was charged with obscene and seditious libel. The proclamation angered a large group of noisy supporters, which led to government troops reading them the Riot Act of 1714. This authorised local authorities to declare any group of 12 or more people to be unlawfully assembled, thus compelling them to disperse or face punitive action (the modern Criminal Justice and Public Order Act (1994) has a similar clause about assembly of 20 or more persons).

A warning had to be read out to the gathering concerned, and had to follow the precise wording detailed in the Act. If the group failed to disperse within one hour of the proclamation, the Act provided that the authorities could use force to break them up.

In this case soldiers ended up firing on the crowd and six or seven people were killed. The event became known as the Massacre of St George's Fields. One of the victims, William Allen, shot in the yard of the Horse-shoe Inn, was buried just opposite what is now the St Mary Newington churchyard in Newington Butts, and a monument was erected to his memory, although it has since disappeared. The inscription read: 'Sacred to the memory of WILLIAM ALLEN An Englishman of unspotted Life and amiable Disposition who was inhumanly murdered near St. Georges Fields on the 10th Day of May 1768 by Scottish Detachments from the ARMY.'

In the 1840s the King's Bench prison was amalgamated with Marshalsea (see page 32) and renamed Queen's Bench. It held mainly debtors from this time and once arrest for debt was outlawed it was used as a military prison from 1862, before being closed and then demolished in 1880.

15. The Curse of Brink's-Mat

◉ Creedon House
⌂ 72 Verney Road and Lynton Road, SE1
⊜ Bermondsey Tube *(Jubilee Line)*

On 16 November 2001, 63-year-old Brian Perry left his wife and children at home in Kent and drove to his minicab office in Verney Road. Perry always parked in the same spot, making it very easy for the hit man who was waiting for him. Perry was shot three times in the back of the head. An investigation by the *Observer* revealed that his murder was the eighth to claim a victim linked to the £26m Brink's-Mat gold bullion raid at Heathrow airport in 1983 (see page 134).

After that robbery, a share of the gold had fallen into Perry's hands. He brought in petty criminal Kenneth Noye to help smelt it. Noye, in turn, contacted John Palmer, a gold dealer whose firm could provide the necessary equipment. Once smelted, the gold was sold on the scrap market.

Noye and Perry's attempts to move the large amounts of money produced eventually came to the attention of the police and Noye was put under surveillance. Unfortunately, one of Noye's guard dogs spotted the officers and, thinking a criminal gang had come to murder him, Noye stabbed a detective 11 times, killing him. A jury acquitted Noye of murder, accepting that he had acted in self-defence, but 11 gold bars – the only ones ever recovered from the robbery – were found at Noye's home, and he was jailed for conspiracy to handle stolen goods.

In 1987 John Palmer was also tried for knowingly handling gold from the Brink's-Mat raid. He was acquitted; he admitted to smelting the ingots but maintained that he was unaware they had been stolen. Brian Perry himself was arrested and sentenced to nine years for his role in laundering the gold. After his release he focused on his cab firm. The motive for his murder remains a mystery, although the underworld suspects it had something to do with Brink's-Mat.

Another supposed victim of the Brink's-Mat 'curse' was career criminal George Francis, who owned a haulage firm just two streets away from here, in Lynton Road. Francis's history of wrongdoing spanned 55 years; he knew everyone from the Krays to Frankie Fraser, the Great Train Robbers – and the Brink's-Mat robbers. Francis once said, 'I would rather die quickly by the bullet than slowly in some old people's home that stinks of cabbage water.'

On the morning of 14 May 2003, at the age of 63, he got his wish.

Professional killers John O'Flynn and Terence Conaghan had been paid £30,000 to murder Francis – they shot him four times as he leaned into his Rover 75 car. The law eventually caught up with the two men after DNA evidence (a dropped cigarette) linked them to the scene. They were sentenced to life.

As with the shooting of Perry, underworld rumours abound that the killing was linked to Brink's-Mat – Francis was once questioned over allegations that he helped launder money from the heist. His murder brought the number of homicides with some connection to the robbery to nine.

These suspicions have never been proven, but the so-called 'curse of Brink's-Mat' has nonetheless made its way into the press, books and documentaries. And with more than £10m still unaccounted for, the heist itself remains a subject of continuing speculation and fascination.

16. Kings of the Castle

◎ **Elephant and Castle, SE1**

⊖ **Elephant and Castle Tube** *(Northern and Bakerloo Lines)*

The Elephant and Castle has been a traffic junction for almost 400 years. The area was devastated by bombs in World War II and redeveloped in 1961–62 around two giant roundabouts with a covered shopping arcade, a cinema and market. Today, the area is often described as 'depressing' and 'confusing' thanks to its mess of pedestrian tunnels and one-way traffic systems.

It also has a long history of wrongdoing. From the start of the 20th century one of London's main criminal gangs, involved in protection rackets and organised violence, was the 'Elephant Boys' led by Charles 'Wag' McDonald. On the other side of the gender divide, Aggy Hill was the 'Queen of the Forty Elephants', a team of women shoplifters who travelled from here to work in the West End in chauffeur-driven cars.

After World War II, the area was home to Teddy Boys who dressed in an Edwardian style. The self-styled 'King of the Teds' in the late 1950s was Eddie Richardson, brother of the future South London gang leader Charlie.

Born in nearby Wyndham Road, Charlie (1934) and Eddie (1936) rose to run an empire of fruit machines, fraud, protection rackets and stolen goods in the 1960s. Charlie's scrap-metal firm at 50 New Church Road in Camberwell was a front. It was also where they tortured rivals. James Moody (see Brixton prison, page 331) and Mad Frankie Fraser (see Cabbell Street, page 191) were part of this team, although Mad Frank denies torturing anyone. The Richardsons' rivalry with the Krays came to a head in March 1966 at Mr Smith's Club in Rushey Green, Catford, after a fight over control of the fruit machine market left Richard Hart, a member of the Kray gang, dead. Ronnie Kray retaliated by shooting George Cornell in the Blind Beggar pub (see page 89), a murder that eventually helped the police to put Ronnie away.

Charlie Richardson was arrested the day England won the World Cup in 1966. The following year, Eddie – who was already in prison serving five years for affray – and Charlie were found guilty of fraud, extortion, assault and grievous bodily harm. Charlie was sentenced to 25 years while Eddie got another ten on top of the five he was already serving.

Charlie was released in July 1984. Eddie hadn't been free long when he was sent down again, this time for 25 years for conspiring to import drugs in 1990. He was released on parole in 2001. After discovering a love for art while inside Eddie has since made a legitimate living selling his paintings.

17. Elephant's Graveyard

◎ New and Old Kent Roads

⬆ Running east from Elephant and Castle, SE1

⊖ Elephant and Castle Tube *(Northern and Bakerloo Lines)*

The New and Old Kent Roads bring us to the southernmost tip of this sightseeing tour. Old Kent, which follows the line of a Roman road, is not the place for a pleasant stroll. It is famous for being the cheapest property on a Monopoly board, and for featuring at the beginning of George Orwell's *Down and Out in Paris and London*.

Once the Cockney heartland where Charlie Richardson had his first tangle with the law – he was stopped driving a stolen car near here – the Old Kent Road was also home to the Downham pub (it has since been demolished, but the Lord Nelson at No. 386 is of the same period and one of the few old boozers still remaining).

If you aspired to become an armed robber, or needed guns for hire or men for a job, then from the 1970s through to the late 80s, the Downham was the place to go. It was also where robbers went to celebrate a successful job. A Flying Squad detective observed: 'More Moët was drunk in the Downham than in the Ritz.'

Many infamous names were regulars: Mickey McAvoy (see page 134), Mad Frankie Fraser (see page 191) and local bank robbers turned drug importers, the Arifs.

The Arifs, led by Dennis, Mehmet and Dogan, were at the top of their game in the 1980s when newspapers described them as 'Britain's No.1 Crime Family'. They left Cyprus in the 1950s for South London and settled in the Old Kent Road where they became known as the 'Wild Bunch'. Their reign ended after a series of successful police operations: Dennis and Mehmet were imprisoned following their arrest during the attempted armed robbery of a Securicor van in November 1990, and Dogan was sentenced to fourteen years for his part in a multimillion-pound drug-smuggling plot. But although many of the Arif gang are now in jail, their influence is still strongly felt in this area.

Also off the Old Kent Road is the North Peckham Estate, scene of the murder of ten-year-old Damilola Taylor, stabbed in the leg with a broken glass by two brothers and left to bleed to death on a lonely stairwell in a condemned housing estate on 27 November 2000. It took six years and three trials to identify and convict the killers of manslaughter.

The Heygate Estate on New Kent Road, which opened in 1974, has become a symbol of the death of the Utopian idea of the mass housing estate. From the moment the first tenants moved in, the Heygate developed a reputation for crime, helping drug dealers by providing them with somewhere to operate and to hide from the police. Now used for film locations (*Attack the Block* and *Harry Brown*) the Heygate has been condemned to demolition. However, progress has been slowed by asbestos, so the estate will remain standing until 2015, when it will be replaced by 'friendlier' housing developments.

BETHLEM HOSPITAL

Moore   Fields

d in the Year 1246, to be a Priory of Canons an
have occasion to travel hither, H. Henry 8
harge converted it to an Hospital for Lunaticks.
recieve the number of Patients brought thither,
pleasant Airy Scituation. It is a commodious
ly Adorn'd with Ornaments and Carving &c. it
he Gardens before; it and contains Appartments

18. Home for the Criminally Insane

◉ Bethlem (Bedlam) Lunatic Asylum (now the Imperial War Museum)

⌂ Lambeth Road, SE1

☎ 020 7416 5000

🖥 www.iwm.org.uk

🕐 Daily 10am-6pm

🎟 Free (there may be charges for special exhibitions)

⊖ Elephant and Castle Tube *(Northern and Bakerloo Lines)* and
   Lambeth North Tube *(Bakerloo Line)*

Today's Imperial War Museum used to be a 'lunatic asylum', part of which housed the criminally insane from 1815 to 1864 (after which time they were moved to what is now Broadmoor Hospital in Berkshire).

The State Criminal Lunatic Asylum was housed in two detached wings at the back of the main building. Two patients spent a total of over 80 years between them in here for trying to kill the same man.

In 1800 James Hadfield tried to shoot George III (who himself became insane and was kept in isolation in Windsor Castle from 1811 until his death in 1820) at the Theatre Royal, Drury Lane, during the playing of the national anthem. Hadfield's first shot missed, after which he said to the King: 'God bless your royal highness; I like you very well; you are a good fellow.' Hadfield spent much of his 39 years in Broadmoor writing verses on the deaths of his cats and birds, his only companions in the hospital. He died here in 1841, from tuberculosis.

Margaret Nicholson spent 42 years in solitary confinement for attempting to stab the same king in 1786, as he alighted from a carriage at St James's Palace. Nicholson, who believed she was the rightful heir to the throne, attempted to murder the King with an ivory-handled dessert knife.

Perhaps the most famous resident in Bethlem was the artist Richard Dadd (1817–86). In July 1842, Dadd travelled through Europe to Greece, Turkey, Southern Syria and finally Egypt on a commission to paint an expedition. He became delusional and increasingly violent while on the Nile, believing himself to be under the influence of the Egyptian god Osiris.

Less than a year later, Dadd became convinced that his father was the Devil, killed him with a knife and fled to France. He then tried to kill a tourist with a razor, but was overpowered by police, after which he was committed.

Sir William Charles Hood had recently become Bethlem's resident physician and instigated a period of reform, improving comfort while reducing the prison-like atmosphere. Hood encouraged Dadd to continue painting. Within these walls Dadd painted his masterpiece, *The Fairy Feller's Master-Stroke*, which he worked on between 1855 and 1864. Dadd was eventually moved to Broadmoor, where he died in January 1886 'from an extensive disease of the lungs'.

Increasingly unpopular with Bethlem's governors, the wings for the criminally insane were always overcrowded and from 1864 such inmates were held at a new institution at Broadmoor in Berkshire, which today is home to nail bomber David Copeland (see page 232), Peter Sutcliffe, aka The Yorkshire Ripper, and Kenneth Erskine, aka the Stockwell Strangler.

19. The Murder Bag

◎ Left Luggage Office
⬡ Waterloo Station, SE1
☎ 020 7401 8444
🕐 Mon-Sun 7am-11pm
⊖ Waterloo station *(Mainline, Jubilee, Bakerloo and Northern Lines)*

In 1924, Patrick Mahon's wife became so concerned about her husband's constant disappearances that she decided to search through his things. Mahon, a 35-year-old travelling salesman, was good-looking and charming – and his wife thought he might be having an affair.

She found a ticket for Waterloo's left luggage locker in his suit pocket. A small leather bag was in the locker. Mrs Mahon was expecting to find love letters or betting slips but inside was some underwear, a blue scarf, two pieces of white silk and a cook's knife – all covered in blood.

She informed the police, who asked Mrs Mahon to replace the ticket and then waited for Patrick to collect the bag. When he did, the police arrested him and took him to Scotland Yard where he was asked how he had come to possess the items inside. Mahon told them that the answer lay inside an isolated Eastbourne bungalow. Once there detectives found that the pleasant seaside house had been used as a butcher's shop – of human flesh.

When eminent pathologist Sir Bernard Spilsbury (1877–1947) entered the house, he found a detective using his bare hands to collect pieces of bloodied flesh. When Spilsbury demanded to know why he wasn't wearing rubber gloves, the officer replied that they didn't have any.

Spilsbury proposed a standardised kit to be provided to officers in the field, a major development in police forensics. Equipped with everything needed to collect evidence, it was christened the 'Murder Bag' and contained rubber gloves, tweezers, evidence bags, a magnifying glass, compass, ruler and swabs.

Inside the house, Spilsbury found two large saucepans of boiled flesh, more flesh in a hatbox, a biscuit tin stuffed full of human organs and a trunk with the initials 'E.B.K.', containing pieces of torso. Spilsbury discovered that the victim had been pregnant.

Mahon admitted that his mistress, Emily Kaye, had died at the house, but claimed she had fallen and hit her head during a lovers' quarrel. The head in question was missing. Mahon was found guilty of murder and hanged on Wednesday 3 September 1924.

Mahon's hanging at Wandsworth (see p327) did not go smoothly. After he was placed on the trapdoor and the executioner was about to pull the lever to open it, he jumped forward to avoid falling to his death. Unfortunately for Mahon, he swung backwards and smashed his spine on the inside of the trapdoor before the hanging reached its inevitable conclusion.

20. The Battle of Waterloo

◎ **The Wellington Hotel**

⌂ **81–83 Waterloo Road, SE1**

☎ **020 7928 6083**

ⓦ **www.wellingtonhotelwaterloo.co.uk**

🕐 **Mon-Sat 11am-11pm, Sun 12pm-10.30pm**

⊖ **Waterloo station** *(Mainline, Jubilee, Bakerloo and Northern Lines)*

Charles 'Wag' McDonald (1877–1943) and his gang the Elephant Boys ruled South London's criminal underworld for more than 30 years. Named after the Elephant and Castle, they were at their strongest in the 1920s and 30s when they dominated the southern, eastern and northern parts of central London.

Named Wag after 'Charley Wag the Boy Burglar', a mischievous character from the so-called penny-dreadfuls, Charles and his four brothers ran protection rackets in the West End and controlled bookmaking south of the Thames. His sisters Ada and Annie were expert shoplifters who targeted expensive West End shops (see also Elephant and Castle, page 43).

The Elephant Boys' main rivals were the Sabini gang from Clerkenwell's Little Italy (see page 137), led by the ruthless Charles 'Darby' Sabini, who was one of the first organised criminals to make use of police bribes. In March 1921, in the interests of making money, Sabini organised a peace talk with McDonald but, predictably, a fight broke out. In June the same year, the Elephant Boys beat up a group of bookies at Epsom who were under the protection of the Sabinis. This effort at intimidation backfired when 17 of the Elephant Boys were jailed for the attack.

Pitched battles between McDonald's and Sabini's gangs broke out across London, reaching a climax in 1927. The fights would often take place at railway stations, as the gangs would run into each other as they travelled to the races. On this occasion a full contingent of gang members met outside Waterloo Station and a full-on riot ensued, at the end of which eight men were dead. After this, public concern was so great that the Home Secretary introduced a raft of new police powers.

The Sabinis and Elephant Boys battled on regardless, continuing their struggle for control of allocation of bookmaking pitches on racecourses and the provision of 'services' to bookmakers who were terrorised into paying for them.

Once his power started to wane with the growing strength of the Sabinis, McDonald left London for Los Angeles, where he became bodyguard to many Hollywood celebrities, including Charlie Chaplin and Mafia boss Jack Dragna.

Today it is well worth stopping for a drink at the Wellington Hotel and looking out at the streets where McDonald and his rivals once fought. The pub itself boasts a striking mural of the more famous Battle of Waterloo and cites 'Buster' Edwards of the Great Train Robbery (see Greet Street, page 52) as a former punter.

21. A Great Train Robber Departs

◎ Ronald 'Buster' Edwards
◑ Junction of Greet Street and Brad Street, Waterloo, SE1
◒ Waterloo station *(Mainline, Jubilee, Bakerloo and Northern Lines)*

Shortly after Great Train Robber Ronald 'Buster' Edwards was freed in 1975, after serving nine years for his part in the 1963 heist, he opened a flower stall in Waterloo Station. He kept his goods in one of the arches along this street.

On 28 November 1994, Buster, who was 63 and married with one daughter, asked a friend to mind the stall for a short while. He then walked to Greet Street, passing Graeme Bradley, a worker on the Jubilee Underground line extension: 'When I saw him,' Bradley told newspapers later, 'he looked very poorly, very ill-looking. I asked him what he was doing for Christmas and he didn't seem to know.'

Buster was found at midday by his brother Terence, hanging from a steel girder, inside one of these arches, below the train tracks leading to Waterloo Station. A small bottle of vodka — one-third full —was found next to his body.

The infamous raid on the Glasgow to Euston mail train in 1963 netted the robbers £2.6m. The train driver, Jack Mills, was badly beaten in the process. He never returned to work and died in 1970. Some claim that Edwards was the man who hit him — which he denied. Edwards, who was born in Lambeth, surrendered to police three years after the robbery, claiming he was getting violent demands for money from fellow criminals.

Speaking from Rio de Janeiro, where he was still on the run, after Buster's death fellow train robber Ronnie Biggs promised to 'have a couple of beers' for Edwards. 'I always remember him as a jolly fella.'

The funeral, held at a crematorium in Streatham, was a who's who of London criminals, including two of the nine surviving train robbers and Charlie Kray, elder brother of the Kray twins. Two wreaths in the shape of trains were in one of the funeral cars.

Many suspected that it was the boredom of a nine-to-five job that drove him to suicide: 'It's so dreary compared with the life I used to lead,' he once said. 'It wasn't even the money. I've been on jobs that haven't netted me a penny but, oh, does the adrenaline flow.'

One of Buster's locals was the Kings Arms in Roupell Street, one street north of this location — a miracle of survival in that the late-Georgian Grade II listed houses, which back onto Brad Street, were the only ones in this area to make it through the Blitz. The Kings Arms (020 7207 0784, open 7 days a week) is worth a visit; old, quirky, packed full of knick-knacks, it serves good food, an award-winning selection of ales and — unlike many other venues in the area — it's quiet at the weekends.

22. The Umbrella of Death

◎ Waterloo Bridge
⬆ Viewed from the Victoria Embankment
⊖ Waterloo station *(Mainline, Jubilee, Bakerloo and Northern Lines)*

Bulgaria had been under the Soviet jackboot since the end of World War II and Todor Zhivkov (1911–98) – who took power from 1954 – became the longest serving leader of any Eastern Bloc nation by doing everything Moscow told him.

Bulgarian dissident and writer Georgi Markov (1929–78) fled his homeland for London after he'd started criticising the Zhivkov regime through his writing. His play, *The Assassins*, which featured a plot to kill a general in a police state, was singled out for censure in a newspaper article signed by Zhivkov. Markov defected in 1969, aged 40, shortly afterwards.

Markov proved to be a much bigger problem for Zhivkov in London than he had in Bulgaria. The writer gave a series of weekly talks broadcast by the Munich-based station Radio Free Europe from the BBC's World Service office in Bush House on the Strand. Five million Bulgarians – half the population – tuned in to listen to Markov's satirical and critical summaries of the regime.

Markov also helped expose a number of illegal practices and atrocities carried out by Zhivkov's government, not least of which was illegal arms dealing. The power and influence of Markov's broadcasts was unquestionable. As far as Zhivkov was concerned, Markov had to go.

On the morning of 7 September 1978 (Zhivkov's birthday), in front of a crowded London bus stop on the southern side of Waterloo Bridge, just a two-minute bus journey from Bush House, Markov suddenly felt a sharp pain in his right thigh. He turned to see a heavy-set man carrying an umbrella. 'I am sorry,' the man muttered, as he climbed into a taxi.

In the early hours of the following morning, Markov awoke feeling sick. He told his wife: 'I have a horrible feeling that this may be connected with something which happened yesterday.' He was rushed to hospital but died on 11 September.

Doctors at Porton Down, a government facility for military bio-chemical research, examined Markov's body and found a small platinum pellet, 1.5mm across, embedded in his leg. Further examination revealed it contained traces of the super-toxin ricin. It had been injected into Markov's leg using a mechanism concealed in the tip of the assassin's umbrella.

The assassin, codenamed 'Agent Piccadilly', escaped. The case is still open and British police visited Bulgaria as recently as 2008 to try and uncover new evidence. Markov, survived by his wife Annabel and daughter Sasha, was buried in the village of Whitchurch Canonicorum in Dorset. His gravestone epitaph read that he died 'in the cause of freedom'. Zhivkov resigned in 1989 as the Berlin Wall was being torn down and while his people were rioting. He died while under house arrest in 1998.

23. Murder over the Thames

◉ Hungerford Bridge

⌂ Southbank, SE1

⊜ Waterloo station *(Mainline, Jubilee, Bakerloo and Northern Lines)*

Hungerford Railway Bridge was built in 1864, replacing Brunel's suspension bridge that carried trains across the Thames to Charing Cross Station. A narrow walkway with a four-foot-high railing was also introduced for pedestrians, connecting Waterloo with Charing Cross, but by the 1970s it was poorly lit and rundown, so pedestrian traffic was light after dark.

In January 1974, 21-year-old serial killer Patrick Mackay found himself on Hungerford Bridge just a few hours after stabbing a woman and her four-year-old grandson to death in Hadley Green, Hertfordshire. He passed an elderly tramp. It was late. No one else was around. Mackay, a deranged, clinical psychopath, decided to throw the tramp over the side and into the Thames, which he promptly did.

For some reason, Mackay, perhaps the UK's most savage and cold-blooded serial killer, is rarely talked about these days — especially when compared with murderers like Christie and Nilsen (see pages 180 and 235).

Mackay was born on 25 September 1952 to a violent father. By the time he was ten — when his father died — Mackay was preoccupied with death. He tortured cats and rabbits and once roasted a tortoise alive.

By the age of 13 he was in a mental hospital. By 15, six-foot-tall Mackay had a long record of violent offences. He'd tried to strangle his mother and almost beat a younger boy to death. Despite being diagnosed as a 'cold, psychopathic killer', he was released from care.

His first murder took place in July 1973, when he threw a 17-year-old German au pair from a train near New Cross in Southeast London. He then beat an Irish woman to death in her Kentish Town apartment. Later he murdered the aforementioned grandmother, followed by the tramp on Hungerford Bridge. In February 1974, Mackay strangled and stabbed a fourth woman in her Chelsea home.

He then bludgeoned a 62-year-old tobacconist to death with a piece of lead pipe in Finsbury Park and punched a 92-year-old to death on her Hackney doorstep. In Southend he murdered the proprietress of a local café and followed this by strangling an elderly widow on 10 March 1975.

Eleven days later, he visited a priest who had tried to befriend him when he was a teenager, in Gravesend. Mackay split his head open with an axe. Arrested two days later, Mackay was charged with the priest's murder, convicted, and given a whole-life tariff.

In 1999, two 24-year-old students were thrown into the Thames from Hungerford Bridge after being beaten unconscious. One survived, but the other's body was discovered a day later. Six people were sentenced to life for the murder in 2000.

In 2002 two new footbridges were completed but another killing took place in 2004 when a survivor of the 1999 nail bombing at the Admiral Duncan pub (see page 232) was beaten unconscious by a gang and died in St Thomas's Hospital.

24. The Lambeth Poisoner

◉ St Thomas's Hospital (medical school entrance)
⬥ 103 Lambeth Palace Road, SE1
⊖ Vauxhall station *(Mainline and Victoria Line)* and Waterloo station *(Mainline, Jubilee, Bakerloo and Northern Lines)*

In 1891, when police received an anonymous letter accusing two respectable and innocent doctors of 'The Lambeth Poisonings', they quickly realised that it must have been written by the murderer –the letter writer knew too much about the crimes.

Around this time a London doctor, Thomas Neill Cream (1850–92), met a policeman from New York City who was visiting London. The policeman mentioned that he had heard of the Lambeth Poisoner, and so Cream showed him the victims' homes. The American then reported this to a British policeman, as he found Cream's detailed knowledge of the case suspicious.

Scotland Yard put Cream under surveillance and soon found that Dr Cream, of 103 Lambeth Palace Road (close to the site of the entrance to St Thomas's Hospital medical school), liked to consort with the prostitutes of Lambeth.

The victims of the Lambeth Poisoner included 19-year-old Ellen 'Nellie' Donworth, 27-year-old prostitute Matilda Clover (although her death was at first put down to alcoholism) and Alice Marsh (21) and Emma Shrivell (18), who both died in agony in the flat they shared.

The police investigation took officers to America where they found that Cream, who had lived in Quebec, Edinburgh and Chicago, had poisoned at least one person to death in each city before being convicted for murder by poison in 1881. Cream was sentenced to life but was released in July 1891 after his brother pleaded for leniency – allegedly bribing the authorities for good measure.

When a detective arrived at Lambeth Road to arrest Cream, he spotted a bottle full of strychnine pills – the method by which the victims had died. As he was arrested the doctor said: 'You have got the wrong man; fire away!'

Cream was convicted and sentenced to death. However, his motivation has never been clearly established. He was perhaps a sadist and was certainly greedy, trying to extort money from wealthy people by writing to them accusing them of the murders and offering his silence in return for a fee.

Less than a month after his conviction, on 15 November 1892, Dr Thomas Neill Cream was hanged on the gallows at Newgate prison by James Billington. Billington claimed that Cream's last words on the scaffold were 'I am Jack the –' but this attempt by Billington to claim that he had executed Jack the Ripper failed when it was established that Cream was in a US prison at the time of the Whitechapel murders.

The statue in the photo is of Sir Robert Clayton (1629-1707) a former Lord Mayor of London who was president of St Thomas's Hospital from 1692 until his death. The statue was erected in 1871, when St Thomas's Hospital moved here from its original home in Southwark. Cream would have passed it often (it is visible in the grounds of St Thomas's Hospital, from the Thameside walk of the Albert Embankment). A great deal of the rear section of the hospital dates back to the Victorian era.

25. The Peer of Perjury

◎ Peninsula Heights

◔ 93 Albert Embankment, SE1

⊖ Vauxhall station *(Mainline and Victoria Line)*

Peninsula Heights, a bland 15-storey 1960s tower block, previously known as Alembic House, was built for the United Nations Association in 1965 before it appeared as a location in the 60s classic *The Italian Job* and then the 70s not-so-classic *Sweeney!* – the film version of the television series.

Sometime in the 1970s, it was rumoured to be the home of certain MI6 departments (now based at No. 85, see page 308). The block was converted into flats in 1996, with film composer John Barry (*James Bond, Out of Africa*) originally in the penthouse, followed by Bernie Ecclestone and finally the former Tory politician, peer and current bestselling author (*Not a Penny More, Not a Penny Less, Kane and Abel, First Among Equals*), Jeffrey Archer.

In 1987, Jeffrey Archer appeared in lucky Court 13 in the Royal Courts of Justice in the Strand (see page 295), suing Express Newspapers for libel after the *Daily Star* newspaper alleged that Archer, then Deputy Chairman of the Conservative Party, had paid £70 to have sex with 35-year-old prostitute and devoted single mum, Monica Coghlan.

Even though an intermediary had been photographed handing Coghlan £2,000 in cash with which 'to go abroad' at Victoria station, and even after Coghlan identified him in court ('I had no difficulty seeing his face. I was lying on top of him the whole time'), the judge described Archer as 'worthy and healthy and sporting', and Archer won the case. He was awarded a record £500,000 in damages.

Fast-forward to 2001 and, by now a Lord, Archer was the Conservative candidate for London Mayor. Then Ted Francis, a TV producer and former friend of Archer's, claimed that the Tory candidate had asked him to provide an alibi for the night that the *Daily Star* alleged the Coghlan meeting took place.

The *News of the World* backed this up with taped discussions between Archer and Francis, in which Archer 'confessed' to not being with the other man on the specified date. In court, Francis said his alibi was intended to cover up Archer's affair with a former assistant. It was also alleged that Archer had a blank diary retrospectively filled in to 'prove' the alibi – a diary that was used in evidence during the 1987 libel action.

Archer was charged with two counts of perverting the course of justice, two counts of perjury and one of using a 'false instrument' (the supposedly bogus appointment book). Found guilty of the first four counts he was sentenced to four years in jail. Francis was cleared of perverting the course of justice.

In prison, Archer made the acquaintance of the would-be getaway-boat driver Kevin Meredith from the Dome Diamond robbery (see page 72). They got on so well that Archer gave him a mention in his book *A Prison Diary*. The disgraced politician recalls his barrister's advice never to believe anything he is told in prison, but adds: 'Kevin is so courteous and kind that I really do want to believe him.'

26. 72kb Supercomputers

◎ **Tintagel House**

◐ **Lambeth Palace Road/Albert Embankment , SE1**

⊖ **Vauxhall station** *(Mainline and Victoria Line)*

Tintagel House and Camelford House were both built in 1960 with contrasting stone and horizontal brick banding, and large rectangular windows, an effort designed to resemble the area's former waterside warehouses.

Tintagel House has been home to several of Scotland Yard's specialist units, including Child Protection, Counter-Terrorism and the National Public Order Intelligence Unit. It's also acted as the Yard's disciplinary wing, where officers accused of wrongdoing are brought before a board made up of the senior ranks who decide their fate.

Shortly after it opened it was used by the team — led by 'Nipper' Read — that had been brought together to put the Kray twins behind bars. Among the 20 or so members were head of the Murder Squad John du Rose, Superintendent Harry Mooney, Superintendent Don Adams and Chief Inspector Frank Cater.

The team was based here, as it was believed the Krays' influence was pervasive enough to reach into Scotland Yard — that corrupt officers might leak information. It would take the Kray Squad longer than they thought to bring the twins to justice, but they were ultimately successful (see page 90). It was from here that the dawn raid that would finally bring down the Krays was launched.

This building was also home to Scotland Yard's computer department, which was bombed by the Angry Brigade (see page 252) on 22 May 1971. However, the bomb barely caused any damage to the UK-designed, bungalow-sized, 5-tonne ICT 1301 mainframe. For the time this was a cutting edge piece of kit: it had an internal memory of about 72 kilobytes (about the same as the average Microsoft Word document) with the tape units holding just under 10 megabytes of information (equivalent to two digital music tracks).

Today, the police have come to rely on HOLMES2, a searchable database that sifts through millions of pieces of information looking for connections, patterns and, hopefully, a likely suspect. HOLMES2 can sometimes perform the work of a thousand investigators in the hunt for a suspect and help solve cases that would otherwise have been impossible.

27. The Thames Torso Murders of 1887–89

◎ Vauxhall Bridge (looking towards Pimlico and the Houses of Parliament)
◎ Vauxhall station *(Mainline and Victoria Line)*

In 1882, ferrymen, passers-by and the marine police pulled 544 corpses from the river Thames, of which 277 cases resulted in open verdicts. The majority of the remainder were suicides (see page 98).

The work of those trying to identify and pinpoint the cause of death of bodies pulled from the river is complicated by the river's movement, pollution and by wounds caused postmortem.

This was never more evident than when, in May 1887, a female torso was washed up on the shores of Rainham in Essex. In the following week, more body parts started to appear on other parts of the Thames shore, until the body was almost complete – although the head was never found.

Police surgeon Dr Thomas Bond – who would work on the Jack the Ripper case a year later (see page 164) – stated that whoever had dismembered this woman had a rough anatomical knowledge, but was not a medical man. Because of the level of decomposition, Dr Bond was unable to conclude that a 'violent act' had occurred, so at the inquest the unknown woman was recorded as being 'Found Dead'.

The following year, as Jack the Ripper fever gripped London, a woman's arm was recovered from the shore of Pimlico, barely a mile from the Houses of Parliament. Then, on 28 September, another arm was found on the opposite bank in Lambeth before finally, on 2 October, a female torso was discovered in the cellar of the construction site for Norman Shaw's New Scotland Yard building on the Embankment (see page 300). The press called the discovery the 'Whitehall Mystery'.

Dr Charles Hibbert, who examined one of the arms, stated, 'I thought the arm was cut off by a person who, while he was not necessarily an anatomist, certainly knew what he was doing – who knew where the joints were and cut them pretty regularly.'

In June 1889, parts of another woman were fished out of the Thames. One of her arms was later found thrown onto the riverside grounds of the house that had belonged to Mary Shelley, author of *Frankenstein* – a novel about a monster built from the amalgamation of various body parts. Although – like the others – the head of this victim was never found, her identity was revealed from other clues: Elizabeth Jackson, a suspected Chelsea prostitute.

On 10 September 1889, Constable William Pennett was on his beat when he found a female torso under a railway arch in Pinchin Street, Whitechapel. '[I]t was naked,' he told the inquest. 'I noticed that the head had been taken from the body, and that the legs were missing.'

This murder was eventually attributed to the Thames Torso Killer but, like the Ripper, the case was never solved.

28. A Short-Lived Agency

◉ Serious Organised Crime Agency (SOCA)

◓ Citadel Place, Spring Gardens, off Tinworth Street, Vauxhall, SE1

☎ 0370 496 7622

⊖ Vauxhall station *(Mainline and Victoria Line)*

Created on 1 April 2006, SOCA is an agglomeration of 4,200 officers from the investigative and intelligence sections of HM Customs Investigations into serious drug trafficking, the National Crime Squad (NCS) and the National Criminal Intelligence Service (NCIS).

Its aims are to gather more and better intelligence and to tackle major crime. SOCA spends 40 per cent of its operational effort on drug trafficking, 25 per cent on organised immigration crime, 10 per cent on fraud and 15 per cent on other organised crime. The remaining 10 per cent is devoted to supporting other law enforcement agencies. A key part of the agency's work is asset recovery – recovering money from organised crime.

The results so far have not been great. After its inception, SOCA's annual spend rocketed to £521m (for the financial year 2008–09). This was despite the fact that when SOCA started, no operations were in place for its 4,200 staff to investigate. Until then, there had just been a small group of senior managers trying to get things set up – an impossible task. There was no infrastructure and to many of its officers it seemed as if there was no plan.

To start with, an outdated list was produced of 'core nominals' (top criminals) and officers were instructed to go after them. Unfortunately, the list was so out of date that some of the criminals on the list had retired or died.

Figures were released in 2009, which showed that for every £15 of public money SOCA spent, just £1 was recovered from criminals.

In 2010, the government announced the abolition of SOCA in favour of a new UK-wide National Crime Agency (NCA), which was launched in 2013. The NCA's remit includes organised crime and border policing. It will also join forces with the child exploitation and online protection centre (CEOP). Officers will have far-ranging powers to fight crime but this is the third major revamp of organised-crime policing in 13 years – a sign of the problems the UK authorities have faced in tackling cross-border criminal networks.

29. The Prime Minister's Stowaways

◎ Government Car and Despatch Agency (GCDA) and Metropolitan
   Police Garages
◑ Ponton Road, SW8
⊖ Vauxhall station *(Mainline and Victoria Line)*

This high-security facility has been photographed from the north side of the
Thames to avoid making any accidental security breaches. It sits behind a
large modern unmarked building in front of the Post Office Depot and next to
Christie's Fine Art Auctioneers high security storage warehouse, and provides
vehicles to UK Government and Ministry of Defence VIPs, including Cabinet
Ministers. Carefully vetted drivers also transport sensitive official documents
across the UK. The facility also provides secure confidential waste handling and
destruction.

The area, which has attracted several high security storage facilities, will soon
be home to the new US Embassy, which is moving from its current location in
Grosvenor Square in Mayfair to Ponton Road.

In September 2007, an adapted dark-grey BMW 7 Series car – destined to
transport the then Prime Minister Tony Blair on official visits – arrived in the
Metropolitan Police Garages, just next door to the GCDA. With bullet-proof
windows, reinforced doors and several top-secret modifications, the car cost
£100,000. The Met Police's Counter-Terrorism Command had ordered the 7 Series
from the German car giant's HQ in Munich.

The car was in a container but when counter-terrorism officers opened it they
found four asylum seekers inside. A source later said: 'They had a nasty surprise
when they realised they were in a police yard. We had an even worse surprise
when we saw how they had arrived.' The lorry and its container should have been
impregnable. But the asylum seekers – from the Indian subcontinent – somehow
got inside in northern France.

The police arrested the asylum seekers and the car was returned to BMW, as
its security had been compromised.

30. A Serial Killer Leaves His Fingerprint

◎ Battersea Power Station
⊕ Kirtling Street, SW8
⊖ Battersea Park *(Mainline)*

After Identikit (see page 243) came Photo-Fit, invented by facial topographer Jacques Penry. Photo-Fit used photographs instead of line drawings, providing witnesses with a better selection of pictures from which to draw when recalling the crime.

Photo-Fit was first used after the murder of James Cameron in Islington in October 1970. The suspect's Photo-Fit was broadcast on the TV show *Police 5* and the face was recognised by a shop assistant. A customer had bought an umbrella from his shop in Victoria using a bad cheque, but had produced a firearms certificate to verify his identity. This led to the arrest of John Ernest Bennett, who was convicted of the murder.

The next stage was E-Fit, launched in October 1988, which allowed the police artist to alter features, using special software, to match a witness's description. This method was instrumental in catching London serial killer Colin Ireland.

In 1993, 39-year-old Ireland made a New Year's resolution to become a serial killer. A petty criminal and one of life's losers, he was fascinated with serial murderers. In March he travelled from his Southend-on-Sea home to the Coleherne pub in London's Old Brompton Road (261 Old Brompton Road, SW5 – now the Pembroke). At that time it was popular with gay men who went there looking to pick up sexual partners. Posing as a 'top' (the dominant partner in sado-masochism), it was here that Ireland met his first victim – a 45-year-old choreographer.

Together they returned to the other man's flat in Battersea, a short distance from the power station, where the choreographer willingly allowed Ireland to gag him with knotted condoms and bind him with cord to his four-poster bed. Ireland then beat the man before eventually pulling a plastic bag over his head. He left two teddy bears in an approximation of a '69' position on the bed next to his body.

The police assumed it was a sex game gone too far. At the time they generally had poor relations with the gay community, indeed they were accused of ignoring gay-related abuse and crime. Also, the day before Ireland's first victim's body was found, a new ruling had made sado-masochism between consenting adults illegal (British law does not recognise the possibility of consenting to bodily injury).

Ireland, who travelled with a 'murder bag' to assist him, evaded capture until he'd killed five men (four within 17 days of each other) – the number necessary to become classified as a serial killer. Finally, frustrated at the police's lack of progress, Ireland contacted them anonymously to tell shocked detectives that the murders were all linked.

On 21 July, Ireland turned himself in after seeing a remarkably accurate E-Fit image on a wanted poster. He initially tried to explain away his contact with his final victim, a 41-year-old chef, as entirely innocent, but confessed when told that his fingerprint had been found at the scene of his first murder.

Ireland died of natural causes in Wakefield prison on 21 February 2012.

31. We're Only Here for De Beers

◎ **Millennium Dome (O₂)**
🜨 **Greenwich Peninsula, SE10**
☏ **020 8463 2000**
ⓦ **www.theo2.co.uk**
🕐 **Daily from 9am, last admission is at 1am**
⊖ **North Greenwich Tube** *(Jubilee Line)*

At an unveiling ceremony in De Beers' Charterhouse Street HQ (see page 130), the 11 blue diamonds that made up the £200m De Beers Millennium Diamond collection orbited the Millennium Star, a 203.04-carat, internally and externally flawless pear-shaped jewel. Indeed, it was so perfect that, uniquely, De Beers decided not to 'spoil' it with any branded security.

De Beers announced that the diamonds would be displayed in the Millennium Dome's Money Zone throughout 2000 (this was in between what is now the O₂ Bubble and entrance G to the O₂).

Putting one of the world's most valuable diamonds in what turned out to be a poorly guarded tent in Greenwich (after announcing it was unmarked) turned out to be too much of a temptation for a gang of South London criminals who decided to crash their way into the Dome on a JCB.

After a couple of false starts the raid went ahead at 9.30am on 7 November 2000 when the JCB, driven by 38-year-old Ray Betson, crashed through a gate to the north of the main entrance, heading for the Money Zone.

With Betson on the JCB were William Thomas Cockram (48), whose job was to break the security glass using a nail gun, Bob Adams (55), who would then finish the job with a sledgehammer, and Aldo Ciarrocchi (29), armed with smoke bombs, who would keep onlookers back.

Outside on the Thames in a speedboat was Kevin Meredith, waiting near The Slice of Reality (an art installation, which is still there) to whisk the gang away across the Thames where Terry Millman (56) was in turn waiting in the getaway van near Bow Creek.

As the men launched their attack on the diamond display, the people who were near the vault reacted very strangely – they pulled guns from prams and rubbish bins before throwing stun grenades at the vault area. 100 armed officers from the Flying Squad had been lying in wait. They'd also replaced the diamonds with very good fakes. Outside, Meredith was trapped by three boatloads of armed officers who then spotted Millman.

At the Old Bailey, Ray Betson, the leader of the 'Diamond Geezers', who'd grown up on the Walworth Road near the Elephant and Castle (see page 43), was sentenced to 18 years (reduced to 15 on appeal), as was Cockram. Ciarrocchi was given 15 years (reduced to 12 on appeal). Meredith was sentenced to five years. Millman, who had cancer, died while awaiting trial. Adams, also sent down for 15 years, died from a heart attack while in prison.

As to who wanted to buy the diamonds – well, the intelligence suggests that a Russian gem smuggler based in Spain would have cut and resold them on the black market for several million pounds.

32. London's New Prison

◉ **Belmarsh Prison**

⌂ **Western Way, Thamesmead, SE28**

⊖ **Plumstead station** *(Mainline)*

This 933-capacity prison, covering 60 acres (47 acres are inside the mile-long perimeter wall) and costing £100 million, opened in 1991, and was the first London prison to be built in the 20th century – the first new prison, in fact, since Wormwood Scrubs in 1874.

All cells are en-suite and there's a gym, indoor tennis and an all-weather football pitch (some more conservative critics have described Belmarsh as a 'holiday camp'). It serves as both a local prison for Southeast London and a Category-A area for high-risk remand prisoners, including members of the IRA and the extremists behind the plot to blow up British aircraft using liquid bombs in 2006.

A Crown Court and a Magistrates' Court are connected to the prison by an underground tunnel. In 2010, a separate Young Offenders Institution contained within Belmarsh's perimeter, named Isis, was opened.

Former Conservative Party Chairman Jeffrey Archer, a member of the House of Lords, was brought here after being sentenced to four years for perjury and perverting the course of justice (see page 60), as was former Tory MP, Jonathan Aitken (see page 303).

Other notable inmates have included child murderer Ian Huntley and the 'Night Stalker', Delroy Grant, one of the UK's most prolific sex offenders. Grant spent almost two decades stalking the streets of South London, burgling, raping and sexually assaulting the elderly. He struck more than 200 times.

Barry George, wrongly convicted of the murder of TV presenter Jill Dando, spent time here before he was retried and acquitted in 2008. Dando was shot dead on the doorstep of her Fulham home in West London in 1999. The search for her murderer continues.

On 22 August 2012, 71-year-old former fugitive tycoon Asil Nadir was convicted of ten counts of theft amounting to £28.6 million. After the guilty verdict was pronounced, Nadir was taken to Belmarsh – quite a change from the Mayfair house he'd been renting for £20,000 per week during the trial.

Nadir fled Britain for Northern Cyprus in 1993 and was found to have plundered millions from his Polly Peck International business empire between 1987 and 1990. Beginning his career selling clothes in the East End, Nadir transformed Polly Peck, a failing ladies' fashion group, into a multi-million pound conglomerate and Stock Exchange star. It crashed in 1990 with debts of £550 million.

As Nadir was sentenced to ten years, he may have regretted returning to London earlier that year to, as he said, 'Clear his name'. However, he maintains his innocence and has said that he will appeal.

No one has yet escaped from Belmarsh, although in 2010 three inmates were caught with a rope they were planning to lob over the perimeter wall.

On the Bloody Trail
of the Kray Twins

10

Bethnal Green

A107

Three Colts Lane

Cambridge Heath Road

11

Barnsley Street

Collingwood Street

Whitechapel Road

Whitechapel

01

13

12

It's hard to see why these two psychopathic thugs who raped, pillaged and murdered throughout their adult lives, abusing people without a second's thought, taking advantage of the weak to make a dishonest living, have been so long lionised.

Perhaps their fellow East Enders, who had been – over the past couple of centuries or so – left to fester in their own poverty by the establishment, were pleased to see that someone was at last striking back on their behalf, someone able to penetrate the sick heart of this other world and start to destroy it, while remaining untouched by the law.

Ronald 'Ronnie' and Reginald 'Reggie' Kray began their violent careers by running several protection rackets from their base, a run-down local snooker club. They were soon involved in hijacking and armed robbery and used stolen cash to buy clubs, pubs and houses. In 1960, they acquired Esmeralda's Barn, a Knightsbridge nightclub, which attracted celebrities.

The Krays also grew rich – assisted by banker Alan Cooper – and their money, along with their notoriety, helped bring them into contact with some of the era's biggest political and showbusiness names, turning them into celebrities of a sort. Friends included the artist Francis Bacon, Tory peer Lord Boothby (a neighbour of Lord Lucan, see page 320) and actress Barbara Windsor.

By the mid-60s Ronnie and Reg Kray were of great concern to police and government alike. 'The Firm', as their gang was known, was more than a loose, rag-tag group of criminals; members were loyal and prepared to do anything to advance the Firm's aims.

Worst of all, as far as the authorities were concerned, they were well organised. It looked as though the Krays' criminal network could last for generations. Fortunately, because Ronnie was as mad as a box of frogs, with Reggie not far behind, Scotland Yard's job was eventually made easier than it might have been and both brothers were put behind bars.

01. Turn right out of Whitechapel Tube station and walk to the site of the Grave Maurice at 269 Whitechapel Road.

Established in 1723, rebuilt and moved a short distance to this location in 1874, the Maurice closed in 2010 and most recently operated as a bookies. Sadly nothing of the interior remains – the table where the Krays sat lasted until the early 1990s, as did most of the 1950s furnishings.

For decades, jazz played at night for the doctors and consultant surgeons from the Royal London Hospital across the road. Actress Diana Dors – a friend of the Krays – once signed the visitors' book.

When Detective Chief Superintendent Leonard 'Nipper' Read, head of the Murder Squad and the man tasked to put the Krays out of business (see Tintagel House, page 63), found out that Ronnie Kray was about to give a TV interview here, he was curious to see his opponent in the flesh.

Read snuck into the pub beforehand and sat sipping his pint near the window. He later recalled how a large American car drew up and a smart, besuited bodyguard with a gun-shaped bulge against in his chest climbed out, checked the pub, checked the street and then, deciding all was well, opened the rear door of the car. Ronnie emerged, every inch the image of Al Capone, dressed in a full-length cashmere coat.

The Grave Maurice was a regular meeting place for the Krays. It was where they met George Cornell, a childhood friend of Ronnie's. Cornell had moved to South London, where he joined rivals the Richardsons (see page 43) acting as the gang's enforcer. He was also the Richardsons' negotiator.

At the meeting, an argument broke out between Cornell and car dealer Thomas 'Ginger' Marks. Ronnie said he acted as 'peacemaker' that night, but he would eventually shoot Cornell dead at the Blind Beggar.

02. **Exit Whitechapel Road turning right into Vallance Road and walk south, passing under the railway bridge. On the right just after the bridge is a row of new-ish housing association buildings. These are on the site of 178 Vallance Road, the Kray twins' family home.**

In 1939, when the twins were just six, the Kray family moved from Shoreditch to 178 Vallance Road. The house was tiny, with no bathroom, and the toilet was in the garden. The streets around here were a ghetto, with gambling dens, dodgy pubs, smoky billiard halls and brothels tucked away in the side streets. Unemployment, poverty and crime were all around; in many ways little had changed from the days of the Ripper.

'Mad' Jimmy Kray, the twins' paternal grandfather, was a stallholder in Petticoat Lane and was renowned for his drinking and fighting.

Their maternal grandfather, Jimmy Lee, the 'Southpaw Cannonball', had in his youth been a bare-knuckle boxer and then a music-hall entertainer. Jimmy's son Charles, the twins' father, was a 'pesterer', a travelling trader who went up and down the country buying and selling silver, gold and clothing. He made a decent living and was able to provide his sons with a better lifestyle than most other families in the neighbourhood.

Charles was away a lot, so the twins were raised almost solely by their mother, Violet. A local beauty, Violet was a warm and softly spoken generous woman and she built her life around her three sons (Charlie junior was born six years before the twins) – about whom she was extremely possessive.

Apart from Charles, the Krays were close-knit. Violet's sisters Rose and May were her neighbours, and her brother Jimmy slept in the living room.

When the twins had grown up, No. 178 became 'Fort Vallance', where they kept a gun and sword armoury under the floorboards. It remained their gangland headquarters until 1966, when the council pulled the row of crumbling houses down.

03. Facing the railway arches, turn right off Vallance Road into Dunbridge Street and carry on until the junction with Ramsey Street, where the former Cheshire Street Public Baths building still sits.

The Public Baths and Wash Houses Act of 1846 led to the establishment of public baths such as this one. They quickly became essential public services, remaining in use well into the 20th century. Before World War II, they recorded 800,000 visits each year. The twins went here most days.

Even after the War, many Londoners continued to live in old Victorian sub-standard buildings. As late as 1971, over 500,000 Greater London households had access only to a shared bathroom or none at all. Public baths and washhouses like this provided hot water and laundry facilities. A hot bath with towel cost one penny. Today, as is the way with many public buildings in East London, the building has been converted into flats.

Next door to the bath house is Repton Amateur Boxing Club, the most famous amateur boxing club in Britain. Founded and funded by Repton College in 1884, it was an East London mission for the underprivileged boys of Bethnal Green and surrounding areas until the college withdrew its support in 1971. Despite this, it remains a boxing club today. Olympic champion Audley Harrison trained here.

The Kray twins learned to box here as boys. They made the finals of the London Schools Boxing Championship three times – and appeared on the same bill in December 1951 when they had the distinction of boxing in a middleweight boxing championship held at the Royal Albert Hall. The twins even fought one another in an exhibition match when a fair came to Bethnal Green. In total, Ronnie fought six professional bouts and won four of them, while Reggie won all six of his. Their boxing careers came to an end when, on 2 March 1952, they were called up for national service (see page 94).

In January 1965, local villain Freddie 'Brown Bread Fred' Foreman (involved in the 1983 Security Express robbery, see page 149) shot Ginger Marks dead outside the club. Foreman claimed that this was in retaliation for Marks shooting Foreman's brother in the legs. Marks died instantly. His body was never found. It's rumoured he's in the foundations of the Hammersmith Flyover.

Although Foreman was later arrested and brought to trial, he was acquitted of the murder, after which he later admitted he was guilty in an ITV documentary. Under the double jeopardy rule he could not be tried for the same crime twice – something that has since been changed.

04. **Wood Close School (now William Davis Primary School) is a little further along Cheshire Street.**

The twins went to school here until they were 11 years old and by all accounts caused little trouble. Being, in the school board's words, one of the 'poorest and least accessible parts of London', the school was considered of 'special difficulty'. In consequence, teaching staff sent here received an extra allowance.

Although the area still has problems with poverty and social exclusion, today's 200-pupil school was recently judged 'outstanding' by the schools inspectors Ofsted.

You adored and loved me from the start
From the day I was born you gave me your heart
For the years you loved and nursed me with care
I'm really so thankful and very much aware
That without you, no life would be there

From the first verse of a poem the young Krays wrote in honour of their mother, Violet.

05. **Next to the school is the Carpenters Arms, a great place for refreshments.**

Now a small, cosy and only slightly fashionable pub, serving around 50 different ales, the Carpenters was once London's most notorious pub, thanks to its owners, Reggie and Ronnie Kray.

The twins bought it in 1967 for Violet and hung their boxing gloves over the Carpenters' crest behind the bar. The bar counter (still there) was said to have been made from coffin lids. The pub was papered in a faux Regency style with striped burgundy wallpaper, matching their West End nightclub.

On 28 October 1967 the twins had been drinking at the Carpenters when they left for a house in Evering Road, Stoke Newington. They waited for the arrival of Jack 'The Hat' McVitie, a local villain with whom the twins had fallen out. Two friends had told McVitie to expect a party – instead he arrived to find the twins and asked: 'Where's all the birds, all the booze?'

Reggie replied by pointing a gun at McVitie's head, but it jammed. McVitie lost his hat as he tried to escape through a window but he couldn't squeeze through and was dragged back into the room.

'Why are you doing this, Reg?' he shouted.

Reggie grabbed a carving knife and stabbed McVitie in the face, and then repeatedly in the chest, then the stomach and, after he fell to the floor, through the throat, impaling him to the floorboards. By the time he was done McVitie was so cut up, his liver slid out from his body.

Members of the Firm wrapped McVitie's body in some bedding and carried him out into a car. Kray associate Tony Lambrianou drove, followed in another car by his brother Chris and another man.

They decided to leave the body south of the Thames in the hope that the police would immediately suspect the Richardsons. They left it near the home of a close friend of the Krays, however, so their brother Charlie, with the help of Ronnie Hart and Freddie Foreman, removed and disposed of McVitie's body. It was never found. Reggie, meanwhile, threw the gun and knife into the Regent's Canal from a humped-back bridge known as Suicide Bridge.

→ **06.** Turn right immediately after the Carpenters into St Matthew's Row and St Matthew's Church is on the right.

The funerals of Violet, Ronnie, Reggie and Charlie Kray were all held in St Matthew's Church.

In 1982, when they were 49, the twins were let out of prison for their mother's funeral – Violet had died of cancer, aged 72. It was the first time they'd been out since they were sent down for life in 1969. Among the mourners at the funeral was family friend, the actress Diana Dors, dressed in black, wearing sunglasses and carrying a bouquet. The brothers arrived separately, both handcuffed to a prison guard and surrounded by police officers.

Ronnie Kray, who had by then been declared criminally insane, had to be brought from Broadmoor. Reggie, who was brought in from Parkhurst on the Isle of Wight, was still being held as a maximum-security Category 'A' prisoner.

Ronnie died of a heart attack in Broadmoor on 17 March 1995.

Reggie died from bladder cancer on 1 October 2000, aged 66 – by then he'd served 32 years for murder. Although never officially released, he was allowed out of prison on compassionate grounds to receive treatment at the Norfolk and Norwich hospital. His wife Roberta, 41, was at his bedside.

Charlie died a few months before Reggie in Parkhurst in April 2000, aged 73, while serving a 12-year sentence for masterminding a cocaine-smuggling operation.

The Krays are all buried together in the family plot at Chingford Mount cemetery in East London. Reggie was buried to the sound of Frank Sinatra singing 'My Way'. At his funeral, Mark Goldstein, the Krays' solicitor, told the congregation that the man they had come to remember was 'an icon of the 20th century' who possessed 'an amazing sense of humour'.

Hundreds of people braved the cold weather to listen to the service, which was piped outside to the churchyard. The male mourners sported long black coats, black leather jackets, dark glasses, tattoos, chunky gold rings and stern expressions.

Police motorcycle outriders provided an escort for the nine-mile journey to the family plot at Chingford Mount cemetery.

07. Continue past the church and cross Bethnal Green Road into Turin Street. Walk all the way to the end of the road, turn left onto Gosset Road. On the left is the Bethnal Green Academy, formerly the Daniel Street School.

The twins were 11 when they started school at Daniel Street. It was here that they got into their first scrap and realised that boxing would be a useful skill. Their older brother Charlie, who was already boxing in the Navy, initially trained them using one of his kitbags, stuffed and strung up upstairs at Vallance Road.

It was also here that the twins pretended to be one another to confuse their teachers, something they repeated as adults to great effect.

In 1958 Ronnie was sentenced to three years for an assault and a short while later developed 'prison psychosis' and had to be put in a straitjacket after he learned that his Aunt Rose had died. He was declared insane and sent to Long Grove in Surrey, a Victorian lunatic asylum a mile from Epsom. When Reggie came to visit him, they wore the same clothes and Ronnie simply put on Reggie's coat and walked out of the asylum, leaving Reggie to tell the officers who only noticed an hour later: 'It's not as if I've done anything wrong, I've just been sitting here waiting for a cup of tea.'

08. **Return down Turin Street, turn left into Bethnal Green Road and stop at St James the Great Church on the junction of Pollard Row.**

Reggie married 21-year-old Frances Elsie Shea here in April 1965. She'd known him since she was 16. They spent their honeymoon in Athens, where the marriage was not consummated. Once back in London, Reggie sent his young wife to live with his mother. The marriage lasted eight weeks – although it was never officially annulled. Frances changed her name back to Shea before she committed suicide two years later. Her funeral service was held here before she was interred in the Kray family plot.

A confidential Home Office file revealed that Frances' mother wanted official approval to remove the remains of her daughter from the 'showpiece' Kray family plot in Chingford cemetery so she could be reburied in a different grave under her maiden name. Reggie, who owned the plot of land, refused.

Ronnie never married – it was well known that he preferred men – and he made no attempt to keep this fact a secret.

While Violet was comfortable with her son's homosexuality, his father and older brother were horrified. Ronnie had a number of regular sexual partners and strong friendships with other homosexual men – including Conservative politician Lord Boothby, for whom he obtained youths and received political favours in return.

09. **On the other side of Bethnal Green Road, opposite St James', is a London institution: Pellicci's Café.**

This tiny 'caff' has stood here for 112 years and has even been given Grade II listed status thanks to the ornate handiwork of regular customer and carpenter Achille Capocci, back in 1946.

Owned by Nevio Pellicci (born above the shop 86 years ago), the caff has been in the family since it was built.

The inspectors who listed it lovingly described it as having a 'stylish shop front of custard Vitrolite panels, steel frame and lettering as well as a rich Deco-style marquetry panelled interior... an increasingly rare example of the intact and stylish Italian café that flourished in London in the inter-war years'.

Around 2,000 Italian-owned cafés and coffee bars sprang up in the UK after the end of World War II. Most of them have gone now, thanks to high rents and the invasion of the coffee chains.

Pellicci's was a favoured meeting place of the Krays and the Firm and has since attracted many celebrities thanks to its king-sized breakfasts and down-to-earth charm. Pellicci remembers the Krays as 'gentlemen', once telling a journalist: 'They were children when I started serving them. They were very respectful, charming. If my mother was behind the counter and someone swore they would ask them to show some respect.'

→ 10. Stay on the same side of the road and walk east towards Bethnal Green Tube station. W. English and Son, Funeral Directors, is just before the railway bridge.

This is the undertakers where all the Krays lay at rest before being taken on a procession through the area they once lorded over.

For the last Kray, it was quite a show. Reggie's funeral on 11 October 2000 began at 10am with the hearse being drawn by six black stallions with feathered head plumes. The carriage was adorned with elaborate wreaths. Behind the hearse followed a procession of 16 black funeral limousines. One carried a wreath from Barbara Windsor, the actress, whose card said simply 'With love'.

It was a small affair compared to the funeral of the twins' mother, Violet. When she made the same trip in 1982 it is said more than 60,000 people lined the route from the undertakers to St Matthew's Church, a mile away. At Reggie's, the minders outnumbered the mourners. The Krays' star had truly faded.

Reggie had been allowed out of jail to lead two funeral processions (accompanied by three guards) for his brother Ron and then for Charlie. His own funeral was a traditional, respectful East End send-off but one can't help recall how the Firm used to get rid of the bodies of dead gangsters. They'd be put in a coffin with an innocent body before the lids were hammered down. Grieving relatives never knew they were burying a complete stranger with their loved one.

→ 11. Walk back along Bethnal Green Road and turn left down Wilmot Street. Cross the junction with Three Colts Lane into Tapp Street, walk underneath the railway arches and stop at No. 8, formerly the Lion Pub, now residential flats.

The Lion was commonly known as the 'Widow' to the Krays, named after the landlady, whose husband had recently passed away.

It was at this typical East End boozer, on 9 April 1966, that Ronnie heard South London gangster George Cornell was having a drink at the Blind Beggar pub in Whitechapel. Outraged, he summoned a driver and one of his henchmen, Ian Barrie, aka Scots Ian.

Ronnie wanted revenge for the murder of Richard Hart, who had been killed in a fight over the control of the fruit machine market with the Richardsons (pictured below, see page 43) in March 1966, at Mr Smith's Club in Rushey Green, Catford. Ron went home to get his gun and then made his way to the Blind Beggar.

⟶ 12. Continue south down to the end of Tapp Street and follow the road round into Barnsley Street. Turn right into Collingwood Street and follow this road into Darling Row before turning right into Cambridge Heath Road and then right again into Whitechapel Road until you are within sight of the Blind Beggar at No. 337.

Cornell, who had previously angered Ronnie Kray by calling him a 'fat poof', was sitting on a stool beside the small, U-shaped bar and supping a light ale. When Ronnie Kray and Scots Ian walked in, the jukebox was playing the Walker Brothers' 'The Sun Ain't Gonna Shine Anymore'.

Cornell turned round, saw Kray and exclaimed, 'Well, look who's here then.' They were his last words. Ron took careful aim and put a bullet between Cornell's eyes. At that moment the needle of the jukebox stuck in the middle of the song on the word 'anymore … anymore … anymore …'

At first, intimidation prevented any witnesses from cooperating with police. But the Met, led by Nipper Read, later came close to nabbing the Krays after they questioned their financier Alan Cooper about his involvement in an attempted car-bombing (see page 272). Through Cooper the police thought there might be enough evidence against the Krays to convict them.

The twins were arrested at their flat in Bunhill Row, EC1, on 9 May 1968 and taken to West End Central police station in Savile Row (see page 259). Once in custody, witnesses slowly started to emerge and give evidence to the police team.

The Old Bailey trial at Court No. 1 – for the murder of McVitie – lasted 39 days, a record for a murder trial (it was also the most expensive). Throughout the trial, police with walkie-talkie radios patrolled the Old Bailey and guarded all the entrances and exits. Sixty policemen kept a 24-hour watch on the jury, following them home from court and even down the pub, making sure they couldn't be intimidated.

The Krays remained calm throughout and at one point Ronnie told the judge that if he had not been required in court he would 'probably have been having tea with Judy Garland'.

The jury deliberated for almost seven hours before returning the unanimous guilty verdict for the murder of Jack McVitie. Charlie Kray was found guilty of being an accessory to the murder of McVitie – helping to dispose of the body – and was jailed for ten years. Ronnie was also found guilty of the murder of George Cornell.

The Kray twins were both sentenced to life imprisonment with a recommendation they should be detained for a minimum of 30 years – the longest sentences ever passed at the Old Bailey for murder.

13. **Whitechapel station is a little further west down Whitechapel Road and the tour ends here.**

Today and too often, the East End is seen as the 'friendly face' of crime, with films, books and television programmes displaying the criminal fraternity of the Krays' era as 'rough diamonds' who abided by a criminal code. East End gangsters were tough but fair, charismatic and sometimes glamorous, attracting celebrities and gossip columnists alike.

Recent books spawned by retired East End gangsters like Mad Frank reinforce these ideas, as does the national press. They are wrong to do so. The East End criminals were just as greedy and callous as any other criminal, putting their own interests above anyone else's. The Krays were the embodiment of this and that is how they should be remembered.

The tabloid newspapers, in particular, were never able to resist the criminal allure of the Krays. Some years after the twins had been imprisoned one well-known red top ran a story which featured a photograph, smuggled out of prison, showing Reggie enjoying a cup of tea. The headline read: 'I Could Murder a McVitie!'

EAST

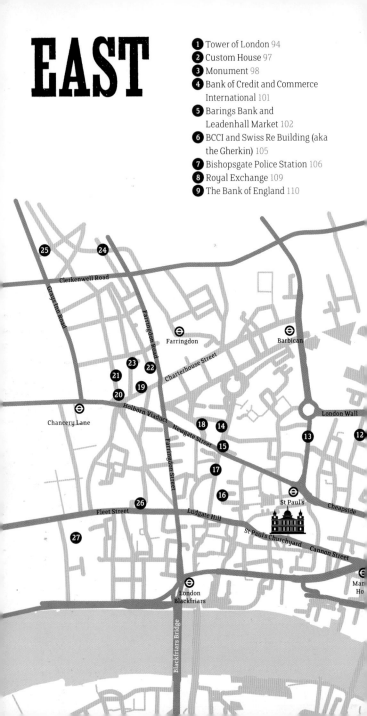

1. Captain Blood and Krays Incarcerated

◎ Tower of London

⌂ Tower Hill, EC3

☎ 0844 482 7799

🖥 www.hrp.org.uk/TowerOfLondon

🕐 1 Mar-31 Oct: Tues-Sat 9am-5.30pm, Sun-Mon 10am-5.30pm; 1 Nov-29 Feb: Tues-Sat 9am-4.30pm, Sun-Mon 10am-4.30pm

💷 Adult £19, Child £9.50, Concessions £16, Family £50. Discounts are available by booking online.

⊖ Tower Hill Tube *(District and Circle Lines)* and Tower Gateway station *(Docklands Light Railway)*

William I originally built on this patch of land shortly after 1066, so it has been used by British monarchs for almost a thousand years. Today, this 18-acre space is home to the most perfect medieval fortress in Britain. The Tower of London has been a palace, prison and a place of execution, and still guards the Crown Jewels.

In 1671 Irishman Colonel Blood tried to steal the Crown Jewels after befriending the keeper and his family – suggesting their daughter might marry his wealthy nephew. On 9 May 1671, Blood arrived with his 'nephew' and some friends and was let into the Tower. He knocked out the keeper with a mallet, grabbed the crown and flattened it with said mallet before stuffing it down his trousers – turning it into a magisterial codpiece.

The keeper quickly regained consciousness and began to shout, 'Murder, Treason!' Blood and his accomplices scarpered, but he was arrested by the Iron-Gate, after trying to shoot one of the guards.

In custody, Blood stubbornly demanded: 'I'll answer to none but the King himself.' He knew the monarch had a reputation for liking bold scoundrels and when he was finally brought before King Charles II, Blood told him that the Crown Jewels were not worth the £100,000 they were valued at, but only £6,000. Charles was highly amused.

The King then asked Blood, 'What if I should give you your life?'

'I would endeavour to deserve it, Sire!' Blood replied.

Not only was Blood pardoned, the King gave him Irish lands worth £500 a year. Blood became a familiar figure around London and made frequent appearances at Court until his surprisingly mundane death from an illness in 1680.

A notable 20th-century prisoner was Sir Roger Casement, held in the Tower during World War I, after planning, with German help, the Easter Rising of 1916 against British rule in Ireland. John Ellis hanged Casement at Pentonville prison on 3 August 1916 (see page 180).

The Kray twins also spent a week locked up in the Tower in 1952 after Ron knocked out their corporal, who'd foolishly tried to stop them going home on their first day of compulsory national service. Young Ronnie and Reggie's military service ended with a court martial and six months in a Shepton Mallet prison – where they learned a great deal about a life of crime from their fellow inmates.

2. **Hunting Drug Dealers**

◎ Custom House

⬤ Lower Thames Street, EC3

⊖ Monument Tube *(Circle and District Lines)*

The first Custom House was built around 1275 to collect duties on imported goods. It was replaced by a larger building in 1378 during which time Geoffrey Chaucer (1343-1400), author of *The Canterbury Tales*, was Controller of Customs. In 1559 it had to be rebuilt after a fire. This building perished in the Great Fire of 1666. Like so much of the City, it was rebuilt by Sir Christopher Wren. Wren's Custom House, completed in 1671, was the grandest yet.

The current version is a replica of Wren's, which was destroyed in another fire in 1714 and the photograph here shows the grottier side of the Grade I listed building, built with Portland stone, which faces Lower Thames Street. The interior is unremarkable except for the severe-looking Long Room, with Doric pilasters on 15-foot-tall pedestals, an oval, panelled ceiling and corniced doors and windows. This room, 190 feet in length used to be the main public office of the Customs Service, where officials processed all paperwork regarding customs duties payable on cargoes from behind lamp-lit desks. Below it are fireproof cellars, originally built to store gunpowder and alcohol seized by Customs, which exploded during yet another fire in 1814, leading to a detonation so large that debris was blasted as far as Hackney Marshes.

More recently, this rather dirty-looking building has been home to some of the most elite and secretive crime-fighting teams in the UK. Among them was Alpha, which used phone-intercept technology to trap some of Britain's biggest drug dealers. When the new Serious Organised Crime Agency (see page 67) came into existence in 2006 Alpha was disbanded and its officers were absorbed into the new crime-fighting agency.

Specialist investigative teams that hunt major heroin and cocaine dealers are still based here. The profits to be made from drugs, particularly Class A drugs, are phenomenal, so dealers never stop trying to smuggle them through London's airports. In 2009 Customs officers based here were behind the discovery of around 165kg of heroin in freight at Heathrow, believed to be the biggest seizure of its kind ever at the airport. The detection led to an international investigation, a number of arrests and further large seizures in the UK and South Africa. In total, £25m worth of heroin and cannabis destined for UK streets were seized.

3. Suicide Was Easy – and Illegal

◎ Monument
🜊 Fish Street Hill, EC2
☎ 0207 626 2717
Ⓦ www.themonument.info
🕐 Daily 9.30am-5.30pm (last admission 5pm)
💷 Adults £3, Concessions £2, Child £1.50
⊜ Monument Tube *(District and Circle Lines)*

Erected in memory of the Great Fire of 1666, the 61.5-metre column containing a 311-step spiral staircase was built between 1671 and 1677 and is the tallest 'isolated stone column in the world'.

Just before 10am on 11 September 1839, 23-year-old Margaret Moyes approached the porter at the Monument and told him she was going to meet friends there, but after a 20-minute chat she paid her sixpence and ascended alone. Moyes took the quick way down, crashing into an ornament on the side of the building as she fell, before severing her arm when she hit the surrounding railing.

Murder usually caused sensation among the Victorians, while suicide – tinged with disgrace – was less talked about. Families tried to hide a relative's suicide for a number of reasons. It was illegal, considered immoral, and the Crown took any property belonging to a proven suicide.

News about Moyes spread quickly. The *Observer* wrote:

> Her left arm, near the shoulder, came in contact with the bar, and was so violently severed that the part cut off flew over the iron railings several yards into the square. After striking the bar, the body fell in a tub containing a lilac plant, which it broke in pieces, as well as several flower pots, placed on the right side of the door. Not a sign of life, except some contortions of the muscles of the legs and arms, was discernible on the body when it was picked up.

Crowds flocked to the scene for days afterwards, wanting to know why Moyes had committed suicide. There was no straightforward answer.

A few weeks later, in October 1839, Richard Hawes, a 15-year-old servant-boy, was fired from his job at the home of a surgeon. He went to the Monument and leaped to his death. Hawes had talked about Moyes to the other servants. It took one more suicide, that of Jane Cooper, a servant-girl, on 19 August 1842, before demands to enclose the viewing area in an iron cage were met.

Suicide remained a crime in England and Wales until 1961. *The Times* reported that 5,387 failed suicide attempts were recorded in 1956 and that 613 people were prosecuted – 33 were sent to prison. Hangman John Ellis (see page 180) was spared punishment for attempting suicide in 1924. 'If your aim had been as true as the drops you have given it would have been a bad job for you,' the court told him. 'Your life has been given back to you, and turn it to good use in atonement.' Ellis hung on for another eight years, until 1932, when he cut his throat with a razor.

4. Bank of Crooks and Cocaine International

◎ aka Bank of Credit and Commerce International

⦿ 100 Leadenhall, EC3

⊖ Liverpool Street station *(Mainline, Central, Circle and Hammersmith & City Lines)* and Aldgate Tube *(Metropolitan and Circle Lines)*

Agha Hasan Abedi founded the Bank of Credit and Commerce International in Luxembourg in 1972. Abedi was born in India in 1922 to a lowly rent collector and worked his way up through the banking system until in the late 1960s he struck gold when Sheikh Zayed, the ruler of Abu Dhabi, entrusted Abedi with the billions made from his newly found oil reserves.

Abedi persuaded Sheikh Zayed to become one of BCCI's founding investors. Abedi pitched his new bank to the Muslim world as an alternative to the 'Jewish-dominated' banks of New York. He knew that wealthy Arabs liked to regard their bank as a home of sorts and so the BCCI branches were luxuriously furnished. By the mid-1980s there were branches all over the world, including a prime spot in London's Park Lane (taken over by squatters after the bank's collapse).

At its peak in the 1980s, the bank had 14,000 employees, 400 offices in 72 countries, 1.3 million depositors and more than $20 billion in assets, at least on paper. Its high interest rates drew in many surprising investors, from local UK councils (including Westminster) to presidents and prime ministers. Abedi mixed with world leaders, including the Pope and UK Prime Minister James Callaghan – and made donations to their favourite charitable causes.

In 1989, the BCCI was found to have engaged in drugs money laundering for General Noriega of Panama. Then it was revealed it had trafficked in arms for Abu Nidal. And in 1990, US authorities acted against the bank when they suspected it had taken control of First American Bank of Washington by stealth. The pressure took its toll on Abedi, who had had a heart attack in 1988, and in 1990 he ceded power to his assistant, Swaleh Naqvi.

In July 1991 the bank was forcibly shut down by regulators around the world. It owed $16 billion and the battle over whose fault this was – between the Bank of England and the bank's creditors – lasted almost ten years. The court case made history for the two longest opening speeches – 199 days for the Bank of England, 80 for Deloitte, BCCI's liquidators. The case became so complex that the two sides were separated by a stack of files five feet high, dubbed the Berlin Wall, and the legal bills rose to over £100m. However, most of the money was recovered – the creditors have so far been repaid 81p for every £1 they lost.

The Serious Fraud Office (see page 142) investigated and successfully prosecuted a number of people. Although Abedi faced criminal charges in several countries, including the United States, and was convicted in absentia in the United Arab Emirates, Pakistani authorities refused to extradite him. He died in 1995 seven years after he underwent a heart transplant – disappointed, ill and in obscurity. The BCCI was later dubbed 'Bank of Crooks and Cocaine International'.

5. How to Blow a Billion

◎ Barings Bank and Leadenhall Market
◐ Formerly of 8 Bishopsgate EC2, junction of Leadenhall Market, 1a
   Leadenhall Market, Gracechurch Street, EC3
Ⓦ www.leadenhallmarket.co.uk
◐ Public areas of Leadenhall Market are normally open 24 hours a day,
   market stalls operate Monday to Friday
◉ Liverpool Street station *(Mainline, Central, Circle and Hammersmith &
   City Lines)*

Established in 1762 by John and Francis Baring in nearby Queen Street, this was London's oldest merchant bank (it helped fund the Napoleonic Wars and its more recent customers included Queen Elizabeth II). It was famous for its 'My word is my bond' approach to banking. Barings moved to Mincing Lane and Devonshire Square before settling in Bishopsgate in 1805, where it remained until 1995.

In early 1994 Nick Leeson, Barings' 25-year-old chief trader on the Singapore Monetary Exchange, started losing money on the futures market. By the end of 1994 Leeson had lost the bank $500 million but instead of coming clean he hid the losses in a secret account (its number was 88888) and was wired more funds from his head office so he could keep trading. Two months later Leeson's losses amounted to $1.3 billion – more than everything the bank owned.

In February 1995 Leeson went on the run while the bank went into meltdown. Investors lost their savings, 1,200 employees their jobs, including those executives who should have been watching Leeson. After the scandal broke a photo of Leeson was published of him in an old magazine wearing the blue and gold Barings jacket with the caption: 'It is cost effective to have positions in Singapore.'

Leeson was eventually captured in Germany and extradited to Singapore (which was where he'd committed the crime) and he was eventually sentenced to six-and-a-half-years for forging documents and deceiving the bank's auditors. Barings was bought by ING for £1 and they ditched the name soon after.

Leeson was reunited with his old boss, Peter Norris, 16 years after the debacle when the two were brought together for a BBC radio programme. Norris recalled how he felt towards Mr Leeson as he saw him taken into custody: 'I think I wanted to punch your lights out,' he said.

'I wouldn't have blamed you if you had,' Leeson replied.

This entrance to Leadenhall, which served as a meat and dairy market from the 15th to the 20th century, is just opposite the side entrance of what was once the Barings building. It's now full of shops and restaurants and is a popular place for City workers to dine.

6. The Towering Innuendo

◉ BCCI and Swiss Re Building (aka the Gherkin)

⬥ 30 St Mary Axe, EC3

⊖ Liverpool Street station *(Mainline, Hammersmith & City, Metropolitan, Central, and Circle Lines)* and Aldgate *(Metropolitan and Circle Lines)*

Looming over 100 Leadenhall Street is 30 St Mary Axe, aka the Swiss Re building – known to all as the Gherkin. It opened in 2004, 40 floors and 180 metres high, and it stands on the site of the Baltic Exchange building, which was severely damaged on 10 April 1992 by a Provisional IRA bomb.

The fertiliser bomb, which was hidden in a large white truck, killed three people: Paul Butt, 29, a Baltic Exchange employee, Thomas Casey, 49, and 15-year-old Danielle Carter. It caused £800m-worth of damage, an estimated £200m more than the total damage caused by the 10,000 explosions that had occurred during the Troubles in Northern Ireland up to that point.

Another IRA bomb exploded near the same spot the following year. A medieval church, St Ethelburga's, collapsed; another church and Liverpool Street Underground station were also wrecked. The bomb killed 34-year-old Ed Henty, a freelance photographer working for the *News of the World*. He was married with two children. In 1996, after a year-long ceasefire, the IRA planted a bomb in Canary Wharf in the Docklands area. Two died and many more were injured.

This marked a new tactic by the IRA of targeting the UK's financial centre, rather than military and police bases and personnel. The huge payouts by insurance companies contributed to a crisis in the industry, including the near-collapse of the world's leading insurance market, Lloyd's of London (opposite the Gherkin at 1 Lime Street, EC3). Some have argued that this sped up the peace process and helped secure favourable terms for the IRA, including the release of all political prisoners – including the man who helped make the Bishopsgate bomb. It certainly changed the way the City of London was policed.

In July 1993 the police introduced the 'Ring of Steel', which left only eight routes into the City, each with checkpoints manned by armed police. Over 70 police-owned CCTV cameras that recorded registrations and drivers' and passengers' faces were introduced. The City Police also encouraged companies in the Square Mile to invest in their own CCTV cameras – at that time only 12 per cent used them. Today there are 619 police and council-owned cameras in the Square Mile and several thousand owned by private companies (although no precise data exist for privately-owned cameras). Taken together they make the Square Mile one of the most heavily watched areas in the world.

7. The Birth of Forensic Photography

◉ Bishopsgate Police Station

⬤ 182 Bishopsgate, EC2

◉ Liverpool Street station *(Mainline, Central, Circle and Hammersmith &*
City Lines)

Bishopsgate Police Station was first constructed in 1861 and rebuilt on this
site in 1939. One year later, in September 1940, it was almost demolished by a
German bomb. No police officer was killed but the night-duty nurse, who had
been in the basement, was badly injured. The bombing of the City reached its
peak on 29 December 1940 when 1,400 fires were burning in the Square Mile
alone. It became known as 'Red Sunday'.

A pioneer of police photography, Constable Arthur Cross, was based in
Bishopsgate's basement. Up until this time, just a few albums of criminal
photographs were stored at Old Jewry (see page 113) and the police didn't have
a studio, so instead relied on local photographers' shops (the Houndsditch
murderers were photographed this way, see page 153). Cross, an amateur
photographer, was given a basement room in Bishopsgate and a budget of
just ten shillings a month. His duties included taking portraits of every police
officer in the City Police, as well as criminals and crime scenes.

During World War II, Cross was asked to take photos of bomb damage to
the City in the Blitz. He often scaled St Paul's Cathedral for the best view. He
was eventually given an assistant, Constable Fred Tibbs. More than 350 of
their photos were used to help with the rebuilding of the City after the war.
Tibbs and Cross were usually on the scene within minutes of the All-Clear
sounding. Arriving soon after one bombing to photograph the falling front
of the Salvation Army headquarters in Queen Victoria Street, Tibbs stepped
back and disappeared into a bomb crater. The constable was unhurt but the
photograph is slightly out of focus.

In 1951 the new Police Commissioner, Arthur Young, visited Cross's
basement room. He was so impressed by Cross's work that he gave the
delighted photographer a purpose-built darkroom and studio and increased
his annual budget to £1,000.

8. Fagin's Kitchen Crew

◎ Royal Exchange
🏠 Threadneedle Street and Cornhill, EC3
🌐 www.theroyalexchange.com
🕐 Mon-Fri 10am-11pm. Some restaurants are open at weekends.
　Check website.
🚇 Bank Tube *(Central and Northern Lines)*

The Royal Exchange (under the Gherkin in the photograph), a Grade I listed building just across the road from the Bank of England, dates back to 1565. In 2001, after extensive renovations, it reopened as a high-end shopping centre with several exclusive stores, including De Beers, Omega, Gucci, Hermès, Cartier and Tiffany & Co.

Just after 10pm on a Saturday in August 2010, raiders stormed the building, using bolt-cutters to break through the ornate wrought-iron gates before crashing a stolen car into a metal bollard, knocking it over and then smashing the shop windows of De Beers and Omega. They grabbed dozens of rings, necklaces, watches and fled. They were the first such gang to strike in the City — and on a Saturday night, a time when the City, the centre of global finance, is usually deserted.

The smash and grab raid has been on the rise in recent years. In May 2010, the De Beers and Tiffany & Co stores in the Westfield shopping complex in West London were raided by a gang that battered through a fire door to grab gems worth over £2m. Also in 2010, valuables worth more than £4m were snatched from stores including Dolce & Gabbana, Cartier and Watches of Switzerland. In a raid at the Mozafarian store in Knightsbridge in August 2009, jewels worth over £1m were stolen in less than a minute. Other Tiffany and De Beers branches have also been targeted by thieves riding stolen mopeds and armed with sledgehammers.

In recent years a gang of about 50 teenagers, known as Fagin's Kitchen Crew, have been targeting the jewellery shops in the West End and designer stores in the City. The teenagers — many of whom are based in the old Sabini stomping ground of Clerkenwell (see Saffron Hill, page 137, and Hockley-in-the-Hole, page 141) — use Italian scooters and ride away with millions in jewellery and computer equipment each year. They've even targeted Mappin and Webb, silversmiths to the Queen.

The City of London Police are now using scooters to pursue them. In one case, a gang member threw a hammer at an officer, writing off his Vespa. Five members of the gang were recently jailed, but unfortunately an undercover operation after a raid at Tiffany's, off Sloane Street, resulted in the death of a 21-year-old, who crashed his scooter as he sped away from police.

Two of the Royal Exchange thieves were jailed after an Old Bailey trial, but keep your eyes peeled ... it is very likely that Fagin's Kitchen will strike here again.

9. The World's Biggest Mugging

◎ **The Bank of England**

⌂ **Threadneedle Street, EC2**

☎ **020 7601 5545**

ⓦ **www.bankofengland.co.uk**

🕐 **The Bank of England Museum is open Mon-Fri 10am–5pm**

ⓕ **Free**

⊖ **Bank Tube *(Central and Northern Lines)***

In 1990 an estimated £30 billion was carried in bearer bonds by messengers through these streets each day. A messenger might carry several hundred million pounds on their person – at least until 2 May 1990, when a 58-year-old messenger, with money broker Sheppards, was mugged at knifepoint at 9.30am on a quiet side street near the Bank of England. The messenger was taking Bank of England Treasury bills and certificates of deposit from banks and building societies. The bonds were in bearer form and as good as cash to anyone holding them. The mugger escaped with 301 Treasury bills and certificates of deposit, mostly in values of £1m each. The thief's total haul was £292m.

The Bank of England told the press that the bonds were worthless to whoever had stolen them. But this was untrue; all you need to cash in a Government bond is your driving licence, or some proof of identity, and after that the cash is all yours.

The City of London Police formed a 40-strong team determined to get the bonds back. Far from being a 'lucky' mugging, the attack was discovered to be part of an international fraud and money-laundering ring, with organised crime links in the United States.

Two months after the securities were stolen, Mark Osborne, a Texan businessman, attempted to sell some of the bonds to an undercover FBI operative in New York. He was arrested, 'turned' and used to trap other members of the gang, including ringleader and conman Keith Cheeseman from Bethnal Green, East London. In the months after the robbery, detectives tracked down all but £2m of the £292m. They arrested 25 people but only Cheeseman – who was captured at his luxury flat in the Barbican, in November 1990 – has ever been successfully prosecuted.

Cheeseman subsequently jumped bail and fled to Tenerife, where he was recaptured and extradited to the US and sentenced to 6½ years. He claims he fled because he feared a Mafia godfather had put a contract out on him. This may well have been true: fellow conspirator Mark Osborne was murdered. His body was found in the boot of a car parked in Houston, Texas, with two bullets in his head.

Police believe the City mugging was carried out by Patrick Thomas, a petty crook from South London, but he was never charged with the robbery. Thomas too was found dead from a gunshot wound to the head in December 1991. Not long after the mugging, the Central Moneymarkets Office was established so that the £30 billion or so that whizzes around the City every day can now do so via wires rather than pieces of paper.

10. From Ex-Convict to Police Commissioner

◎ City Police Commissioner's Official Residence

◯ 26 Old Jewry, EC2

⊖ Bank Tube *(Central and Northern Lines)*

Bought by the City of London Police for £6,500 in 1841, this building underwent a number of refurbishments, until it was completely rebuilt by the City of London Corporation's Chief Architect, Sydney Perks (see also Snow Hill, page 129), in neo-Georgian style, and extended back to a rear entrance on Ironmonger Lane between 1926 and 1930.

Purchased in 1841, it was the official residence of the first Commissioner of the new City of London Police force, Daniel Whittle Harvey (1786–1863). Harvey, who was elected MP for Colchester and later Southwark, also founded *The Sunday Times* newspaper in 1822. The following year he was sued for libel when his paper alleged in the 9 February edition that George IV was mad, like his father. He was found guilty, fined £200, and imprisoned for 12 months in the King's Bench.

Upon being appointed Commissioner he was forced to stand down as an MP. The founder of the police, Sir Robert Peel, warned against the danger of a police commissioner sitting in the Commons and challenging the home secretary on police matters. Since then the police have (with one or two exceptions) remained politically neutral.

The first murder of a City policeman occurred when Detective Sergeant Charles Thain was bringing back a prisoner, Christian Sattler, from Hamburg where he had chased him for a theft from a City stockbroker. The two men shared a cabin on the journey back and it was while they were at sea that Sattler, even though he was handcuffed, managed to get hold of a gun and shoot the detective three times in the chest. There was no doctor on board and the ship was three days from land. Thain died ten days after landing and on 9 February 1858 Sattler was publicly hanged outside Newgate (see page 125). Surrounding the scaffold was a ring of City policemen whose job it was, until 1868, to maintain order on execution day.

Daniel Harvey was buried in the grounds of the Unitarian chapel in Hackney (39 Newington Green). The City police paid for a monument to be erected over his grave, which is still there. During his life he handed over part of the Commissioner's residence to what became the first detective department, or CID (Criminal Investigation Department). The building ceased to be the Commissioner's official residence in 1863 and became the administrative headquarters of the City of London Police, until it was vacated in 2001. Although the view pictured here is not accessible to the public, part of the old police building, on Gresham Street, is now a restaurant from where it is possible to see this courtyard through the rear windows.

11. The Smithfield Stake

◎ Guildhall Buildings and Smithfield

○ Guildhall, Basinghall Street, EC2, Smithfield, Long Lane, EC2

Ⓦ www.guildhall.cityoflondon.gov.uk, www.smithfieldmarket.com

◐ The markets at Smithfield are open Monday to Friday from 3am but
are closed on Saturday, Sunday and Bank Holidays

◉ Guildhall: **Bank Tube** *(Central and Northern Lines)*, Smithfield:
Barbican Tube *(Hammersmith & City, Circle and Metropolitan Lines)*

Guildhall has been the administrative headquarters of the City of London, the Square Mile's local authority, for over 800 years. Although damaged by fire in 1666 and bombed by the Luftwaffe in 1940, its medieval core has survived. Within the precincts of the Guildhall is the Mayor's and City of London Court, the oldest local civil court in England, having sat for over 700 years, virtually without a break. The City of London Court's present building was erected in 1888.

In medieval times, the Guildhall used to be a place of trial, including that of noblewoman Ann Askew for heresy in 1546. Protestant Askew, who was about 25 years old, had left her Catholic husband, whom she had been forced to marry and from whom she sought a divorce. Askew was racked in the Tower and tied to the Smithfield stake, a short distance from Guildhall, ready for burning, where she was given the chance to go free if she repented. She refused and was burned to death.

Smithfield, the site of the meat market opposite St Bartholomew's Hospital, a short distance from the Guildhall, was a place of execution for 400 years until the gallows were moved to Tyburn (see page 271) in the reign of Henry IV. Smithfield executions were particularly gruesome. Scottish hero William Wallace was hanged, drawn and quartered here in 1305. In 1538, Friar John Forest was roasted alive for failing to acknowledge the King's supremacy. More than 200 Protestants were burned at the stake during Queen Mary's reign in the 1550s.

Even as late as 1652 a woman was burned at the stake here for poisoning her husband. In the late 17th century Smithfields was so troubled by riot and duellists that it became known as 'Ruffians Hall'. After it was fully converted into a market, herders often stampeded their cattle through London to get them to the market on time.

Today Smithfield is still a meat market and has its own tiny police force, the Market Constabulary. With only eight officers, they're the smallest 'force' in the UK. Their wages are paid by the City of London Corporation, the owners of the market, based in Guildhall.

12. The Birth of the City Police

⊚ City Police Headquarters and City Police Museum

⌂ 37 Wood Street, EC2

☎ City Police Museum: 020 7601 2328

ⓦ www.citypolicemuseum.org.uk

🕐 Tues-Wed 10am-4pm, Fri 2-6pm (telephone beforehand as these times are subject to change)

💷 Free (donations welcome)

⊖ Moorgate Tube *(Northern, Circle, Hammersmith & City Lines)* and St Paul's Tube *(Central Line)*

In the 17th century, London was known as the 'city of gallows' as there were over 200 crimes (from graffiti to murder) that merited hanging. The London Watch, an early version of the police, was fairly ineffectual and by 1828, just 400 watchmen policed a city of a million souls. It wasn't until 1839 that the City of London Police came into existence. Their first police station was a converted pub by Bart's Hospital (see also 26 Old Jewry, page 113). Today the City of London Police is the smallest constabulary in the UK. This is because it polices such a small area – the Square Mile as well as the Middle and Inner Temple (see page 146). The rest of London is under the jurisdiction of the Metropolitan Police, the UK's largest police force.

The City Police, as well as safeguarding the Square Mile and its 9,000 residents, 320,000 workers and many sightseers, specialises in economic crime but it will deal with any crime committed on its patch, from murder to jewellery raids (see Royal Exchange, page 109).

Although the Wood Street headquarters are new (2002) the building rests on the site of a Roman fortress, which may have been home to the Roman equivalent of the City Police. The tall building in front of the station is all that remains of St Alban's Church, designed by Sir Christopher Wren. The rest of the church was destroyed in the 1940 Blitz. Inside the station is a small but fascinating museum dedicated to the history of crime and policing in the City of London, covering Jack the Ripper, the siege of Sidney Street and, of course, the men and women who have guarded the City of London since 1839 – featuring uniforms, badges, warrants, criminal tools and so on.

The City of London police entered a tug-of-war team in the 1920 Olympics and won the gold medal. As the event was never held again at the Olympics they remain reigning champions.

13. A Time-Saving Device

◎ Police Call Box and Postman's Park
◑ St Martin's Le Grand, EC1
◒ St Paul's Tube *(Central Line)*

Police posts like this – no longer in use – were once a common sight in London. Much of a constable's time was wasted travelling to and from his police station – for example, a half-hour refreshment break called for a visit to the police station (or any other suitable place), and then a return to beat duty. This meant that up to a quarter of a constable's patrol time could be wasted.

Each kiosk contained a telephone linked directly to the local sub-divisional police station. Officers on the beat could make reports to their sergeants from them and, if the light was flashing, then they knew to call the station. They were also there for public use. Larger police boxes contained, for the use of officers, a stool, a table, brushes and dusters, a fire extinguisher and a small (often very inadequate) electric fire.

The earliest boxes (now world famous as the exterior of the TARDIS in the BBC's time travel adventure series *Doctor Who*) were designed by Gilbert Mackenzie and made of wood. At their peak in 1937, 700 were in use. They were phased out at the end of the 1960s, after the introduction of personal police radios. The last one to go was in Barnet in 1981, but a souvenir remains in the grounds of the Peel Centre police training school in Hendon and a replica has been erected outside Earls Court Tube station. A few authentic police posts like the one pictured remain. There's one in Piccadilly Circus and one – still working as of 2011 – in Grosvenor Square, near the American Embassy.

Just behind this police post is a former burial ground, now Postman's Park, which is well worth a visit. It's the largest park in the City of London and gets its name from the nearby former grounds of the headquarters of the Post Office.

In 1900 the park became the location for artist and sculptor George Frederic Watts' 'Memorial to Heroic Self Sacrifice', a memorial to ordinary people who died saving the lives of others and might otherwise have been forgotten. Watts hoped to see memorials like this in every town in England and provided space for 120 plaques in Postman's Park. One of the plaques is to a policeman, PC Alfred Smith, who saved 150 women working in a factory from a German bombing raid in 1917, but was himself caught in a blast.

The last memorial was installed in 1931 and, by the time George Watts' widow, Mary died in 1938, 68 spaces remained unfilled – until 2009, when the name of Leigh Pitt, who died on 7 June 2007 rescuing nine-year-old Harley Bagnall-Taylor from a canal, was added. A spokesman said that the Diocese of London (who manage the park) will consider adding more names to the memorial in future.

14. Execution Song

◎ St Sepulchre Without Newgate
⌂ Holborn Viaduct, EC1
☎ 020 7236 1145
ⓦ www.st-sepulchre.org.uk
🕐 Mon-Fri 10am-2pm
ⓕ Free (donations welcome)
⊖ St Paul's Tube *(Central Line)*

Named after the Holy Sepulchre in Jerusalem, this church, the largest in the City of London, was first mentioned in 1137. Damaged in the Great Fire of 1666 – scorch marks can still be seen inside the building – it was rebuilt by Christopher Wren's masons in 1670–71. Within sight of the Old Bailey, St Sepulchre's bells are mentioned in the famous rhyme 'Oranges and Lemons'.

Inside the church is the execution bell, which from 1605 was rung at midnight on the eve of an execution at Newgate prison. It would be carried via a tunnel that passed below the street to the condemned's cell and 12 double tolls would be rung in front of the prisoner, while the ringer recited a macabre rhyme.

All you that in the condemned hole do lie,
Prepare you for tomorrow you shall die;
Watch all and pray: the hour is drawing near
That you before the Almighty must appear;
Examine well yourselves in time repent,
That you may not to eternal flames be sent.
And when St Sepulchre's Bell in the morning tolls
The Lord above have mercy on your soul.

Among many others, the bell was rung for François Courvoisier, a valet who had cut the throat of his master, former MP Lord William Russell, after Russell caught him stealing silverware. Courvoisier was hanged outside Newgate prison on 6 July 1840. Among the 40,000 people who turned up to watch was novelist William Makepeace Thackeray, writing: 'I came away that morning with a disgust for murder, but it was for the murder I saw done... I feel myself shamed and degraded at the brutal curiosity that took me to that spot.'

Courvoisier's body was most likely turned over to nearby St Bart's Hospital (now nearly 900 years old and London's oldest functioning hospital) for medical study – at the time doctors were only allowed to study the corpses of people who had been executed. Although this didn't deter the 'resurrection men' who robbed St Sepulchre's graves before taking the bodies to the Fortune of War pub, where they were laid out for surgeons to inspect and a price to be negotiated.

Overlooking St Sepulchre's churchyard, in Giltspur Street EC1, is the Watch House, originally built in the 17th century. Families would pay the watchmen to keep an eye on the bodies of their newly departed until such time as they were unfit for study.

15. The Giltspur Prison Cells

◎ Viaduct Tavern
◔ Holborn Viaduct, EC1
☎ 020 7600 1863
🕐 Mon-Fri 11am-11pm
⊖ St Paul's Tube *(Central Line)*

The Viaduct Tavern opened in 1869, at the same time as the Holborn Viaduct – the world's first flyover. It is claimed that the tavern's cellars were once part of Newgate prison (see page 125), and if you ask the bar staff they'll take you downstairs for a look – as long as it's not too busy.

The cells' location – and a plaque at 2 Giltspur Street – suggests that they were more likely to be part of Giltspur Street Compter (compter is another term for prison), mainly used to hold debtors. This small jail was situated in Giltspur Street between 1791 and 1853. It was demolished to make way for the King Edward Buildings Royal Mail Sorting Office, which eventually became the General Post Office Headquarters.

Quite possibly, these were the smallest prison cells London had ever seen – not a place for claustrophobes. Hepworth Dixon, a journalist, historian and traveller wrote:

In Giltspur Street Compter, the prisoners sleep in small cells, little more than half the size of those at Pentonville, though the latter are calculated to be only just large enough for one inmate, even when ventilated upon the best plan that science can suggest. But the cell in Giltspur Street Compter is either not ventilated at all, or ventilated very imperfectly; and though little more than half the dimensions of the 'model cells' constructed for one prisoner, I have seen five persons locked up at four o'clock in the day, to be there confined till the next morning in darkness and idleness, to do all the offices of nature, not merely in each other's presence, but crushed by the narrowness of their den, into a state of filthy contact, which brute beasts would have resisted to the last gasp of life...

Inside the pub, three pictures of maidens represent agriculture, banking and the arts. However, the 'Maiden of Arts' was either shot or bayoneted by a World War I soldier, and the damage is still there to see. Small busts depict 15 hanging judges from the Old Bailey.

Respectable enough now, it was once a rough pub – a prostitute was murdered in the ladies' lavatory. Previously, punters had to buy tokens from a secure area behind the bar before they were allowed to buy a drink – the records of the Old Bailey detail many cases of bad coins being passed over the bar, including by 24-year-old Daniel Murphy, who was given 18 months' hard labour for passing over a dodgy half crown to barman Patrick Tutte while Detective Frederick Haywood was in the same bar.

16. A Prototype of Hell

◉ Newgate Gaol
⌂ Amen Corner, EC4
⊖ St Paul's Tube *(Central Line)*

Newgate, once London's premier prison, was just a stone's throw away from St Paul's Cathedral. Henry Fielding (1707–54), the novelist and founder of the Bow Street Runners (page 291), described it as a 'prototype of hell' – heaven and hell had never been so close.

Newgate's high and long walls were black and provided a dark view from the Old Bailey. 'Black as Newgate' used to be a popular metaphor. The conditions there were miserable; a lack of water and ventilation helped spread 'gaol fever', a terrible type of fatal typhoid. New prisoners were bullied, beaten and extorted by other inmates and by the turnkey (jailer), who charged fees for almost anything – for loosening chains or proximity to warming fire, as well as providing food, water, wine and prostitutes.

The prison was extended many times, and remained in use for over 700 years, from 1188 to 1902, with minor interruptions for the Great Fire of London and the Gordon Riots of 1780, when it was destroyed by arson and rampage. By 1800 it was one of 19 large prisons gathered in old London and held prisoners prior to execution. After the death sentence was pronounced, the unfortunates had to attend Newgate Chapel to hear the condemned sermon. They sat around a table on which rested a coffin. Then, the night before they were to be hanged, they were awoken at midnight by the executioner's bell as part of a macabre ritual (see St Sepulchre, page 121). After the executions the bodies of the criminals were taken to Surgeons' Hall in the Old Bailey for public dissection.

By 1830, the death sentence could be handed down for over 300 different offences including sacrilege, letter stealing, returning from transportation, sodomy and stealing as little as five shillings (25p). By 1860 however, only four capital crimes remained: murder, treason, arson in the Queen's docks and piracy.

Newgate hangings were extremely popular and crowds of up to 30,000 were common until public executions were abandoned in 1868. Nevertheless, the public still gathered outside the prison to see the black flag raised. Between 1868 and the demolition of the prison in 1902, 1,106 men and 49 women were hanged within Newgate.

Amazingly, a piece of the prison wall – complete with gas lamps – remains. It's hidden in a quiet residential street lined with picturesque 17th-century houses built for the clergymen of St Paul's Cathedral in Amen Corner, and is shown in the photo here. It backs onto the rear of the Central Criminal Court.

17. God Help Us

◎ Central Criminal Court

◑ Old Bailey, EC4

🕐 There is no public access to the precincts of the Central Criminal Court but the public galleries are open each day for viewing of trials in session. The times are Mon -Fri 10am-1pm and 2pm-5pm (approx). The court is closed on Bank Holiday Mondays and the adjacent Tuesday. No appointment is necessary but you will need to arrive without a mobile phone or any other piece of electronic equipment and absolutely no bag.

🅕 Free

⊖ St Paul's Tube *(Central Line)*

The country's most famous law courts – known as the Old Bailey – opened in 1907 to replace those that joined Newgate prison. These have been the setting for most of the UK's most infamous court cases of the 20th and 21st centuries.

All judges sitting in the Old Bailey are addressed as 'My Lord' or 'My Lady' and between them they have handed out tens of thousands of years in prison in the hundred-plus years since the court opened. '*Domine, Dirige Nos*' is imprinted on the court seats. This Latin phrase can be interpreted by the judges as 'Lord, direct us' or – if you are on the other side – as 'God help us.'

Famous attendees include Princess Diana's butler, Paul Burrell, who was acquitted of theft here in 2002; the Kray twins in 1969 (see page 90); Dr Crippen, hanged in 1910 (see page 228); Peter Sutcliffe, the Yorkshire Ripper, in 1981, who murdered 13 women; Ruth Ellis in 1955 (see page 183); and William Joyce, also known as Lord Haw-Haw, who broadcast Nazi propaganda to the UK in World War II and was hanged for treason in 1946.

Peter Scott, the 'king of the cat-burglars' (see page 264), who burgled his way through Mayfair in the 1960s, told a reporter on the Old Bailey's 100th anniversary that during his trial he had been struck by the graffiti carved onto the prisoner's side of the door leading into Court One: 'A boy's best friend is his mother.'

In 1973 an IRA car bomb detonated outside the courts, and a shard of glass is preserved as a reminder, embedded in the wall at the top of the main stairs. Altogether four bombs were planted in London that day – only two were found in time and defused. One man was killed and 238 were wounded, mostly by flying glass. A police photographer, who was taking a picture of the car when it exploded, was badly injured but survived.

At the Old Bailey in 1974 Mr Justice Donaldson sentenced three young men and one 17-year-old woman to life for a series of IRA pub bombings carried out in Guildford and Woolwich that claimed the lives of seven people and injured dozens more. (Although only 17, Carole Richardson received an indeterminate 'At Her Majesty's Pleasure' sentence for murder, but a life sentence for conspiracy.)

Fourteen years later, a detective re-examining the case found that police had manipulated statements to make the so-called Guildford Four appear guilty. They were cleared and released in 1989.

18. Prostitute's Progress

◎ Snow Hill Police Station and Cock Lane
◯ Snow Hill, EC1
⊖ Farringdon Tube *(Mainline, Hammersmith & City, Circle and Metropolitan Lines)*

The City of London Police is divided into two territorial divisions, Snow Hill and Bishopsgate (see page 106). Both stations are fully operational and open 24 hours a day.

Snow Hill police station was built in 1926 by Sydney Perks and is Grade II listed. It was built on the site of the former Saracen's Head Inn, first recorded in 1544 (and mentioned as the coaching station in Charles Dickens' *Nicholas Nickleby*), which was demolished in 1868 to make room for building work necessary to prepare the way for the Holborn Viaduct.

A City of London plaque on the police station's wall commemorates the ancient and infamous tavern, which in 1522 had 30 beds for travellers and stabling for 40 horses. Coaches would pass through a wide gateway into a courtyard surrounded by galleries, which lead to the bedrooms.

Dickens described the tavern's notable signage, '[The] Saracen's head, frowns upon you from the top of the yard; while from the door of the hind-boot of all the red coaches that are standing therein, there glares a small Saracen's head with a twin expression to the large Saracen's head below, so that the general appearance of the pile is of the Saracenic order.'

Unwittingly anticipating the site's future association with the forces of law and order, one of the landladies of the Saracen's, Sarah Ann Matthew, shot a burglar in the leg here in 1833.

The nearby St Sepulchre church (see page 121) dates back to 1137 and was the departure point for many crusaders who wanted to rescue the Holy Sepulchre in Jerusalem from the possession of the Saracens.

John Bunyan (1628–88), author of *The Pilgrim's Progress*, lived in Snow Hill after serving various prison sentences for 'preaching without licence' and died here after catching his death of cold walking through Holborn in the rain.

Spelled 'Cokkes Lane' in medieval times, Cock Lane was the site of legal brothels. It is also famous as the site of the house (No. 25 or 33 depending on the accounts you read) where the supposed Cock Lane Ghost, aka Scratching Fanny, manifested herself in 1762 – to the delight of the landlords of the Saracen's Head, as Cock Lane became thronged with thirsty people hoping to see or hear Fanny in action. The ghost was later proved to be the invention of the family living at the house, who faked one-knock-for-yes and two-for-no during séances.

19. **Diamonds Are For Never**

◎ De Beers' Diamond HQ

⌂ Charterhouse Street, EC1

⊖ Farringdon station *(Mainline, Hammersmith & City, Circle and Metropolitan Lines)*

This building, on the edge of Hatton Garden, London's diamond centre, looks like a fortress with good reason — it is. Behind its concrete walls are huge vaults containing 4 billion rough diamonds. And yes, you did read that correctly: FOUR BILLION DIAMONDS.

Among them in 2000 was the flawless 203-carat Millennium Star, along with 12 spectacular coloured diamonds that together made up the Millennium Collection, which became irresistible to robbers when they were put on display at the Millennium Dome (see page 72).

Hidden among the bricks of this building are cameras powerful enough to record the colour of your eyes. It is a building De Beers' executives describe as 'the most secure in Europe'. So don't go getting any ideas. This is also where De Beers' stolen diamonds are returned and where the work of theft prevention takes place. De Beers use a number of methods to protect their diamonds, enabling the company to identify lost stones should they ever be found. One technique involves firing lasers and X-rays into each diamond. This creates a specific optical response which is recorded and becomes that diamond's 'fingerprint'. Then, using another laser, they cut a serial number, invisible to the naked eye, into each gem.

When a diamond is stolen, police send out bulletins listing the missing jewel to pawnshops, jewellers, cutters and traders. Trying to sell a stolen gem is risky business. All too often the seller is shopped to police by the buyer.

Most robbers would be disappointed to know that diamonds are not as rare as we are led to believe. They were pretty hard to come by until mining practices became super-efficient. Dozens of diamond mines have since been discovered in the world, from Siberia to Australia and, most recently, in Canada.

One reason diamonds are so expensive is because they are only sold by a small number of companies, including De Beers. Indeed, in 2001 CNN reported that for most of the preceding century De Beers had sold over 85% of all the world's diamonds. And in 2004 De Beers pleaded guilty to a US charge that it had colluded to fix the price of industrial diamonds — although it has since legally resumed selling them. However, the company has always denied unlawfully monopolising the supply of the gems and has consented to an injunction which prohibits it from doing so.

Regardless of the cause, prices remain high. So, although it may sound like a catastrophic loss when millions of pounds' worth of diamonds are stolen — De Beers stores across London have been the target of several gem raiders in recent years, including the Royal Exchange (see page 109) and Bond Street (see page 260) — the company needn't be too worried. It still has plenty hidden away in these vaults.

20. Diamond Geezers

⊙ The Gold and Diamond Markets

⌂ Hatton Garden, EC1

⊖ Farringdon station *(Mainline, Hammersmith & City, Circle and Metropolitan Lines)* and Chancery Lane Tube *(Central Line)*

The first jewellers, working in gold and silver, came to Hatton Garden in the mid-1830s. Their numbers were boosted by the arrival of polishers and cutters from Antwerp in the early 1900s.

Today, Hatton Garden is the undisputed centre of Britain's gold and diamond trade, and its tightly knit community of jewellers have hired the protection to match: dozens of giant security guards who communicate with one another via encrypted radios stand on almost every street corner and doorway. It's not an easy place for a jewel thief to strike.

In November 2003 a dapper gentleman in his fifties, dressed in a dark suit, a tie and a homburg hat arrived in the Garden. His name, he said, when he rented four deposit boxes in the basement of the Hatton Garden Safety Deposit (88–90 Hatton Garden), was Philip Goldberg.

His final visit, at 9am on a Saturday in June 2004, went almost unnoticed. It wasn't until Monday that Hatton Garden realised that more than £2m in jewellery and cash had vanished from several customers' boxes, and the gent had vanished too, in what appears to have been one of the most audacious jewel heists ever.

Police have ruled out the use of an inside man, so how did he do it? 'Goldberg' rented four strongboxes, dotted around the vault, meaning he would have a legitimate reason to be lingering in the room. During this time he made conversation with other regulars, winning their trust. However, the safe deposit works on a two-key system: customers have one key and the deposit staff have another. Both have to be used simultaneously for the box to be opened. Even if the culprit had a copy of the safe deposit's master key he would still have to obtain copies of the individual keys for the boxes from which he stole. The case remains open and theories abound – including the use of hypnosis.

Also in Hatton Garden, on the first floor of Nos. 63–66, is the unique and wholly remarkable organisation known as the Art Loss Register. Established in 1991, it maintains an international database of over 350,000 lost and stolen works of art, which it uses to match claims, mediate disputes and recover items on behalf of the rightful owner. In other words they're modern-day treasure hunters who often have to deal with criminal gangs to recover lost masterpieces.

Recent finds include 271 Picassos and a priceless 17th-century bust of botanist and physician Dr Peter Turner, stolen in 1941 from a bombed church, only a mile or so from Hatton Garden (St Olave's in Hart Street, EC3, the resting place of Samuel Pepys). Among the items they're still looking for are James Bond's DB5 Aston Martin, used in the film *Goldfinger* and valued at £29m, as well as Cézannes, Monets and Picassos worth tens of millions of pounds.

21. Who Wants to Be a Bullionaire?

◎ Charles Cooper Ltd
◐ 8 Hatton Garden, EC1
⊜ Chancery Lane Tube *(Central Line)*

Just after 6.40am on 26 November 1983, six armed men charged into the Heathrow depot of security company Brink's-Mat. The robbers disabled the sophisticated security system, tied up the guards, doused them with petrol and threatened to set them alight unless they revealed the combinations to the safe.

The leaders, Mickey McAvoy, a young hardman, and an old blagger called Brian Robinson, had heard there would be £3m in cash in the vault and the plan was to split it six ways. It was only when they were in the vault that they found the gold. They left with 6,800 gold bars worth £26m. It was the UK's biggest ever criminal haul. Once the gold market heard the news it panicked, causing the haul to rise in value by another million.

Officers from the Flying Squad combed Hatton Garden, knowing that this was the only place in the UK where someone might be able to offload nearly 7,000 bars of gold. They spoke to gold dealers, including a company director of Charles Cooper Ltd, Andrew Duncan, asking them to report any suspicious behaviour.

Fifteen days after the robbery, on 11 December, a man in his late thirties strolled down Hatton Garden – the undisputed centre of Britain's gold and diamond trade – before entering Charles Cooper Ltd at No. 8, just next to Ely Court, down which can be found the tiny 16th-century Olde Mitre Tavern. The plump man spoke to Andrew Duncan, telling him (in a strong Cockney accent) that he was after an industrial gold smelter. Duncan replied that it would be possible to get a machine that liquefied 36kg at a time. 'That'll do nicely,' the man said. He wanted to take it with him there and then but this was impossible as it had to be ordered.

Following this visit, Duncan called the Squad and after looking through a book of mugshots, he picked out a face that turned out to be a friend of known robber Mickey McAvoy. This was the Flying Squad's first real lead.

Detectives started following McAvoy and then Robinson – noting that they'd left their council houses for enormous homes in Kent, paid for in cash. McAvoy also bought two Rottweiler dogs and named them Brinks and Mat. Then detectives found out that security guard Tony Black had been the inside man. Black told all and fingered McAvoy in the police line-up. McAvoy head-butted him in response. McAvoy and Robinson ended up with 25 years apiece.

While the criminals were caught, the gold proved much harder to find with only £16m of the original £26m so far recovered. For the concluding part of this story, see The Curse of Brink's-Mat, page 40.

London Borough of Camden

HATTON GARDEN
E.C.1

22. The Sabini Gang

◎ Saffron Hill

⬡ Clerkenwell, EC1

⊖ Farringdon station *(Mainline, Hammersmith & City, Circle and Metropolitan Lines)* and Chancery Lane *(Central Line)*

In the 14th century, fields in this area grew saffron and strawberries. Over the centuries it degenerated into a slum, home to Irish and then Italian immigrants.

In the 1920s and 30s it was the lair of the Sabini Gang, led by Charles 'Darby' Sabini (born in Saffron Hill) and his brothers, George, Fred, Joseph and Harry-Boy. All boxers, they made money by providing security for sporting events and took on any troublemakers, no matter how powerful. When Monkey Benneyworth (from the South London gang the Elephant Boys) purposely ripped the dress of a barmaid in Saffron Hill's Griffin Pub, it was Darby who broke his jaw.

From this moment, the Sabinis' move into organised crime truly began. The Sabinis fought the Elephant Boys for control over racecourses. They extracted money from bookmakers by surrounding them and preventing punters from placing bets until a premium had been paid. Any refusals were dealt with using barbers' razors. The Sabinis also turned to theft, more extortion, illegal gambling and nightclub ownership. They won favours from the police with heavy bribes. At their peak they were 300-strong. As the Sabinis spread across London, reaching Soho, they fought pitched battles with their rivals – reaching a climax in 1927 when at least eight people were killed in the 'Battle of Waterloo', a riot outside the Duke of Wellington pub in the Waterloo Road (see page 51).

The Sabinis were also key players in the 1936 'Battle of Brighton', the fight for control over Brighton's racecourse bookmakers, which inspired Graham Greene's *Brighton Rock*. Darby himself was the inspiration for the fictional gangster Colleoni.

Perhaps Charles 'Darby' Sabini's 'greatest' moment came at Croydon Airport in 1935, when members of his gang stole £12m (at today's value) in gold bullion. At the outbreak of World War II, he was arrested at Hove dog track and subsequently interned under Defence Regulation 18B in April 1940. Despite numerous letters and testimonials to his 'good character' and his work for 'numerous charities', Met Police and MI5 files painted a rather different view. In fact he was detained because he was a 'dangerous gangster and racketeer of the worst type' with fascist sympathies who was 'liable to lead internal insurrections against this country' at the behest of an occupying power.

After World War II, the Sabinis – and Italian gangsters in general (see the Messinas, page 248) – faded away and their enterprises were quickly overtaken by other gangs, including those led by Alf White, Jack Spot and Billy Hill (see page 251).

23. A London Murder Mystery

◎ Bleeding Heart Yard

⌂ Bleeding Heart Yard, EC1

⊖ Farringdon station *(Mainline, Hammersmith & City, Circle and Metropolitan Lines)*

The last piece of advice which I'd have you regard
Is, 'don't go of a night into Bleeding Heart Yard,'
It's a dark, little, dirty, black, ill-looking square,
With queer people about, and unless you take care,
You may find when your pocket's clean'd out and left bare,
That the iron one is not the only 'PUMP' there?
The Ingoldsby Legends by Richard Barham, 1837

Home to a fine bistro and a selection of Hatton Garden jewellery workshops, the cobbled court of Bleeding Heart Yard is certainly one of the more unusually named of London's streets.

In the mid-19th-century this area was home to gangs of thieves and pickpockets of the kind written about by Charles Dickens in *Oliver Twist*, and it gets a mention in *Little Dorrit* as a slum. Its name comes from a gruesome 17th-century legend featuring society lady Elizabeth Hatton, who 'collogued' with the Devil to win favour from Elizabeth I for her husband, Queen's Chancellor, Christopher Hatton.

Christopher did do very well from the Queen, who gave him Ely Place (just over the back wall of Bleeding Heart Yard), which used to be owned by the Bishop of Ely. Ely Place is still subject to the monarch's decree and remains a private road, separate from the City of London. Guarded by a uniformed officer, even the police are forbidden to enter without an invitation.

Unfortunately for Lady Hatton, the legend has it she was murdered in 1626 during a high-society party at her new home. The next part of the story has many different versions – some say the following day her bloody heart was found by the water pump in this yard, while others claim that her body, ripped to pieces, was left in the yard and when the party guests found her, her heart was still pumping out blood.

There is one problem with the story though: Christopher Hatton never married. Some historians believe the legend is more likely to refer to a later Lady Hatton who sought the help of a necromancer for advice on her marriage but ended up dying alone – of a 'bleeding' heart.

24. 18th-Century Blood-Sport, Brawls and an Underground River

◎ The Coach and Horses

⌂ Ray Street, EC1

☎ 020 7278 8990

ⓦ www.thecoachandhorses.com

🕐 Mon-Fri 12pm-11pm, Sat 6pm-11pm, Sun 1pm-5pm

⊖ Farringdon station *(Mainline, Hammersmith & City, Circle and Metropolitan Lines)*

The River Fleet is an ancient river that starts in Hampstead, flows down through Camden and King's Cross, passes down Ray Street and joins the Thames at Blackfriars. It was used as an open sewer in the 18th century and even today it forms part of London's sewer network. If you stand over the drain cover outside the Coach and Horses, you can hear the Fleet rushing past below.

The Coach and Horses sat on the banks of the Fleet for centuries and was next door to the Bear Garden of Hockley-in-the-Hole, an 18th-century purpose-built arena slotted into the natural amphitheatre of the Fleet Valley. The building has lost a floor, which is now below Ray Street. With a network of closets, secret passages and trapdoors that led from the pub to the Fleet, it was an ideal destination for a criminal fleeing from the police. Like other pubs in the area, a plank was kept handy so that the river could be quickly bridged and un-bridged before the police arrived.

Although cock-fighting, bear baiting and sword fighting became unpopular among the middle classes, Hockley-in-the-Hole continued to draw huge crowds keen to witness blood-sport and very often, after filling up on alcohol at the Coach, to join in with an illegal bare-knuckle fight, duel or all-out brawl, providing the police with more riot and disorder than they could cope with. As one observer wrote in the *Illustrated London News* of 22 May 1847: 'Low public houses abound, where thieves drink and smoke.'

A survey of criminal life published in 1861 put Hockley-in-the-Hole at the top of London's murder league table. It also identified the area as a home of pickpockets (who would prey on the rich who'd come to watch a bit of bear baiting), receivers, coiners, and child strippers (women who stole children's clothes).

At the end of the 19th century, Hockley-in-the-Hole was mostly filled in and the slums demolished. What was once the *Guardian* newspaper's car park (they recently moved to swanky new offices near King's Cross) now covers the arena.

25. The 200-Mile Tower of Paper

◎ Serious Fraud Office (SFO)
⬡ Elm House, 10–16 Elm Street, WC1
Ⓦ www.sfo.giv.uk
⊖ Chancery Lane Tube *(Central Line)*

Formed in 1987, the SFO fights against bribery and corruption. It investigates the most serious types of economic crime and at any one time its 300 staff can be working on 100 cases, many of which involve tens of millions of pounds.

In 2010–11, 17 cases involving 31 defendants went to trial (26 were found guilty and received an average jail sentence of 30 months), £10m was recovered in assets and £64m was returned to victims. At the heart of the SFO's work is the paper trail and in 2010–11 they processed 70 million documents of evidence – stacked on top of one another this would lead to a pile of paper 200 miles high.

The SFO uses the Bribery Act (2010), which came into force in July 2011, to prosecute bribery by UK companies in other countries or by foreign companies with a UK presence. If the directors of a company know about bribery and do nothing, then the directors are guilty. Other new offences include inducing someone to act contrary to their obligations and one of bribing foreign public and private sector officials. Recent cases include the successful prosecution of three men who attempted to sell £5m of fake tickets to the 2008 Beijing Olympics and various summer music festivals.

One of the SFO's most famous early cases involved Irish drinks giant Guinness. Rumours circulated in the City that the Guinness bid in 1986 for the Distillers Company was tainted by an unlawful share support operation, which involved Guinness offering protection from loss to those investors who supported the bid. This led to a marked rise in the price of Guinness shares. Guinness chief executive Ernest Saunders, aka 'Deadly Ernest' (he apparently had a habit of droning on), denied any knowledge of this. The SFO opened an investigation that resulted in Saunders and three other defendants (Anthony Parnes, Gerald Ronson and Jack Lyons) being convicted in 1990.

Saunders was sentenced to five years' imprisonment, but the Court of Appeal accepted doctors' advice that he was suffering from the symptoms of Alzheimer's disease and he was released after just ten months. Amazingly, Saunders made a full recovery, later clarifying that the symptoms had turned out to be the result of a cocktail of tranquillisers and painkillers that he was taking at the time.

The government has recently been criticised for only opposing allegedly corrupt practices when the UK's own interests are not at stake. The SFO failed to get to the bottom of allegations of accounting irregularities related to BAE Systems and a £43 billion arms deal with Saudi Arabia, which saw tens of thousands of jobs created for British workers both in the UK and Saudi Arabia. The investigation was stopped in December 2006 amid fears it would threaten national security – it was claimed that the Saudi government had threatened to withdraw cooperation on international security matters.

26. The Murder Gang

◎ The Telegraph Building (1862–1987)

◐ 135 Fleet Street, EC4

⊖ Chancery Lane Tube *(Central Line)* and Temple Tube
   (Circle and District Lines)

Fleet Street was the home of the newspaper industry from 1702 – when the *Daily Courant* was first published – until the end of the 20th century. The *Daily Courant* may have inspired the fictional legend of Sweeney Todd, Demon Barber of 186 Fleet Street, when on 14 April 1785 it reported the murder of a young man by a barber. According to the *Courant*: 'The two men came to an argument, and of a sudden the barber took from his clothing a razor and slit the throat of the young man, thereafter disappearing and was seen no more.'

Fleet Street has a long association with crime – reporting it, that is – and of overstepping the mark to get the story. Perhaps the most notorious Fleet Street crime reporters were Norman 'Jock' Rae of the *News of the World* (its offices were at 30–32 Bouverie Street, just off Fleet Street) and Harry Procter of the *Daily Mail* and later the *Sunday Pictorial*, who operated in the 1940s and 50s.

Armed with their editors' chequebooks, Fleet Street's crime reporters (known as the Murder Gang) paid everyone and anyone to get to the heart of a good crime story; it seems everyone had their price, whether police officer, solicitor – or even a murderer on the run.

Indeed, they scooped the full stories on three serial killers:

John Christie, the landlord who gassed eight people and sexually interfered with their corpses. He was hanged in 1953 – after an innocent man had already been executed for the same crimes (see page 180).

John Haigh, who claimed to have drunk the blood of the six victims he disposed of in vats of acid. Although he tried to plead insanity, Haigh was convicted and hanged in 1949 (see page 324).

Neville Heath, the brutal murderer of two women. He was executed in 1946. When offered a whisky before the hanging, he replied, 'Considering the circumstances, better make it a double.'

Procter met Neville Heath on at least two occasions – *before* Heath committed his first murder – and got face-to-face interviews with John Haigh and John Christie before either was arrested or charged. Astonishingly, Rae managed to meet with Christie while the serial killer was on the run – a time when every police force in Britain was on the lookout for him.

In return for interviews the journalists paid the killers' defence costs – in two cases they made substantial payments to the families of two of the killers after they were executed. The *News of the World* sold 8 million copies every Sunday – they had money to spare.

Although most papers have left Fleet Street for more modern premises in other parts of London, traces remain. You can just make out the old lettering on the *Daily Telegraph* building at No. 135 and the black and silver art deco building of the old *Daily Express* at No. 120.

27. A Temple of Lawyers

◎ Inner and Middle Temple
◒ Between Fleet Street and Embankment, EC4
ⓦ www.innertemple.org.uk
◔ Seven days a week. The remarkable Inner Temple Garden is open to the public 12.30-3pm each weekday
◉ Temple Tube *(Circle and District Lines)*

The warrens of the Inner and Middle Temple are two of the four Inns of Court where London's barristers work – the other two Inns are Lincoln's Inn and Gray's Inn. To be called to the Bar and practise as a barrister in England and Wales, an individual must belong to one of these Inns. This is where you come to search for a defence lawyer should you ever find yourself facing trial at the Old Bailey.

The photograph shows the southern entrance to the Temple from the Embankment and Nos. 1 and 2 Temple Gardens, designed by Edward Manningham Barry, the son of Charles Barry, who designed Westminster Palace (see page 303).

The Temple was originally used by the Knights Templar, an order of French warrior monks founded in 1118 to protect pilgrims travelling to the Holy Land. Turning to finance in later years, they bought the land here in 1162 and over time solicitors (no doubt attracted by the smell of all that money) set up shop and never left. Sadly much of the Temple was destroyed in the Blitz of 1941 (photographed by our friends Cross and Tibbs from Bishopsgate Police Station, see page 106).

Famous members of Temple Inns include Hanging Judge Jeffreys (see page 157), Mahatma Gandhi and the authors John Buchan (*The Thirty-Nine Steps*) and Bram Stoker (*Dracula*). Current members – although not practising – include London Mayor Boris Johnson as well as Prince William, the Duke of Cambridge, and Prime Minister David Cameron (both honorary members).

Even though law is sacrosanct here, a murder took place at 2 Brick Court in the Inner Temple in 1785. The details are slightly sketchy but it seems a certain Miss Broderick grew impatient waiting for her lover – Mr Eddington, who was hours late for their assignation – and was so displeased with his excuse (he was in the pub with friends and forgot the time) that she shot him dead.

Ten years later, if you walked to the top of the Inner Temple and exited at Fleet Street, you would have found, on your immediate right, Mrs Salmon's Waxworks (1795-1816), where some of the Inner Temple's unlucky clients found themselves and their crimes reborn in wax. Among many gruesome displays was that of demon barber Sweeney Todd and his famous chair. The building, at 17 Fleet Street, survived the Great Fire, and still looks the same now as it did in Mrs Salmon's day.

28. Smell the Money

◎ Security Express
⌂ Curtain Road, EC2
⊖ Old Street Tube *(Northern Line)*

The late 1960s, 70s and early 80s were the 'Golden Age' of bank robbery in London. In 1972, the annual total of armed robberies in the Metropolitan district was 380. By 1978, it had risen to 734 and by 1982 it more than doubled to 1,772 (that's five a day) – a 466 per cent increase in a decade. Changing attitudes to authority, the growth of motorways and the arrival of cheap, fast cars, helped robbers stay ahead of the law. Two of the most notorious were Ronnie and John Knight.

The Knight family grew up in Hoxton. Ronnie ran clubs and successfully kept a life of crime secret from Barbara Windsor, his movie-star wife – even though he was spending nearly every night out with Ronnie and Reggie Kray. Ronnie's younger brother John owned a garage and ran the Fox Pub in Shoreditch. In 1983, John masterminded what was then Britain's biggest cash robbery.

The Security Express depot in Curtain Road was known locally as Fort Knox. Knight found an empty building in the alley that overlooked the depot. He broke in and watched the place for more than a year before striking and escaping with five tons of cash, £6 million in total. 'When them doors opened it was beautiful,' John said. 'It was like Aladdin's cave.'

The cash was counted in the basement of the Fox Pub. John's share was £400,000. He buried most of it in his garden and took £100,000 to Ronnie asking him for help to get it out of the UK, to Spain. Then the Flying Squad, the Met Police's robbery specialists, got a tip-off and John was arrested. Ronnie fled for Spain – which, at that time, had no extradition treaty with the UK.

During John's trial, the jury were taken to the Fox to see where the money had been hidden and – in a legal first – to smell it: the smell in the basement matched the smell of the money. In 1985, five men were found guilty of robbery and handling money from the Security Express robbery and sentenced to a total of 66 years. The judge singled out John Knight for the harshest sentence: 22 years.

Ronnie returned to Britain in 1994 after losing most of his money, and after a newspaper agreed to pay him £20,000 for his story. The police were waiting at the airport. He pleaded guilty to handling £384,000 and was sentenced to seven years. Only £2 million of the stolen cash was ever found and the police failed to convict other members of the gang, including drug smuggler Clifford Saxe, the former manager of the Fox. Police arrested Saxe in Spain on Boxing Day 2001 but the 73-year-old died before he could be extradited.

29. **London's Best Loved Robber**

◎ **Spitalfields Market**

◒ **Commercial Street, E1**

ⓦ **www.spitalfields.co.uk**

🕐 **Market: Tues-Fri 10am-4pm, Sun 9am-5pm (including public holidays)**
Shops: Mon-Sun 10am-7pm Restaurants: Mon-Fri 8am-11pm,
Sat-Sun 9am-11pm

⊖ **Liverpool Street station** *(Mainline Rail, Central, Circle,*
Hammersmith & City Lines)

On the morning of 4 September 1724, Jack Sheppard, a lowly, 22-year-old thief from Spitalfields, was due to be hanged at Tyburn for the theft of three rolls of cloth, two silver spoons and a silk handkerchief. But when the door to Newgate's condemned cell was opened, Sheppard was gone.

This was his third break-out in a matter of months. He'd previously escaped via the roof of St Giles' Roundhouse, throwing tiles at the guards who dared to chase him. After that he escaped from Clerkenwell's New Bridewell prison by slipping through a barred window with his girlfriend Elizabeth Lyon, dropping 25 feet to the ground.

Born in Whites Row in Spitalfields on 4 March 1702, Sheppard knew life would be short for the likes of him from the start. Although the market, founded in 1682 under a licence granted by Charles II, was busy and profitable, many of the surrounding streets were home to London's poorest.

In Sheppard's time Spitalfields was a meat, poultry and vegetable market – and a centre for silk weaving. Today, the popular indoor market sells organic food, books, music, clothes, costumes and hats, antiques and art.

Sheppard was named after a dead older brother, and his father and sister both died when he was still an infant. His mother left him at Bishopsgate workhouse when he was six. At 15, he followed in his father's trade and became apprenticed to a carpenter in Covent Garden. It was while he was here that he learned how locks worked – and how to turn tools to his advantage.

Sheppard was recaptured less than a week after his escape from Newgate and was put in a barred and locked cell in handcuffs and fetters, chained to the floor. He escaped again a month later, disguised himself as a dandy and lived every day as if it were his last, partying every moment he could with Lyon. Thief-taker Jonathan Wild finally caught up with Sheppard as he bought everyone drinks at the Clare Tavern in Lincoln's Inn Fields.

Whilst Sheppard was at Newgate for the last time queues formed with hundreds of punters paying four shillings to visit him in his cell. His portrait was painted by Sir Henry Thornhill and he took on James Figg, England's first English bare-knuckle boxing champion, in a drinking competition.

Two hundred thousand people turned out for his hanging. It was only at the last moment that Sheppard's executioners found that the escapologist had a penknife hidden on him. His plan was to cut the cords and leap from the cart into the safety of the surging crowd, whom he hoped would spirit him away from justice. This time, though, with all avenues closed, Jack swung.

30. Anarchy in the East End

◎ H.S. Harris Jewellers

◯ 119 Houndsditch and 100 Sidney Street, E1

⊖ Liverpool Street station *(Mainline, Hammersmith & City, Metropolitan, Central, and Circle Lines)* and Aldgate Tube *(Metropolitan and Circle Lines)*

On 16 December 1910, an eastern European anarchist gang broke into H.S. Harris jewellers at 119 Houndsditch, planning to steal the contents of the safe to raise funds for activists in Russia and Latvia.

The raid was meticulously planned. They rented rooms in a building that backed onto the rear of the shop and took with them an India rubber gas hose 60 foot long (the hose is currently in the London Museum), so they could use gas from their building to burn through the jeweller's safe.

A neighbour, after hearing suspicious noises (it was a Jewish area and the Sabbath, so no one was supposed to be working), alerted an officer from Bishopsgate police station.

Sergeant Robert Bentley (36) was shot dead after entering the house the burglars were using to gain access to the jewellers. Then, fighting their way out of the building, the gang killed Sergeant Charles Tucker (46) and Constable Walter Choat (34). It was the worst incident for the police in British peacetime.

One of the burglars, George Gardstein, was accidentally shot by his friends in the melee and died from his wounds the next day. The gang fled and hid in a flat at 100 Sidney Street, where police discovered them on 3 January 1911. After a tense standoff where 200 officers cordoned off the street, and a series of gun battles with the well-armed terrorists, overseen by Home Secretary Winston Churchill (at one point a stray bullet passed through his top hat), the building caught fire and the anarchists burned alive.

Although police arrested several people who were alleged to have helped the gang, none were convicted. One of them, Jacob Peters, returned to Russia in 1917 and joined the Soviet secret police.

The funeral of the police officers, attended by Winston Churchill, took place in St Paul's Cathedral, on 22 December 1910. All three men were awarded the King's Police Medal and are commemorated by a plaque, which was unveiled in Cutler Street (close to Houndsditch) on the 100th anniversary of the murders.

31. The Long Oar of the Law

◎ Marine Policing Unit

◯ Wapping Police Station, 98–102 Wapping High Street, E1

Ⓦ www.met.police.uk/marine

ⓘ People wishing to visit the Thames Police Museum, inside Wapping
  Police Station, are asked to apply in writing to
  curator@thamespolicemuseum.org.uk

Ⓕ Free

⊖ Wapping station *(Overground)*

Wapping has been the site of the river police's operations since 1798, when a newly formed body of police officers brought some much-needed law and order to the Thames. They were the first of their kind in the world.

The river police used to carry out their duties in rowing boats. On 3 September 1878, the iron ship *Bywell Castle* ran into the pleasure steamer *Princess Alice* in Galleons Reach in East London, downstream of Barking Creek. The paddle steamer had been returning from the coast via Sheerness and Gravesend with nearly 800 day-trippers on board. She broke in two and sank immediately with the loss of over 600 lives. A subsequent inquiry recommended that Thames Division should have steam launches, as rowing galleys were inadequate for police duty. The first two were commissioned in the mid-1880s. The first motor vessels were introduced in 1910.

Just over a century after the *Princess Alice* tragedy, at about 1.50am on 20 August 1989 the dredger *Bowbelle* collided with the passenger vessel *Marchioness* near Cannon Street Railway Bridge. Four police patrol boats were on the scene within six minutes and, with the assistance of the passenger vessel *Hurlingham*, rescued 87 people from the water that night. In the days that followed river police officers recovered a total of 51 bodies, 24 from the wreck and 27 from the river. The Marine Policing Unit were also part of Operation Magician, the plan to apprehend the would-be Dome diamond robbers in 2000 (see page 72). The criminals' plan featured a dramatic escape on speedboats across the Thames.

Today the MPU has several specialised roles. Unit Identification Officers identify corpses recovered from the Thames and can provide specialist advice on all aspects of recovery and identification of bodies found in water. The Underwater and Confined Spaces Search Team (UCSST) is regularly used in major crime enquiries for the recovery of evidence (normally in the form of weapons) and searches for missing persons. The UCSST conducts around 250 searches annually, spending on average 55 per cent of its time diving, 25 per cent wading and 20 per cent in confined spaces. Many searches are security related and are carried out to ensure the safety of VIPs and the general public at many of London's major events.

32. **Execution Dock**

◎ Prospect of Whitby Public House

⚲ 57 Wapping Wall, E1

☎ 02036 034 009

🕐 Mon-Thurs 12pm-11pm, Fri-Sat 12pm to Midnight, Sun 12pm-10pm

⊖ Wapping station *(Overground)*

The Prospect of Whitby is one of the oldest Thameside pubs. Built in 1520, it became known as the Devil's Tavern, thanks to the many smugglers and thieves who were regulars. It changed its name in 1777, after the ship *Prospect* (registered in Whitby) was moored outside. Pepys, Dickens, Whistler and Turner were all customers but its most infamous patron was 'Hanging' Judge George Jeffreys (1645–89), who lived nearby and also drank at the Town of Ramsgate at 62 Wapping High Street.

Jeffreys once sentenced almost 300 men to death in a single session in the West Country after an attempted rebellion against James II. The judge was himself arrested while in the Town of Ramsgate during a more successful rebellion (he was at the time trying to flee the country disguised as a sailor) and was sent to the Tower of London, where he died from kidney disease. An executioner's noose is kept hanging from the back of the Prospect of Whitby in his (dis)honour.

For almost 400 years from the 1400s to the 1800s, Execution Dock (located near Wapping Old Stairs at the end of the cobbled alleyway beside the Town of Ramsgate) was used for the execution of pirates. The condemned were often brought from Marshalsea prison in Southwark (see page 32), over London Bridge and past the Tower. Once here, they were allowed a final speech before being tied to a post in the river and left to the rising tide. The bodies of the most notorious pirates were covered with tar and hung from a gibbet to warn sailors on ingoing and outgoing ships of the price of mutiny and piracy.

The most famous pirate executed here was Captain William Kidd, on 23 May 1701. He was imprisoned at Newgate and on the morning of the execution was plied with rum until he was insensible. Kidd had been sentenced to hang but the rope snapped on the first attempt. The second effort went as it should and his body was left to rot on a gibbet for almost two years. (A pub named after him, the Captain Kidd, can be found a short walk away at 108 Wapping High Street.) Execution Dock's last victims were executed in 1830.

In Search of
Jack the Ripper

➲ Start: Whitechapel Tube *(District and Hammersmith & City Lines)*
Finish: Liverpool Street station *(Mainline, Central, Metropolitan, District and Hammersmith & City Lines)*
✪ Distance: Five miles
🕐 Duration: Two-and-a-half hours

In 1888, policemen neither wanted nor dared to patrol Whitechapel at night. This was a time when the gangs ruled the streets. The Nichol Gang, for example, attacked and sometimes mutilated prostitutes who didn't pay for their 'protection'.

By day, Whitechapel was no less noisy than it is now, but far more crowded, filthier, wilder and poorer. In 1888, 1,000 of its 80,000 residents lived on the streets, sleeping in doorways, staircases and dustbins to keep warm. Men, women and children starved or froze to death in the open, and disease was everywhere, travelling via the open sewers.

Whitechapel was also a centre of commerce. Every week thousands of livestock were driven down the high road to be slaughtered and butchered in the local shops before being sold on the open meat stalls that peppered the maze of alleys and yards.

It was in this labyrinth of poverty and vice that the world's most famous serial killer, 'Jack the Ripper', operated. Preying on female prostitutes from Whitechapel's slums, 'he' committed a series of unsolved murders which were concentrated in the autumn of 1888 – although some 'Ripperologists' have claimed the killer took many more victims over a longer period of time. What is undeniable is that he has inspired miles of newspaper print, libraries of fiction and non-fiction, and hours of documentaries, television dramas and movies – not to mention considerable online debate – all devoted to answering the question: Who was Jack the Ripper?

A definitive answer is almost certainly lost to history. Thankfully, though, many structures from his world still survive and Jack the Ripper-related buildings are visible from the moment you step out of Whitechapel Underground station.

01. Turn left on leaving Whitechapel Tube station onto Whitechapel Road.

The tall building immediately next to the station is the former Whitechapel Working Lads' Institute where the inquests of some of the Ripper's victims took place.

On the opposite side of the road is the Royal London Hospital, opened in 1757. The Royal Hospital Museum, housed in the former crypt of St Phillip's Church (entrance in Newark Street, to the rear of the hospital), is open Tuesday to Friday from 10am to 4.30pm and it's worth a visit if only to see a rather exciting piece of Ripper history on public display: The Openshaw Letter.

The letter arrived at the Royal London Hospital on 29 October 1888 and was addressed to Dr Thomas Horrocks Openshaw. Dr Openshaw had examined the kidney sent in a gruesome package to George Lusk of the Whitechapel Vigilance Committee after the murder of Catherine Eddowes, the Ripper's third victim. Eddowes' body was missing a kidney. The letter reads:

> Old boss you was rite it was the left kidny i was goin to hoperate agin close to your ospitle just as i was going to dror mi nife along of er bloomin throte them cusses of coppers spoilt the game but i guess i wil be on the job soon and will send you another bit of innerds
> Jack the Ripper
> O have you seen the delve with his mikerscope and scalpul a-lookin at a kidney with a slide cocked up.

This was the first use of the nickname 'Jack the Ripper'. Although many claim the letter was a fake, sent by an enterprising journalist to whip up excitement, it remains a fascinating and tangible link to those dark weeks over 120 years ago.

02. Walk back past the Underground station, along Whitechapel Road, passing through the market and turn right into Fulbourne Street. Turn right into Durward Street (called Buck's Row in 1888). Pass the Board School on the right and stop just at the end of the school wall, before the line of houses.

The summer of 1888 had turned out to be one of the wettest and coldest on record. Snow had fallen in July. Thursday August 30 had been yet another day of freezing downpours. Mary 'Polly' Anne Nichols, a 43-year-old prostitute, had spent the night searching for drink, clients and a bed for the night. With her missing teeth and greying hair, Mary could hardly be described as attractive but she had little trouble finding clients. 'I'll soon get my doss money,' she'd boasted to the keeper of a lodging house earlier that evening.

Thousands of women sold their bodies to stave off cold and starvation. The Church and the *Lancet* both estimated that there were as many as 80,000 prostitutes working in London. Women would sell themselves for two or three pence, or for a loaf of stale bread.

In the early hours of 31 August, coffee stall keeper John Morgan served Mary, just a short distance from here. Morgan noted that a thin man dressed in dark clothes was with her.

At 3.40am market porter Charles Cross was on his way to work when he spotted what he thought was a tarpaulin lying on this spot, then the gateway to a stable. It was only when he bent close that he realised it was a woman – Mary Nichols. When Police Constable John Neil arrived, he saw the woman's throat had been cut wide and deep, almost ear-to-ear.

Various witnesses were called to attend the inquest in the Young Working Lads' Institute. The coroner concluded that the frenzied attack had been carried out with a six- to eight-inch blade. The motives were unknown, although blame was first directed at local 'protection' gangs. Two other prostitutes had been stabbed to death not far from where Polly had fallen just a few months earlier.

A nearby building that still survives from the 1880s is the Board School (pictured). Derelict for many years, it was recently converted into luxury flats. It's still possible to see the railings surrounding what was once the rooftop playground.

Buck's Row and White's Row were joined to become Durward Street on 25 October 1892 after the residents complained about living in such an infamous street.

→ **03.** Walk back along Durward Street, turn right again into Vallance Road and take the left turn into Hanbury Street – which is in fact a narrow alleyway.

The building at the junction of Hanbury and Spelman Street was formerly the Alma Tavern. In 1888 it was one of the area's most notorious pubs and pick-up joints.

Forty-seven-year-old Annie Chapman was a regular. On the night of 8 September, a penniless Annie was thrown out of her lodgings and so she went looking for a client. Annie, who was overweight and missing several teeth, was a typical Whitechapel prostitute – if older than average.

At 5.30am Elizabeth Darrell saw Annie talking to a man in dark clothing outside the Cats' Meat Shop (a pet food shop), near the Alma in Hanbury Street.

Elizabeth heard the man ask: 'Will you?'

'Yes,' came Annie's reply.

→ **04.** Keep walking along Hanbury Street until you come across the large brick building on the right – this wall (built in the 1970s) is part of the Truman Brewery. This is the approximate site of No. 29 (the opposite side of Hanbury Street has changed little since 1888).

At about 5.15am Albert Cadoche, a carpenter, stepped out into his backyard at No. 27 to urinate.

He heard a faint cry of 'No!' followed by the sound of something heavy falling against the wooden fence. He ignored the noises; there were always strange goings-on in the neighbourhood. It was left to 56-year-old John Davis to make the grim discovery as he stepped out into the yard of No. 29, also to relieve himself, at 5.45am. At that moment, it was very likely that the murderer was still close by, possibly crouched behind a fence in the next backyard.

Flesh, blood and body parts were scattered on one side of the yard. Annie's body had been 'laid out' with her left arm bent and lying across her breast. Her legs were spread wide open and her dress had been lifted up. Her intestines had been yanked out and were now slung over her right shoulder. A huge jagged gash ran from Annie's rectum up to her breastbone. Her neck had been brutally cut, virtually severing her head.

At the scene, Inspector Joseph Chandler noticed bloodstains on the fences dividing Nos. 25, 27 and 29. A collection of bloody rags found at No. 25 indicated that the killer had stopped there to wipe his hands. Inspector Chandler also observed that not one of the flimsy palings on the slim fences was broken. The killer, whomever he may have been, was as light and as nimble as a cat.

Dr Thomas Bond, surgeon to the Met Police and considered by many to be the world's first offender profiler, suggested that the killer had some amateurish knowledge of anatomy.

Panic started to grip Whitechapel; rumours spread of a murderer who wore a leather butcher's apron, and who might have been an immigrant, possibly Polish, Jewish – or both. With the already chaotic East End now on the brink of racial rioting, the police put every man on the case.

05. Turn left into Wilkes Street and then right into Fournier Street (formerly Church Street). Stop on the corner by the Ten Bells pub.

Fournier Street, which has changed little since 1888, runs alongside Nicholas Hawksmoor's Christ Church (completed in 1729, left derelict in 1960 and restored in 2004, and well worth a visit). In the 1880s its small graveyard was crowded with homeless people, prostitutes and drunks.

Fournier Street ends at the Ten Bells pub at the corner of Commercial Street, a good place to take on some liquid refreshment while admiring its Jack the Ripper display.

It was at the Ten Bells that Mary Kelly — arguably the Ripper's final victim — had spent the night drinking on the evening before she was murdered.

One thing I noticed, and that was that he walked very softly. I believe that he lives in the neighbourhood, and I fancied that I saw him in Petticoat Lane on Sunday morning, but I was not certain.
Statement from labourer George Hutchinson, who saw this man with Mary Kelly on the night of her murder.

⊖ **06.** After stopping at the Ten Bells, return back along Fournier Street and turn right into Brick Lane.

Stop at the junction with Thrawl Street, and look for the gabled Indian restaurant. This used to be the Frying Pan public house and a piece of original pub moulding – a pair of crossed frying pans – remains in one of the upper gables.

This is where the first victim, Mary Nichols, was drinking on the night of her death. Although the current building dates from 1891, records show that the pub itself goes back to at least 1811. When the Frying Pan closed in 1991 it was converted into a restaurant, which also offers bed and breakfast accommodation.

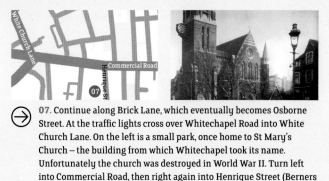

07. Continue along **Brick Lane**, which eventually becomes **Osborne Street**. At the traffic lights cross over **Whitechapel Road** into **White Church Lane**. On the left is a small park, once home to St Mary's Church – the building from which Whitechapel took its name. Unfortunately the church was destroyed in World War II. Turn left into **Commercial Road**, then right again into **Henrique Street** (Berners Street in 1888). **Fairclough** is the first junction ahead.

In the 1880s, a maze of alleyways and narrow streets filled the area around Fairclough Street, which was regarded as 'respectable', with two greengrocers, a chandlery, bakery and chemists. Its inhabitants included dock labourers, shoe-makers and several tailors. At the junction of Fairclough Street and Berners Street, on the western side, stood Dutfields Yard.

On the evening of 30 September, Swedish-born divorcee Elizabeth Stride, 45, aka 'Long Liz', was enjoying a drink in the Bricklayers Arms, about 150 metres from this spot. At 11pm two men saw Elizabeth leaving the Bricklayers Arms and at 11.45pm a witness saw her in the company of a man 'of medium height, wearing decent clothes and who bore the appearance of a clerk'.

At 12.30am PC William Smith turned into Berners Street and caught sight of a man and woman standing together, right at this point, opposite the unlit area of Dutfields Yard. Smith saw that the man was in his twenties, approximately five foot seven, wearing dark clothes, with a dark-coloured felt hat and was of a respectable appearance. He was carrying a newspaper parcel about 18 inches by 6 inches. Seeing nothing untoward, Smith continued on his patrol.

James Brown was passing along Fairclough Street at 12.45am. As he turned and looked down Berners Street, he saw a man who was preventing a woman's passage past him. He heard the woman shout: 'No! Not tonight. Maybe some other night!'

Brown continued on his way home to No. 35. Minutes later, Israel Schwartz, a Hungarian immigrant, spotted the same couple still arguing. The man suddenly grabbed the woman and threw her to the ground. The woman screamed. Afraid for his own safety, Schwartz, who was of small stature, kept walking. The man then called out 'Lipski', an anti-Semitic insult, to another passer-by.

A few minutes later, Louis Diemschutz, a market trader in cheap jewellery, rolled up the street in his horse and cart and began to enter Dutfields Yard. Just above the yard was a Working Men's Club, where Diemschutz also worked as a steward and from which came the sounds of singing. His horse shied away from something on the ground. It wasn't until he climbed down that he saw Elizabeth's body. She was still warm to the touch; her throat had been slit, leaving a huge two-inch-wide gash.

It was quite possible that Diemschutz had disturbed the Ripper, and that the killer was still hiding in the darkness of the yard. As he ran to get help, the Ripper escaped. Despite this close call, he wasn't going to stop. Unsatisfied with his 'work', the Ripper was driven by some terrible madness to finish what he had started.

→ **08–12.** Before moving on it's time for a great British tradition...

A Pub Crawl

08 Walk to the end of Fairclough Street, turn right into Back Church Lane, left onto Commercial Road, left again into Alie Street, passing the Grade II listed **Dispensary pub** (formerly the Old Dispensary, built in 1858 to provide medicine to the poor). Beautifully restored, it's worth stopping here for a classic British lunch or dinner.

09 Cross Leman Street (Leman is old English for lover, sweetheart or mistress) and pass the **Zeppelin Shelter pub** (originally the Black Horse, which opened in 1894, now sympathetically restored to how it looked during World War I).

10 Continue to the end of Alie Street (passing the **White Swan**, on the site of the Half Moon Theatre, which serves excellent traditional ales).

11 Turn right into Mansell Street, then left into Aldgate High Street where the **Hoop and Grapes** (built in 1721) on the left serves many fine ales – including its own, Mendes Gold. Once threatened with demolition, it's now a Grade II listed building. Excavations in the 1990s uncovered a dozen or so graves in the cellar, which were moved to the British Museum.

12 Suitably refreshed, emerge from the Hoop and turn left, down Aldgate High Street, passing St Botolph's Church on the right.

To try and curb the killings and to reduce the Ripper's prey, the police offered prostitutes immunity as long as they worked from the small park surrounding St Botolph's. It was close to here, on the evening of 29 September, that a policeman arrested Catherine Eddowes for being drunk (she had been impersonating a fire engine) and took her to Bishopsgate police station.

Catherine was a popular character locally, known for her happy demeanour and her good singing voice. Her friends also described her as being intelligent but having a fierce temper.

By midnight she had sobered up and was duly released. As she left she cried out, 'Good night, old cock,' and walked in the direction of Houndsditch. Catherine was penniless and so decided to search for a client for fear that her husband would beat her if she returned home broke.

→ **13.** Follow Aldgate High Street around the church and turn left into Duke's Place, then turn left into St James's Passage, which leads into Mitre Square. A small, quiet and enclosed court surrounded in the main by large warehouses and empty buildings, in 1888 it was a regular prostitutes' haunt. Walk to the southwest corner of the square and find the cobblestones, close to the school gate.

This was where, at 1.45am on 30 September, Police Constable Watkins found Catherine's body. She lay in the far corner of the square, on her back with her arms flat against the wet cobbled ground. Her wounds were so deep that it seemed as though the killer had wanted to decapitate her.

Catherine lay with her clothes drawn up exposing her stomach and thighs. Her skin and abdomen had been laid open from her breastbone to the pelvis. Her intestines were laid over her right shoulder; her liver, vagina, and rectum had all been stabbed. Her kidney and part of her uterus were missing. The tip of her nose was cut clean off; one of her cheeks and her lips had almost been sliced away. Several very intricate cuts had been made to her eyes.

The infamous 'Dear Boss' letter was delivered the following day and at this point talk of Jack the Ripper dominated the entire city, from Whitechapel to the West End.

14. Walk to the end of Mitre Street, turn right into Creechurch Lane, crossing Bevis Marks and Houndsditch (the area owes its name to the kennels kept here for City hunts in the Middle Ages, and was also a dumping ground for bodies during the time of the Black Death) into Stoney Lane. Follow this around into Gravel Lane, cross Middlesex Street (Petticoat Market is to the left) and then take the first left into Goulston Street.

A clue was found in the stairway of 48 Goulston Street (what was then the entrance to 108–119 Wentworth Dwellings). At 2.55am Police Constable Alfred Long discovered a bloody rag on the ground – it was a piece of Catherine Eddowes' apron. Above it, scrawled in chalk on the wall were the words: 'The Jews are the men that will not be blamed for nothing.' This was a popular Jewish area with many families working in Petticoat Lane, selling second-hand clothes and shoes.

An inspector was placed on guard to protect the graffiti until it was light enough to take a photograph, but Met Police Commissioner Sir Charles Warren (pictured above) travelled to the street and personally erased the message. The reason, he said later, was for fear of a race riot breaking out.

→ **15.** Walk up Goulston Street, straight ahead into Bell Lane, Crispin Street and left into Brushfield Street (Dorset Street in 1888), opposite Spitalfields Market.

Dorset Street, named in 1867, ends opposite the Ten Bells pub and Christ Church and was one of the most notorious and dangerous streets in the area.

An unusually attractive prostitute, 25-year-old Mary Jane Kelly, lived at 13 Millers' Court, situated between Nos. 26 and 27.

Friday 9 November 1888 was yet another day of rain. The morning papers carried headlines about the forced resignation of the unpopular Police Commissioner Sir Charles Warren. The rubbing out of the chalk writing had been his last mistake as far as the Home Office were concerned. The Ripper had cost him his career.

At 10.45am, rent collector Thomas Bowyer knocked on the door of 13 Millers' Court. There was no answer, so he looked through a broken window. As his eyes adjusted to the dark room Bowyer saw two lumps of flesh lying on the bedside table. Beside them on the bed lay the body of a young woman, covered in blood.

With Mary Jane Kelly, his fifth victim, the Ripper had taken his knife to every part of her, severing her breasts and placing one under her head and the other by her right foot. Her liver was between her feet and her spleen and her intestines had been placed on either side of the body. Mary's neck had been severed down to the spine and her nose, cheeks, eyebrows and ears had been removed. Her left hand lay across her exposed rib cage. Her heart was missing.

> Short of actually skinning his next victim from head to heel, it is difficult to see what fresh horror is left for him to commit.

Inspector Frank Abberline, speaking about the murder of Mary Kelly.

16. Turn left into Gun Street, left into Artillery Lane and pass through the atmospheric Frying Pan Alley on the right to Middlesex Street and left into Bishopsgate. Pass Bishopsgate police station to Liverpool Street station on the opposite side of the road (a subway entrance allows you to pass under Bishopsgate, if you prefer). Here the tour ends.

Who the Ripper was remains a mystery and a full discussion of the many, many suspects is beyond the scope of this book. 'We are inundated with suggestions and names of suspects!' Sir Charles Warren had written to the head of the City Police in October 1888.

Jack the Ripper may have terrorised the city but he left a surprising legacy; improvements were made to policing and, ironically, the attention the Ripper attracted meant that the authorities began to clean up Whitechapel. Doss houses and whole streets were demolished, breaking up the criminal quarters.

The East End never shook off its criminal reputation, however. In 1938, 50 years after the Ripper murders, the year that five-year-old Reginald and Ronald Kray started school in Brick Lane, the East End was still seen as an area of slums and a criminal haven.

NORTH

Kentish Town

Chalk Farm

Camden Road

Camden Town

Mornington Crescent

Regents Park

Marylebone

7 Baker Street

Marylebone Road

Baker Street

Edgware Road

8

Edgware Road

Regents Park

Great Portland Street

Warren Street

Euston Square

BT Tower

1. Death of a Playwright

◎ 25 Noel Road, N1

⊖ Angel Tube *(Northern Line)*

On 9 August 1967, 34-year-old playwright Joe Orton was murdered here by his 41-year-old lover, Kenneth Halliwell.

The two men had met at the Royal Academy for Dramatic Art in 1951. They became lovers and tried to write books together, but had no success, so they worked at a Cadbury's factory on and off from 1957 to 1959 to save money for their own home, moving into a small flat here in 1959.

Annoyed at the lack of good books in their local Islington library, they stole books and modified the cover art and blurbs – creating saucy montages of semi-nude and homoerotic figures – before smuggling them back into the library. They were discovered in May 1962 and sentenced to six months in prison for five counts of theft and malicious damage to more than 70 books. They were fined £262. Orton and Halliwell blamed their harsh sentence on the fact that they were homosexual, or, as they put it, 'queers'.

Prison turned out to be a crucial formative experience for Orton; the isolation from Halliwell allowed him to break free creatively.

After his release, Orton wrote several plays, including *Entertaining Mr Sloane*, which premiered at the New Arts Theatre on 6 May 1964 where it outraged as much as it amused. Established playwright Terence Rattigan made sure it transferred quickly to the West End and it won several awards, garnering Orton second place for 'Most Promising Playwright'. Orton's next play *Loot* won several more awards and established his notoriety. The film rights were sold for £25,000.

As Orton grew in fame and confidence, Halliwell sank into depression, often arguing with Orton and taking antidepressants and barbiturates to help him cope with his sense of failure.

A few days before his murder, Orton had told a friend that he had another boyfriend and wanted to end his relationship with Halliwell, but didn't know how to go about it. It seems Orton was right to be concerned about how his lover would take the news.

The playwright was found, his head pulped, lying in bed with the murder weapon, a hammer, on his chest. Halliwell was found on the floor, naked, and covered with his victim's blood. After murdering Orton, he had taken an overdose of Nembutal.

Orton and Halliwell's vandalised (and hilarious) book covers have since become a prized part of Islington's cultural history and can be seen in the Islington Museum on St John Street, ten minutes' walk south of Angel Tube station.

2. Getting it in the Head

◎ Thornhill Road Gardens

⌂ Junction with Richmond Avenue, N1

⊖ Angel Tube *(Northern Line)* and Highbury and Islington station
   (Victoria Line and Overland)

On 28 July 1977, a police officer was called to this spot, on the edge of a quiet park in Richmond Avenue, where he was shown into a public toilet. Inside, he was greeted by a decapitated, half-rotted, grinning human head wearing a dark-blue woollen balaclava. It was defrosting, having been frozen and wrapped in the pages of the *London Evening News*, dated 16 June 1977.

On that day, a trial (lasting seven months, a record at that time) had ended at the Old Bailey where two men, Bob Maynard and Reg Dudley, who both lived in Islington, had been convicted and jailed for life for the torture and murder of fellow career criminals William Moseley and Micky 'the laughing bank robber' Cornwall.

Moseley's torso was found in the Thames in 1975 while Cornwall's body was found in a shallow grave near Hatfield. The victims' finger- and toenails had been extracted and cigarette burns covered their bodies.

Commander Bert Wickstead, a police legend known as the 'Grey Fox', led the investigation. Incorruptible and loved by his men, the former SAS commando had played a leading role in the probe into Met officers' links to Soho pornographer Bernie Silver and pimp Jimmy Humphreys (see Bent Coppers, page 259).

The jury was told that Dudley and Maynard decided to kill Billy Moseley after he had an affair with the wife of a friend. Then, when Cornwall found out his friend had been killed, he planned revenge, but Dudley and Maynard murdered him first. However, Dudley and Maynard claimed that the 'confessions' Wickstead had produced in court that said they'd shot Moseley in the head were faked.

Indeed, the skull found in the public toilet on the last day of the trial was proven to be Moseley's – and there was no bullet wound. The fact that the head had been left at this spot on the day Dudley and Maynard were convicted suggested that perhaps they were right – who else other than the murderer would know where the head had been kept? The head, however, was ignored.

It wasn't until 2001 that a forensic document examiner proved the contemporaneous statements upon which Dudley and Maynard were convicted could not have been made in the time the police claimed.

Then a key witness, bank robber Tony Wild, retracted his evidence. He'd claimed Dudley had shown a pub landlord Moseley's head and said, 'Your customers are always complaining their beer hasn't got a head on it. Why don't you give them this?' Wild admitted he made this up to help avoid a long sentence for armed robbery.

Thanks to the new evidence, Dudley, 77 and Maynard, 63 had their convictions quashed by the Court of Appeal in 2002. Wickstead didn't live to see Dudley and Maynard freed. He died in 2001 after a long illness.

Dudley, whose mother, sister, two brothers and an ex-wife all died while he was in jail, said he'd become an artist and planned to use any compensation money to open his own gallery.

3. London's Executioners

◎ Pentonville Prison
⬗ Caledonian Road, N7
⊖ Caledonian Road Tube *(Piccadilly Line)* and Caledonian Road and Barnsbury station *(Overground)*

Built from 1840 to 1842 and designed to hold 500 prisoners, Pentonville was modelled on the American penitentiary system, with five separate and light-filled wings, where prisoners were exercised and taught a trade. It became the model for all British prisons and 54 others were built according to its design over the following six years.

Pentonville became the location for North London hangings after Newgate closed in 1902. Though many tried, the week-long Prison Commissioners' Assistant Executioner training course at Pentonville was not something that anyone could apply to take, one had to be invited and recruits were often selected from the prison service.

One hundred and twenty hangings were carried out here between 1902 and 1961, including Dr Hawley Crippen, Roger Casement, Timothy Evans and John Christie. The executioner John Ellis, who hanged Crippen for the murder of his wife, recalled that the doctor smiled as he walked towards him.

Christie murdered at least seven women at 10 Rillington Place (the street is no longer there) in Notting Hill, West London, between 1943 and 1953. He was a witness at the trial of his neighbour Timothy Evans, who, despite his innocence, was convicted and 'swung' for one of the killings. Albert Pierrepoint (see page 236) hanged both men.

One of Pentonville's most prolific hangmen was Robert Orridge Baxter (c. 1878–1961). His career lasted from 1915 to 1935, during which period he carried out 44 hangings and assisted at 53 others. Indeed, Baxter was responsible for nearly every execution carried out in London during his tenure and carried out 24 consecutive hangings at Pentonville prison.

His first job as chief executioner was the hanging of Frenchman Jean-Pierre Vaquier, who'd poisoned his lover's husband, in 1924. Baxter gained a reputation as being quick, calm and reliable until, on 11 December 1928, at Swansea prison, he carried out the execution of Trevor Edwards, who had bludgeoned his sweetheart to death and cut her throat.

Baxter failed to notice that his new assistant, Alfred Allen, had not cleared the trapdoor after strapping the prisoner's legs. When Baxter pulled the lever, Allen fell into the pit along with Edwards. Baxter was completely blind in his left eye – a fact he'd kept concealed – and hadn't seen Allen. As Edwards died instantly and Allen escaped unharmed, he was cleared of any blame and allowed to keep his job.

Before he retired in 1935, Baxter's last execution was Alan Grierson at Pentonville on 30 October. Grierson had murdered an elderly woman for her jewellery. During the hunt for Grierson, the police relied on an artist's sketch, made from descriptions given by people who knew him, the first time in history this technique was used.

4. A Terror to Evil Doers

◎ Holloway Prison

⌂ Parkhurst Road, N7

⊖ Caledonian Road Tube and Holloway Road Tube *(both Piccadilly Line)*

Originally known as the City House of Correction, the original Gothic-style, four-wing prison opened in Holloway in 1852.

Female-only since 1903 (the Moors murderer Myra Hindley was incarcerated here) five women were hanged at Holloway in the 20th century. Amelia Sach and Annie Walters met their end on 3 February 1903. They'd murdered up to 20 infants, given to them by mothers (often servants made pregnant by their masters) who believed that Sach and Walters would pass them on to people waiting to adopt – for a fee of £25 to £30. Instead, the babies were murdered and the pair split the proceeds. They were hanged by Henry Pierrepoint, father of Albert (see page 236).

Before Robert Baxter became chief executioner in 1924, he assisted John Ellis in the hanging of Edith Jessie Thompson in January 1923 at Holloway prison for her role in the murder of her husband, Percy, stabbed to death by Edith's lover, Frederick Bywaters. Thirty-year-old Edith went to the gallows in extreme distress. This execution hit Ellis hard and he resigned in March the following year, having executed a total of 203 people. Before his suicide on 20 September 1932, Ellis wrote a remarkable memoir, *Diary of a Hangman*.

Albert Pierrepoint hanged Styllou Christofi, who had bludgeoned her daughter-in-law to death, on 13 December 1954 and 28-year-old Ruth Ellis – the last woman to be hanged in England – on 13 July 1955. Her boyfriend, David Blakely, caused Ellis to miscarry by punching her. Ellis shot Blakely five times outside the Magdala Pub, 2a South Hill Park in Hampstead (the pub claims that marks left by ricocheting bullets are preserved in the wall). Ellis's counsel attempted to argue that she should be convicted for manslaughter by provocation but she was found guilty of murder instead and sentenced to hang.

Despite a huge public appeal, after three weeks and two days in the condemned suite at Holloway as Prisoner 9656, the execution date arrived. Shortly before her death, Ellis said: 'I am now completely composed. I know that I am going to die, and I'm ready to do so. You won't hear anything from me that says I didn't kill David. I did kill him ... it's a life for a life. Isn't that just?'

Outside, a crowd (pictured) of more than 500 people gathered, singing and chanting.

Ellis was given a glass of brandy just before 9am. Then, Albert Pierrepoint entered, pinioned her hands behind her back and led her 15 feet to the gallows. Ruth said nothing at all during her execution.

Her body was buried within Holloway prison but later disinterred and reburied when Holloway was demolished in 1970, before being rebuilt. The original foundation stone remains, however. Carved into it is the inscription: 'May God preserve the City of London and make this place a terror to evil doers.'

The death penalty in the UK was suspended in 1965 and permanently removed in 1970.

5. The Camden Ripper

◎ The Hospital for Tropical Diseases (now St Pancras Hospital)
and The Hardy Tree

⌂ St Pancras Way, NW1 and St Pancras Old Church graveyard, NW1

🕐 St Pancras Old Church graveyard is open from 7am till dusk daily

⊖ King's Cross station *(Northern, Victoria, Hammersimth & City, Circle
and Metropolitan Lines)*

At about 6.40am on 30 December 2002, a homeless man was found wandering
in the grounds of the Hospital for Tropical Diseases. He was carrying a bin liner.
Inside was a pair of dismembered legs belonging to a middle-aged woman.

He had found them in a nearby bin in Royal College Street. A police search
led to the discovery of the upper part of a torso of a second, younger woman.

The following afternoon more body parts were found in carrier bags in other
bins. Police then raided a ground-floor flat in the nearby Hartland block in
the College Place Estate where they found further cut-up remains of the older
woman's torso.

The flat was occupied by Anthony John Hardy, a grey-haired six-footer in his
forties, described by neighbours as a 'loner', with a history of mental illness. By the
time the police arrived he had gone on the run.

Hardy, the son of a coal miner, had studied engineering at university before
marrying and moving to Australia. Sadly he started to suffer from mental illness
and tried to harm his family. Divorced and diagnosed with manic depression,
Hardy returned to the UK where he began abusing drugs and alcohol. He moved
to his Camden flat in 2000 – a short distance from King's Cross, an area used by
prostitutes to pick up clients, many of whom frequented the nearby St Pancras Old
Church graveyard next to the hospital, home to the Hardy Tree (pictured). He lured
women to his flat by offering them money.

Murder Squad detectives had questioned Hardy a year before the body parts
were found, after discovering the body of a middle-aged woman in his flat. However,
a subsequent inquest ruled that she died of natural causes and he was allowed to go
free. He would later confess to her murder.

On 2 January 2003, a member of the public spotted Hardy at Great Ormond
Street Hospital for children in central London and he was arrested. His victims were
identified as three local prostitutes.

At the Old Bailey in November 2003 Hardy pleaded guilty to the murders and
was given three life sentences, eventually adjusted to a whole-life tariff in 2010.

Hardy – who was under the supervision of a local health authority at the time –
might have killed other women. The mutilated headless body of another prostitute
was pulled from Regent's Park canal – half a mile from Hardy's flat – in February
2001. Her killer has never been found.

The Hardy Tree is named after the author Thomas Hardy who, in 1865, as a
25-year-old trainee architect, was entrusted with the proper exhumation of bodies
in the graveyard to make way for a new railway line to King's Cross. The cemetery
and church have been restored as part of the regeneration of the whole area,
including the new St Pancras Station, and now attract many visitors.

6. **Princess Diana and a Murdered Innocent**

◎ Brill Place Park

⌂ Brill Place, NW1

⊖ Mornington Crescent Tube *(Northern Line)* and King's Cross station
*(Victoria, Piccadilly, Hammersmith & City, Circle, Metropolitan and
Northern Lines)*

In 1994, this small park, now in sight of the new, still-gleaming St Pancras International train terminal, was secretly visited by the most photographed woman in the world.

Princess Diana had come here to pay her respects to a murdered child, 15-year-old Richard Everitt.

The Princess stood with her head bowed in prayer and read messages on bouquets left on the spot where Richard had bled to death, cradled in his father's arms. She told local vicar Brendan Clover that she was deeply worried about racism.

In the early 1990s this area, Somers Town, was the centre of severe racial tensions. The main secondary school in the area was awash with gangs divided by race: Bangladeshi, white and black.

Richard's murder shocked the nation. Popular and friendly, a teenager 'without an ounce of aggression', according to his parents, Richard had spent that summer's afternoon playing football with friends when they decided to get some food. They were passing Brill Place when they ran into a gang of about ten young Asian men who attacked them.

His two friends ran for safety but Richard was stabbed in the back and died here from a wound seven inches deep. The Asian men left, taking the boys' food with them.

Badrul Miah, 19, interviewed by police later that night, was found to have blood on his jeans and trainers. Scientific examination linked that blood with the dead boy. It took 14 months before Richard's devastated parents, Mandy and Norman Everitt, saw Miah jailed. Some of the gang, including the knifeman, were believed to have fled the country. Others were discharged because of insufficient evidence.

But there were cheers and applause in the Old Bailey as Miah was led away to begin his life sentence. Though he had not struck the fatal blow, forensic evidence proved he'd been very close. Mandy and Norman Everitt subsequently left the area and moved to Yorkshire to start a new life.

As has been shown over and over again, racist tensions belie the real cause of urban violence: an unending, hopeless sense of deprivation and social exclusion. In the early 19th century Somers Town used to be a haven for Spanish refugees, who lived here in great poverty, leading to similar explosions of violence.

Public unease following Richard Everitt's murder led to efforts to improve the area – and, with the help of the new British Library (in sight of Brill Place), St Pancras International and the renovation of St Pancras Old Church graveyard, it has improved. But as Shane Meadows' film *Somers Town* depicted in 2008, many residents still live in unshakeable poverty.

7. The Walkie-Talkie Job

◎ Lloyd's Bank

⌂ 185 Baker Street, London, NW1

⊕ Baker Street Tube (*Hammersmith & City, Circle, Metropolitan, Bakerloo and Jubilee Lines*)

At 11pm on Saturday, 11 September 1971, an amateur radio 'ham' called Robert Rowlands contacted Scotland Yard to say that he had overheard a conversation between what sounded like a team of bank raiders and their lookout on a nearby rooftop during a robbery in progress somewhere in central London.

At 2am, a senior officer decided to take his report seriously but by then the 'walkie-talkie' conversations had stopped.

The police checked on 750 banks. They visited Lloyd's Bank on the corner of Baker Street and Marylebone Road on Sunday afternoon, but the 15-inch-thick doors of the vault were intact and secured by a time lock.

The raiders were still inside, however, and had gained access by renting a nearby shop and tunnelling under the Chicken Inn restaurant next door before carving their way up through three feet of reinforced concrete using a thermic lance and emerging inside the vault. As the floor was thought to be impenetrable, it wasn't connected to the alarm system.

The robbers left behind eight tons of rubble, taking with them the contents of 268 deposit boxes and millions in cash (making it the UK's largest bank job). They'd written, 'Let Sherlock Holmes try to solve this' on one of the walls.

Although the press initially reported the theft, they were suddenly and unusually hit with a government gagging order, or D-Notice, imposed to prevent further coverage in the interests of national security.

This suggested that something very sensitive had been taken from the deposit boxes. It was rumoured that photographs and other evidence of illicit sexual encounters implicating influential public figures were held at the bank.

Only four men were convicted in connection with the crime and much of the loot was never recovered. Of the stolen property that police did manage to retrieve, most was never reclaimed by its owners.

The men convicted at the Old Bailey were Anthony Gavin, 38, a photographer from Dalston; Thomas Stephens, 35, a car dealer from Islington; and Reginald Tucker, 37, a company director from Hackney. They all pleaded guilty and received 12 years each. A fourth man, Benjamin Wolfe, 66, a 'fancy goods' dealer from East Dulwich, pleaded not guilty but ended up with eight years.

The story was turned into a film in 2008, *The Bank Job*, starring Jason Statham.

8. The Rise of Mad Frank

◎ Hyde Park Mansions

⌂ Cabbell Street, NW1

⊖ Edgware Road Tube *(Bakerloo, Hammersmith & City, Circle and District Lines)*

Jack Comer, aka Jack Spot (he liked to say he helped people who were in a 'spot', but the nickname more likely came from a facial mole), was Polish and arrived in the East End in the 1930s. He established himself as a player in gambling and black-market rackets and, with partner in crime Billy Hill, dominated Soho. His power waned in the 1950s after a falling-out with Billy Hill, a failed heist at Heathrow Airport (which would have netted him £1.25m) and with the legalisation of bookmaking.

After a short spell in prison, Billy Hill decided it was time to make a move on Spot. He sent diminutive 'Mad' Frankie Fraser and six others to deal with Spot at his home at Hyde Park Mansions.

On 7 May 1956, Spot's wife Rita was with him when the gang – armed with razors and iron bars – launched their attack. Fraser, who was keen to make his gangster name, slashed Spot's face before stabbing him with a butcher's chopper. As Spot fell, Rita tried to block the attackers but received a series of punches and kicks for her trouble.

Mad Frank was one of two people charged with carrying out the attack. His 15 previous convictions counted strongly against him and he went down for seven years.

His reputation as a no-nonsense gangster was sealed, however. He went on to spend over 40 years inside, 10 years for being part of the Richardsons' torture gang (see page 43). It has been alleged that he pulled teeth with a pair of pliers, something he strongly denies.

In the 1960s, the control of Soho and the West End slipped from Billy Hill, Jack Spot and the Messinas, among others, to the Kray twins and the Richardson brothers, Charles and Eddie. Fraser became the Richardsons' enforcer (see Elephant and Castle, page 43). Fraser earned his 'Mad' nickname after the authorities decreed he should be confined in Broadmoor, the hospital for the criminally insane.

Fraser claimed he beat up the executioner Albert Pierrepoint in Wandsworth prison on the day he hanged teenager Derek Bentley for the murder of a police officer. He said it was 'the best thing I ever done'.

In August 1991 Fraser was shot in the head as he left Turnmills club in Clerkenwell. He was with his then girlfriend, Marilyn Wisbey, daughter of the Great Train Robber, Tommy.

'I was really legless,' Fraser said. 'When the first shot hit me in the head, I went for where the flash come from. Marilyn … slung her arm round me head, pulled me back and the next shot flew by because she pulled my head out of the way … no question but she saved my life. The next morning she said to me, "That was a powerful shot of vodka we had last night. What proof was it?"'

The London of Sir Arthur Conan Doyle

Although of course fictional, Sherlock Holmes is perhaps the world's leading detective. The *New York Post* once carried out a poll to 'find the most famous character in English literature'. They asked 1,000 people of all ages and found that in second spot, after Harry Potter, came Sherlock Holmes.

The author of the Holmes adventures, Sir Arthur Conan Doyle, is no less fascinating than the master detective, so this themed walk, dedicated to the writer who ensured London's status as the capital of crime, follows in the footsteps of Sherlock Holmes and his creator, taking in some examples of real-life Victorian crime along the way.

01. Exit Baker Street Tube station via the south entrance onto Marylebone Road and you'll see a statue erected in honour of the great detective. Turn right into Baker Street and head north. The museum is on your left.

The Sherlock Holmes Museum is the first stop after exiting the Underground for any Holmesian pilgrim. The curators have faithfully recreated Holmes's and Watson's apartments (up 17 steps as Conan Doyle described in *A Study in Scarlet*), situated above Mrs Hudson's restaurant.

Mrs Hudson was, of course, Holmes and Watson's long-suffering landlady who, in *The Adventure of the Naval Treaty*, serves a curious breakfast of curried chicken. Mrs Hudson receives a mention in 16 of the stories and usually appears armed with a tray of food or a telegram, or makes the announcement that a client has arrived with yet another mystery for the crime-fighting duo.

She was fond of Holmes, as she went into 'violent hysterics' upon his return from the grave in *The Empty House* and was even persuaded by Holmes in the same story to take part in an adventure which involved the careful manipulation of a dummy to deceive a would-be assassin: 'We have been in this room two hours, and Mrs Hudson has made some change in that figure eight times, or once in every quarter of an hour. She works it from the front, so that her shadow may never be seen.'

> 'Mrs Hudson has risen to the occasion,' said Holmes, uncovering a dish of curried chicken. 'Her cuisine is a little limited, but she has as good an idea of breakfast as a Scotchwoman.'
> *The Adventure of the Naval Treaty*

➔ **02.** Head south down Baker Street to 221, also known as Abbey House.

Conan Doyle was amazed by the British public's interest in Sherlock Holmes; by the time he had completed the first series of adventures, his work was more widely read than Dickens. The fact that many readers believed Holmes was real was a constant amusement to Conan Doyle who, in an audio recording made on 14 May 1930, seven weeks before his death, said: 'With regard to Sherlock Holmes, for many, he seems to be a real person and I have had numerous letters from time to time addressed to him from all parts of the world, and the most quaint request involved what was virtually an offer of marriage.'

The first letter addressed to Sherlock Holmes at 221b Baker Street arrived in 1890, when a tobacconist from Philadelphia wrote asking for a copy of Holmes's exhaustive monograph on tobacco ash.

The owners of the building, the Abbey National Building Society, eventually decided to provide a secretary to Sherlock Holmes to respond to the 40 letters that continued to arrive from all over the world every month. After Abbey House was closed and converted into flats in 2005 (by the Baskerville Group), the Sherlock Holmes Museum took over.

Some fans ask quite specific questions about Holmes: 'Why did you never marry?' 'What type of tobacco do you smoke?' or 'Would you care to give me some advice on setting up in practice as a consulting detective?'

Many actually request Holmes's assistance in solving real crimes, mysteries and problems; everything from lost pets (including German budgies, a pet rabbit called Thumper and a kidnapped tarantula) to how to overcome shyness with boys and how to understand English newspaper headlines.

Holmes has also been asked to locate the kidnapped heiress Patty Hearst, to investigate the Watergate scandal, to end the nuclear arms race, to recover a stolen Rolls-Royce and locate a giant ball made of foil. On one occasion he received a letter from a kidnapped Dr Watson demanding a $5,000 ransom (a Christmas card from the good doctor arrives every year, without fail).

Dear Mr Holmes, I am at my wit's end. I dare not give particulars here ... a small fortune in gold coins and the good name of a kindly African heiress hang in the balance.
Excerpt from letter addressed to 221b Baker Street, sent in 1904

$\rightarrow$ **03**. From Baker Street, turn right into Marylebone Road and then the first left to Gloucester Place.

This stop, should you wish to make it (it is by no means essential), will take some preparation. This is the home of the Sherlock Homes Collection and is available to view by appointment only (Tel. 0207 641 1206 or see www.westminster.gov.uk/services/libraries/special/sherlock).

The Collection includes stories, information about Conan Doyle, photographs, cuttings and journals as well as the original manuscripts of *The Dying Detective* and *The Lion's Mane*, securely held in the library's purpose-built archives repository. Copies are available to view, while the delicate originals are restricted to those serious scholars whose work demands they scrutinise the original.

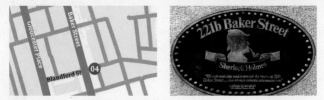

04. Return to Baker Street, this time staying on the south side of Marylebone Road, and then turn right into Baker Street, heading south towards Oxford Street.

In Doyle's day 221b Baker Street didn't exist – the section north of Marylebone Road was called Upper Baker Street and the upper part of Baker Street south of Marylebone Road was called York Place. Baker Street began where York Place ended at the junction with Paddington Street.

So which house inspired Doyle to house the famous detective? This has excited debate among Holmesian scholars but it's generally agreed that the best clue to 221b's real location comes from *The Empty House*, the 'sequel' to *The Final Problem*, where Holmes returns to life after having supposedly fallen to his death into the Reichenbach Falls while fighting his arch-enemy Professor Moriarty.

To fool a would-be assassin, Holmes rigs a waxwork dummy, the shadow of which can be seen through the window. With Dr Watson, Holmes embarks on a long and winding journey through the West End, until: 'We emerged at last into a small road, lined with old, gloomy houses, which led us into Manchester Street, and so to Blandford Street. Here he turned swiftly down a narrow passage, passed through a wooden gate into a deserted yard, and then opened with a key the back door of a house. We entered together, and he closed it behind us.'

Once they exit the front of the house, Holmes asks: 'Do you know where we are?'

'Surely that is Baker Street,' Watson replies.

Holmes confirms that, and informs Watson that they are in Camden House, 'opposite to our own old quarters'.

Following these instructions today leads one to a modern office block, but just across the road, Nos. 32 and 34 (pictured on previous page) could pass for Nos. 221a and b.

Other Sherlock-connected aspects to Baker Street include The Park Plaza Sherlock Holmes Hotel (entrance in Chiltern Street), which contains a Moriarty restaurant and a Dr Watson bar, with many Holmesian prints on view. Sherlock Mews, off Paddington Street, is named after the great detective.

05. Continue down Baker Street and turn left into George Street, then first right into Manchester Street. Turn left at Manchester Square for the entrance to the Wallace Collection.

'To some extent,' he answered thoughtfully. 'My ancestors were country squires, who appear to have led much the same life as is natural to their class. But, none the less, my turn that way is in my veins, and may have come with my grandmother, who was the sister of Vernet, the French artist. Art in the blood is liable to take the strangest forms.'
The Greek Interpreter

At the southernmost end of Baker Street, in Manchester Square, sits the fantastic stately home which holds the Wallace Collection, an unusual museum containing one of the finest private collections of art and artefacts ever assembled by a single family.

Sir Richard Wallace, who died in 1897, bequeathed the house and its contents to the nation on condition that the collection will always be displayed in central London. The museum opened in 1900. Among its treasures are one of the best collections of French 18th-century pictures, porcelain and furniture in the world, a remarkable array of 17th-century paintings and a superb armoury.

Inside, among the suits of armour, swords, Canalettos and Van Dycks, lies a singular clue as to the ancestors of Sherlock Holmes. Doyle revealed little about Holmes's family. Apart from his brother Mycroft, mentioned for the first time in *The Greek Interpreter,* and the distant relation, young Dr Verner mentioned in *The Norwood Builder,* the only other clue we have is the reference to Vernet in *The Greek Interpreter.*

Many of the paintings by Emile Jean Horace Vernet (1789–1863), including *Storm with a Shipwreck* and *Arabs Travelling in the Desert,* currently reside in the Wallace Collection. Comparing Vernet's self-portrait (once you get past the shock of his enormous handlebar moustache) with the famous illustrations of Holmes by Sidney Paget, it is easy to believe – thanks to the high forehead and the shape of the nose – that the two men could be related.

Vernet, who became director of the French Academy in Rome at 38, enjoyed boxing and fencing, and featured these sports in his paintings. These were the same two sports that Holmes revealed he enjoyed while at university in *Gloria Scott*: 'Bar fencing and boxing I had few athletic tastes.'

→ **06**. Walk around Manchester Square and turn left into Hinde Street. Stay on this road, crossing Thayer Street/Mandeville Place, at which point it becomes Bentinck Street.

As I passed the corner which leads from Bentinck Street on to the Welbeck Street crossing a two-horse van furiously driven whizzed round and was on me like a flash. I sprang for the foot-path and saved myself by the fraction of a second.
The Final Problem

Certainly the most traumatic of all cases recorded by Dr Watson, one that caused massive public uproar, *The Final Problem* details the struggle between Sherlock Holmes and the dastardly Professor Moriarty.

After defeating Moriarty's latest criminal project, Holmes realises he needs to flee, and sure enough he is soon being chased through London by teams of criminals intent on only one thing: the murder of the great detective. Holmes was attacked the same day in Vere Street and then when he left his brother's house in Pall Mall.

Holmes and Watson travel to the Continent with Moriarty hot on their trail and their fatal confrontation takes place in Switzerland at the Reichenbach Falls.

07. Continue to the end of Bentinck Street, turn left into Welbeck Street and immediately right into Queen Anne Street, then first left into Wimpole Street. Upper Wimpole Street is straight ahead.

In April 1891, 31-year-old Dr Arthur Conan Doyle took up residence on the first floor as a practising ophthalmologist. Business was slow. So slow in fact that most of his time here was spent writing Sherlock Holmes stories.

On Friday, 3 April 1891, his diary records that he sent *A Scandal in Bohemia* – the first of the Sherlock Holmes short stories – to his agent A.P. Watt. Watt sent it on to the *Strand Magazine* (see page 215), where the manuscript, signed 'A. Conan Doyle / 2 Upper Wimpole Street / London W.' was stamped as being received on 6 April.

His diary entry for 10 April notes: 'finished *A Case of Identity*'. More quickly followed. The first five of the Holmes short stories were written and sent from here (the post box across the road, although not original, is in the same location).

Doyle ended up making £1,500 that year from writing, which was three times the salary of an in-demand doctor, and he was able to quit his practice to write full-time.

08. Head south on Upper Wimpole Street and turn into Weymouth Street, Harley Street is second on the right.

It was, then, in the spring of the year 1897 that Holmes's iron constitution showed some symptoms of giving way in the face of constant hard work of a most exacting kind, aggravated, perhaps, by occasional indiscretions of his own. In March of that year Dr Moore Agar, of Harley Street, whose dramatic introduction to Holmes I may some day recount, gave positive injunctions that the famous private agent lay aside all his cases and surrender himself to complete rest if he wished to avert an absolute breakdown. The state of his health was not a matter in which he himself took the faintest interest …

The Devil's Foot

Harley Street is renowned for its private and expensive medical specialists. Number 84 was once home to John St John Long, aka 'King of the Quacks'. In the 1820s, Long ran a practice here, attracting wealthy female clients who paid him a whopping £13,000 a year to treat them for consumption using a variety of unusual methods, including massage and the inhalation of strange and potent gases. Long was exposed as a quack in 1830, after two patients died. He was found guilty of manslaughter and escaped with a £250 fine, but, somewhat ironically, the handsome doctor died of consumption at the age of 36. His loyal and wealthy patients paid for a grand tomb at Kensal Green Cemetery.

The 'occasional indiscretions' that Dr Watson refers to in *The Devil's Foot* are probably Sherlock's abusive relationship with the drug cocaine, which was quite legal at the time and is mentioned in five of the stories. In 1884, the American surgeon Dr William S. Halstead was the first person to use cocaine as an anaesthetic by injection. Unfortunately, Halstead also became the world's first intravenous cocaine addict. Holmes too prefers to inject the drug for a stronger 'hit', using a 7 per cent solution. However, he was not so addicted that he was distracted from his work – in fact it seemed as if the stupor the drug induced saved him from his overactive mind during long periods of inactivity. As Watson observed: 'Save for the occasional use of cocaine, he had no vices, and he only turned to the drug as a protest against the monotony of existence when cases were scanty and the papers uninteresting.'

→ **09.** Continue south on Harley Street and turn left into Queen Anne Street. Follow this road into Chandos Street then take the left into Langham Place, where you will find the Langham Hotel.

The King of Bohemia (*A Scandal in Bohemia*), Captain Morstan (*The Sign of Four*) and Phillip Green (*The Disappearance of Lady Frances Carfax*) all stayed at the Langham.

In Doyle's time, the Langham was a relatively new addition to Regent Street. Built in 1864 at a cost of £300,000, it was intended to represent a seven-floor Florentine Palace, with 600 rooms and several private suites. The Langham was the essence of Victorian pride and respectability; regular clients included Napoleon III and Mark Twain.

In 1889, Conan Doyle was invited by Joseph Marshall Stoddart, managing editor of the American-based *Lippincott's Monthly Magazine*, to dine at the Langham. Stoddart was interested in putting together an English edition of the magazine and wanted to commission work by England's brightest new talents.

Doyle was not the only guest; they were joined by a promising young writer called Oscar Wilde. Doyle recorded the meeting in his autobiography: 'It was a golden evening for me.' At this historic dinner, Oscar Wilde was commissioned to write *The Picture of Dorian Gray*.

Doyle dashed off the 40,000-word story in under a month – his haste showed, for *The Sign of Four*, as it was finally called, contained many errors, including the most famous of all: Watson's 'magic bullet', his leg wound from *A Study in Scarlet* mysteriously transforming into a shoulder wound.

Nevertheless, upon its publication one reviewer declared it to be 'the best story I ever read in my life'. It certainly had everything a dramatic adventure needed: a locked-room puzzle, a blow-gun-toting dwarf, a love story for Watson and a climactic boat chase on the Thames.

While Doyle's story received critical acclaim, Wilde came under attack for having produced an 'immoral' work. He famously defended himself by saying: 'There is no such thing as a moral or immoral book ... Books are well written, or badly written. That is all.'

→ **10.** Pass by the Langham, turn right into Regent Street and continue to Oxford Circus.

> He quickened his pace until we had decreased the distance which divided us by about half. Then, still keeping a hundred yards, we followed into Oxford Street and so down Regent Street.
> *The Hound of the Baskervilles*

Oxford Street is mentioned in nine of Sherlock Holmes's adventures. At the time they were written it was full of small shops yet to be pushed aside by the first department stores. It was also on Oxford Street that Holmes purchased his tobacco, from the fictional Bradly's Tobacconists.

Holmes knew a fair bit more about tobacco ash than the average tobacconist, as described in *The Boscombe Valley Mystery*: 'I found the ash of a cigar, which my special knowledge of tobacco ashes enables me to pronounce as an Indian cigar. I have, as you know, devoted some attention to this, and written a little monograph on the ashes of 140 different varieties of pipe, cigar and cigarette tobacco.'

In *The Disappearance of Lady Frances Carfax* Watson shopped for his boots from another fictional shop called Latimer's. While neither of these places existed, the Capital and Counties Bank, Holmes's bank, is now Lloyd's at No. 399.

In *The Adventure of the Priory School* Holmes displayed some temerity when asking for payment from the Duke of Holdernesse upon finding his son. 'I should be glad if you would make me out a check for six thousand pounds. It would be as well, perhaps, for you to cross it. The Capital and Counties Bank, Oxford Street branch, are my agents.'

11. Continue down Regent Street, past Oxford Circus until reaching No. 68, on the western side of Regent Street, close to the junction with Air Street.

> We learn with regret that Mr Sherlock Holmes, the well-known private detective, was the victim this morning of a murderous assault which has left him in a precarious position. There are no exact details to hand, but the event seems to have occurred about twelve o'clock in Regent Street, outside the Café Royal … the thugs escaped the bystanders by passing through the Café Royal and out into Glasshouse Street behind it.
>
> *The Illustrious Client*

Conan Doyle and Oscar Wilde were both regulars at the Café Royal at 68 Regent Street (directly south of the Langham), which was the preferred dining spot of the literati of the day.

In March 1894, the year that *The Memoirs of Sherlock Holmes* was published, it was subject to a murder mystery worthy of the great detective himself when a young night porter, Marius Martin, was found lying at the entrance in a pool of his own blood. He had been killed by two bullets to the head. Two men were seen escaping via the rear exit into Glasshouse Street. They were never apprehended and the motive remained a mystery.

The Café Royal opened in 1865 and consisted of three floors. In the basement were a wine cellar and billiard room. A café, luncheon bar and grill room were on the ground floor and on the first floor private rooms could be hired by customers.

From the 1890s to early 1900s, the Domino Room with its marble-topped tables and red velvet seats (later the Grill Room restaurant) was a famous meeting point for artists and writers. Apart from Doyle, patrons included the artist Whistler and satirist and caricaturist Max Beerbohm.

The Café Royal closed in 2008 – after 143 years – and the owners of the building, the Crown Estate, are planning a £500m redevelopment to open up the southern end of Regent Street, creating an open space to rival Trafalgar Square.

The frontage of the Café Royal and the public rooms overlooking Regent Street are still there and all Grade I listed, so will be preserved, but the inside of the building has been converted into a hotel.

12. Continue south on Regent Street, pass Piccadilly Circus and head for the statue of Eros, just in front of the Criterion Theatre and Criterion restaurant.

> On the very day that I had come to this conclusion, I was standing at the Criterion Bar, when someone tapped me on the shoulder, and turning round I recognised young Stamford, who had been a dresser under me at Barts.
>
> *A Study in Scarlet*

There is a plaque on the wall opposite the main bar in the Criterion restaurant to commemorate the historic starting point of Holmes and Watson's many adventures because it is here, in 1881, in *A Study in Scarlet*, that Watson first learned of Holmes's existence from Stamford, an old hospital colleague.

The 'conclusion' that Watson had reached was that he could no longer afford to stay in a private hotel in the Strand, and did not have enough funds to rent an apartment on his own, so needed someone suitable with whom he could share the cost. Financial hardship was something Doyle himself had to endure for much of his early life. When he began writing the first of the Holmes adventures, *A Study in Scarlet* in 1886, the memories of his sparsely furnished house and surgery in Southsea near Portsmouth would have still been fresh in his mind (on more than one occasion, his rations dwindled to bread and water).

Doyle's financial life was precarious until 1891, when he found success with *The White Company*, which sold more copies than *A Tale of Two Cities* and *Treasure Island* and has never been out of print. It relates the adventures of Alleyne Edricson, who joins the White Company, a band of skilled archers that fought during the Hundred Years' War. Also in 1891, *A Scandal in Bohemia* was published in the *Strand Magazine*.

13. Continue south on Regent Street into Waterloo Place and stop at the junction of **Pall Mall**, looking east.

> We had reached Pall Mall as we talked, and we were walking down it from the St James's end. Sherlock Holmes stopped at a door some little distance from the Carlton, and, cautioning me not to speak, he led the way into the hall.
>
> *The Greek Interpreter*

Pall Mall – home to Holmes's brother Mycroft – is a road that takes its name from an Italian game something like croquet (*pallo a maglio*), popular during the reigns of Charles I and Charles II.

During Conan Doyle's time, Pall Mall became famous for its 23 private gentleman's clubs, including the Reform Club, of whom Phileas Fogg of *Around the World in 80 Days* fame was a celebrated, if fictional, member. The Carlton Club was founded in 1832 and was a place where members of the Conservative Party could meet and discuss tactics. The club still exists today and most Conservative Prime Ministers have been members, including Winston Churchill, Anthony Eden, Harold Macmillan and Edward Heath.

14. Continue a short distance to the end of Waterloo Place, to the Duke of York Memorial.

> We shall expect you early tomorrow, and when you get that signal-book through the little door on the Duke of York's steps, you can put a triumphant finis to your record in England.
> *His Last Bow*

The Duke of York Steps are a fine flight of public steps that sweep down from Waterloo Place to the Mall, the avenue that runs from Trafalgar Square to Buckingham Palace.

The Duke of York Column, finished in the 1830s, built in honour of George III's second son, Frederick, towers over them. This 124-foot column cost £25,000 and was paid for by stopping the pay of the army for one day. Until this, the Duke had been a popular figure with the troops. The Duke had debts of £2m at his death and it was suggested that the column was a sufficient height for him to keep out of the way of his creditors.

In *His Last Bow*, the great detective is lured from happy retirement on the Sussex Downs to serve England by penetrating a dangerous spy ring headed by one of the Kaiser's greatest operatives, Von Bork. The master spy's house on the English coast was the centre of a vast web, penetrated ingeniously by Sherlock Holmes under the guise of the Irish-American agent Altamont.

The story itself details the final closing of the net around Von Bork, and involves an exchange of papers through a mysterious doorway in the wall that borders the Duke of York Steps. No such doorway exists, although it's rumoured that the cellars of nearby Carlton House have a secret passage that emerges somewhere on the Duke of York Steps.

His Last Bow contains one of Holmes's most quoted and patriotic statements:

There's an east wind coming all the same, such a wind as never blew on England yet. It will be cold and bitter, Watson, and a good many of us may wither before its blast. But it's God's own wind none the less, and a cleaner, better, stronger land will lie in the sunshine when the storm has cleared.

$\longrightarrow$ **15.** Descend the Duke of York Steps and turn left into the Mall. Continue into Trafalgar Square, turn right (passing the junction for Whitehall) and then turn right into Northumberland Avenue and at the first left into Northumberland Street is the Sherlock Holmes pub.

He laid an envelope upon the table, and we all bent over it. It was of common quality, greyish in colour. The address, 'Sir Henry Baskerville, Northumberland Hotel', was printed in rough characters; the post-mark 'Charing Cross', and the date of posting the preceding evening.
The Hound of the Baskervilles

Previously known as the Northumberland Arms and the Northumberland Hotel, the Sherlock Holmes pub is now a shrine to all things Sherlock Holmes. The walls are covered in mementoes, from portraits of Doyle to film stills from the many movies made about Holmes and Watson.

In the upstairs restaurant there is a reconstruction of the front room at 221b Baker Street, complete with a dummy of Sherlock Holmes (as used in *The Empty House*), reading his *Times* in front of the fire.

Bottles of noxious-looking chemicals line the shelves; Holmes's violin and Persian slippers sit by the fireplace and on the mantelpiece are piles of letters, which are no doubt full of requests for the great detective's help.

16. Face the front of the Sherlock Holmes pub. Just to the right is a small passageway. Head down here and on the right is the sign for Neville's Turkish Baths.

> Both Holmes and I had a weakness for the Turkish bath. It was over a smoke in the pleasant lassitude of the drying-room that I have found him less reticent and more human than anywhere else. On the upper floor of the Northumberland Avenue establishment there is an isolated corner where two couches lie side by side, and it was on these that we lay upon September 3, 1902, the day when my narrative begins.
> *The Illustrious Client*

A terrible tragedy befell the man who introduced the Turkish bath to London in 1858. David Urquhart thought that Turkish bath houses would contribute to a 'war waged against drunkenness, immorality, and filth in every shape'. But in his time he was generally regarded as an eccentric – he refused to shake hands with anyone, declaring it unhygienic – and the decision to place his 18-month-old son William in a Turkish bath to help with his teething was seen by many as bordering on madness. William died and the Urquharts escaped a manslaughter charge by the skin of their teeth.

Despite this, Turkish baths were a very popular pastime for many ladies and gentlemen. By 1861, there were more than 30 baths in London. It is not difficult to see the attraction of a long, slow afternoon moving through heated rooms, often decorated in an Eastern style, followed by relaxation in towels with sherbet, tobacco and fruit provided by attendants.

Apart from cocaine, a Turkish bath seemed to be the only thing that would relax the tightly wound mind of Sherlock Holmes. The bath that Holmes and Watson visited in *The Illustrious Client* was called 'Neville's' and although the bath has long gone, the ladies' entrance remains.

→ **17.** Continue along Craven Passage and turn left into Craven Street, then right on the Strand. Charing Cross Station is on the right.

'Come, Watson, come!' he cried. 'The game is afoot. Not a word! Into your clothes and come!'

Ten minutes later we were both in a cab, and rattling through the silent streets on our way to Charing Cross Station.
The Adventure of the Abbey Grange

I would come to you abroad, but it would excite remark if I left the country at present. Therefore I shall expect to meet you in the smoking-room of the Charing Cross Hotel at noon on Saturday. Remember that only English notes, or gold, will be taken.
The Adventure of the Bruce-Partington Plans

The terminal of Charing Cross train station runs parallel with Craven Street. The station was built in 1864 on the site of the old Hungerford market (from which Hungerford Bridge, the metallic red structure that carries the trains across the Thames, takes its name, see also page 56).

The Charing Cross Hotel was built at the same time as the station and has 218 bedrooms. In 1905, during maintenance, the roof of the station collapsed killing six people and destroying an adjoining theatre, The Avenue. It remains the station nearest to the heart of London. Above the right entrance, there is a small pediment with shield, lion, griffin and motto 'Onward'.

Charing Cross station was mentioned in ten of the Sherlock Holmes adventures; it was often the scene for Holmes and Watson's departure to some suburb or hamlet where an anxious or resentful local policeman awaited their assistance. Also near Charing Cross were the papers of Dr Watson, something he mentioned in *The Problem of Thor Bridge*:

Somewhere in the vaults of the bank of Cox and Co., at Charing Cross, there is a travel-worn and battered tin dispatch-box with my name, John H. Watson, M. D., Late Indian Army, painted upon the lid. It is crammed with papers, nearly all of which are records of cases to illustrate the curious problems which Mr. Sherlock Holmes had at various times to examine.

18. The Adelphi Theatre is located further east along the Strand, on the corner with Bedford Street.

In 1910, Doyle wrote and produced a play called *The House of Temperley*, a complex story about a gambler who has to risk the remains of his fortune on a boxing match. To stage it Doyle took a six-month lease on the Adelphi Theatre (see also page 284).

Unfortunately the play bombed, partly because it was so violent (Doyle hired real boxers and one broke a finger and rib in rehearsals) and therefore alienated the female audience. As most men liked to take their wives or girlfriends to see a play, the theatre remained only half full. *The House of Temperley* closed after only two months, leaving Doyle with a big financial headache. He had spent £5,000, a huge sum at the time, on its production.

Undaunted, Doyle adapted his favourite Sherlock Holmes story, *The Adventure of the Speckled Band*, for the stage in less than a week. As with the fight scenes in *The House of Temperley*, Doyle strived for realism and for the snake central to the plot found a small non-poisonous python, which he described as the 'pride of my heart'.

It opened on 4 June 1910 and received impressive reviews, although one critic enraged Doyle when he wrote: 'The crisis of the play was produced by the appearance of a palpably artificial serpent.' It turned out that the snake Doyle had chosen liked to spend most of its life asleep, so it was sacked and a more 'realistic' rubber one was hired in its place. The props manager did this without telling Doyle – until the author expressed his delight at the snake's much-improved performance and was forced to agree that the rubber snake was the better actor.

The Adventure of the Speckled Band ran for seven months, toured Britain, the USA, France and Sweden and was revived in 1920. Doyle wrote to his brother Innes about the financial success of the play as it toured the country:

Very busy so excuse card. Play holds up very well. Have determined to run a company in the provinces. It is a bold venture ... also the Princess Royal has new fiancé and they were both much impressed. Cheque has gone to Cox and Co., £1050 that week, £1080 this week. Receipts for previous three weeks are £1116, £1161 and £1180, a profit of £350 each. Best Temperley did was £1090 with profit of £200. If we can do this already so far then we have high hopes after Easter but there is a lot to ward off yet. Bravo, jolly good.

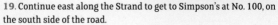

19. Continue east along the Strand to get to Simpson's at No. 100, on the south side of the road.

Watson, you must help me on with my coat. When we have finished at the police station I think that something nutritious at Simpson's would not be out of place.

The Adventure of the Dying Detective

Simpson's is one of the city's oldest restaurants. Situated a few doors down from the Savoy Hotel, it was originally a gentleman's club where members would sit on comfy leather chairs, smoke cigars, drink coffee and play chess. In 1848, the caterer John Simpson joined forces with owner Samuel Reiss to turn it into a grand restaurant, attracting patrons such as Charles Dickens and Benjamin Disraeli.

In 1904 it was reopened with some ceremony as women were allowed to lunch there for the first time, albeit in a separate dining room. Simpson's-in-the-Strand is still going and retains its old-world splendour and club-like atmosphere.

20. Cross the road and continue east along the Strand and take the next left into Burleigh Street. No. 12, once home to the *Strand Magazine*, is on the right at the junction with Exeter Street.

> Under such circumstances I naturally gravitated to London, that great cesspool into which all the loungers and idlers of the Empire are irresistibly drained. There I stayed for some time at a private hotel in the Strand, leading a comfortless, meaningless existence, and spending such money as I had, considerably more freely than I ought.
> *A Study in Scarlet*

The Strand, the road that links Westminster to the City, is just over one kilometre long, with Fleet Street to the northeast and Trafalgar Square to the southwest.

The *Strand Magazine*, which took its name from the street, was first published in January 1891 and was an immediate success, selling 300,000 copies every month. It was aimed at the middle classes and featured a healthy mix of fact and fiction, and a 'picture on every page'.

As well as stories by famous writers, its readers responded to the magazine's campaigning journalism, in particular the exposure of crime and corruption. Indeed, enterprising reporters from dozens of magazines in the Strand area went to great lengths to penetrate the city's underworld – although they didn't have far to travel. In late Victorian London, many of the narrow streets around the Strand were home to pickpockets and prostitutes who made their meagre living preying on pleasure seekers.

Many famous fiction writers contributed to the *Strand Magazine*, including Conan Doyle, whose first Sherlock Holmes story was published here in 1891. Editor of the *Strand Magazine* Herbert Greenhough Smith later recalled receiving Doyle's first Sherlock Holmes stories, *A Scandal in Bohemia* and *The Red-Headed League* and described them as 'a godsend to an editor jaded with wading through reams of impossible stuff! The ingenuity of plot, the limpid clearness of style, the perfect art of telling a story! I at once realised that here was the greatest short-story writer since Edgar Allan Poe.' Before starting what would eventually become *The Casebook of Sherlock Holmes*, Doyle wrote to Greenough Smith, complaining about a lack of good, inspirational stories in the newspapers. The editor responded by recalling a true story about a German man who had tied a stone to a revolver, hung it over the side of a bridge, and then shot himself, the weapon vanishing into the water. Doyle was delighted and set to work on what became *The Problem of Thor Bridge*.

The *Strand* ran for 60 years and Greenough Smith remained editor for 40 of them. Its last edition was published in March 1950.

21. Return to the Strand and continue east until the next left, Wellington Street.

> At the Lyceum Theatre the crowds were already thick at the side-entrances. In front a continuous stream of hansoms and four-wheelers were rattling up, discharging their cargoes of shirt-fronted men and beshawled, bediamonded women. We had hardly reached the third pillar, which was our rendezvous, before a small, dark, brisk man in the dress of a coachman accosted us.
> *The Sign of Four*

As well as a theatre, the Lyceum was also a dance hall in Conan Doyle's time. Built in 1771, it held Madame Tussaud's first London waxwork exhibition in 1802. It was taken over in 1794 by Edgar Allan Poe's great-grandfather, Dr Samuel Arnold. It burned down in 1830 and was rebuilt further west of the original site.

The story *The Sign of Four* has two plot lines. The first is Holmes's investigation into the death of Bartholomew Sholto and the theft of the Agra treasure; the second is the romance between Watson and Mary Morstan, Holmes's client.

At the Lyceum, Holmes, Watson and Morstan are met by a carriage that takes them to a run-down South London estate but then delivers them to the fabulous apartment of Morstan's supposed 'friend', Mr Thaddeus Sholto. Sholto's flamboyant character was thought to be based on Oscar Wilde. *The Sign of Four* also introduces one of the most famous quotes in all detective fiction: '... when you have eliminated the impossible, whatever remains, *however improbable*, must be the truth'.

Conan Doyle was a keen theatregoer, and it was at the theatre that he first decided to bring back Sherlock Holmes, whom he had killed off four years previously in 1893 in *The Final Problem*.

Holmes's death had caused widespread indignation; over 20,000 people cancelled their subscription to the *Strand Magazine* in protest. Newspapers around the world produced obituaries as if Holmes had really lived and for years afterwards Doyle received demands from angry readers, asking that he bring Holmes back from the dead. One letter from a female admirer of Holmes began simply: 'You brute!'

Doyle was shocked by this response (his father had just died and his wife had recently been diagnosed with tuberculosis, so Doyle had expected sympathy rather than outrage). However, he remained steadfast, claiming the detective's death was 'justifiable homicide ... it was him or me'. He wrote of Holmes in 1896: 'I have had such an overdose of him that I feel towards him as I do towards a *pate de foie gras*, of which I once ate too much, so that the name gives me a sickly feeling to this day.'

By late 1897, tired of the pressure from editors, publishers, agents and readers, Doyle started work on a play titled simply *Sherlock Holmes*. It was based loosely on *A Scandal in Bohemia* and *The Final Problem*, except in this story Holmes gets his man (Moriarty is imprisoned) and marries the heroine.

Holmes was played by the American actor William Gillette, who not only looked like the great detective as illustrated by Sidney Paget, but had the personality to match. Gillette eventually took over the writing of the play and sent a telegram to Doyle asking, 'May I marry Sherlock Holmes?' to which Doyle replied, 'You may marry, murder, do anything you like.'

A few days after an anxious Gillette came to England with the finished script, Doyle wrote to his brother Innes, '*Sherlock Holmes* is going to be great. I talked it all over with Gillette and two of his acts are simply grand. There lies the trump card in our fairly good hand.'

Doyle wasn't wrong. *Sherlock Holmes* opened in New York in 1899 and was a great success. Gillette went on to play the great detective for over 30 years, audiences cheering whenever he did something they recognised from the stories, such as taking tobacco from a Persian slipper. The production came to the Lyceum on 9 September 1901. However, the reviews were less than glowing (critics complained that the American spoke too quietly) and many Holmes fans cringed at some of Gillette's lines. The scene in which Holmes declares his love for the heroine while trapped in a gas chamber is especially painful: 'Your powers of observation are somewhat remarkable, Miss Faulkner – and your deduction is quite correct! I suppose – indeed I know – that I love you.'

Nonetheless, the play ran for six months, earning a royal command performance on 30 January 1902 for Edward VII and Queen Alexandra. The King was a great admirer of Holmes and kept Gillette talking so long that the audience were close to rioting by the time the curtain rose.

Gillette and Doyle remained friends for many years and on one occasion the actor had to call on the writer in dire need. At the height of World War I, Gillette was arrested as a spy (the punishment for which was death). The evidence against him was a map of the British Embassy – a stage prop from his production *Secret Service*. Thankfully, Doyle was able to reassure the police that Gillette, the face of Sherlock Holmes, was no threat to national security.

→ **22.** Continue north up Wellington Street into Bow Street. The Royal Opera House is on the left.

Well, Watson, you have one more specimen of the tragic and gruesome to add to your collection. By the way, is it not eight o'clock and a Wagner night at Covent Garden! If we hurry we might be in time for the second act. *The Adventure of the Red Circle*

While not an admirer of the theatre, Sherlock Holmes loved opera and classical music. He was a great fan of Wagner and German music in general and in *The Red-Headed League* he told Watson: 'I observe that there is a good deal of German music on the programme, which is rather more to my taste than Italian or French. It is introspective, and I want to introspect.' Wagner died in 1883, nine years before Holmes and Watson dashed in a hansom to catch the second act of the 'Wagner night'.

In 1892, Walter Paget, brother of Sidney, the famous illustrator who gave Sherlock Holmes his deerstalker, went to the Royal Opera House to see the English premiere of Wagner's *Ring*. As he tried to find his seat a woman cried, 'There goes Sherlock Holmes!' Poor Walter came to regret being his brother's model for the drawings of the detective.

→ **23**. Continue to the top of Bow Street. The former Magistrates' Court is on the right at the junction with Broad Court.

Passing down the Waterloo Bridge Road we crossed over the river, and dashing up Wellington Street wheeled sharply to the right, and found ourselves in Bow Street. Sherlock Holmes was well-known to the Force, and the two constables at the door saluted him.
The Man with the Twisted Lip

Perhaps the most famous person ever tried at Bow Street Magistrates' Court was Oscar Wilde (see also page 316), who was successfully persecuted and prosecuted for his homosexuality (homosexual acts were illegal in Britain until 1967) by the Marquis of Queensberry in April 1895.

After his first fretful night in the cells, Wilde refused prison rations and ordered a breakfast of tea, toast and eggs from the nearby Tavistock Hotel. It was brought to him on a silver tray.

Conan Doyle was quick to point out that his correspondence with Wilde had always been impersonal and professional. He regarded homosexuality as a pitiable but detestable abnormality and did not want in any way to be associated with the 'disreputable behaviour' of the great playwright.

However, Wilde's death in Paris in 1900 did not, it appears, mark the end of their association. On 2 September 1923, an extraordinary letter written by Conan Doyle was published in the *New York Times*. He claimed to have been visited by the spirit of Wilde who told him, 'Being dead is the most boring existence in life.'

Wilde had then, apparently, gone on to dictate a play (unfortunately, Conan Doyle didn't show it to anyone). Doyle was often criticised for his enthusiastic support for and involvement in spiritualism. Lord Alfred Douglas, the former lover of Oscar Wilde and the cause of Wilde's imprisonment, was moved to write to Doyle calling him 'a disgusting beast' whose 'blasphemous ravings' merited 'a good horse-whipping'.

24. Turn left from Bow Street into Floral Street and then first left down the pedestrianised area and into Covent Garden Piazza. The market is in the building at the centre.

We passed across Holborn, down Endell Street, and so through a zigzag of slums to Covent Garden Market. One of the largest stalls bore the name of Breckinridge upon it, and the proprietor a horsy-looking man, with a sharp face and trim side-whiskers, was helping a boy to put up the shutters.

The Adventure of the Blue Carbuncle

Covent Garden Market was London's best-known fruit and vegetable market, beginning in 1656 with a few temporary stalls. It remained a rather ramshackle affair for almost 200 years and became famous for the amount of rubbish and trouble it produced. Slipping on banana skins, rotten fruit and horse dung was an occupational hazard for the seven policemen who were eventually installed to try and cope with thieves, pickpockets and muggers, plying their trades in among the stalls and in the narrow unlit side-streets.

The market would be at its busiest at dawn as dozens upon dozens of heavily laden wagons rolled in from the city's docks. As they unloaded, the homeless and drunk were kicked awake from their doorway slumbers by the police and spilled out into the congested square full of its exotic marvels. Indeed, many a foreign fruit made its British debut at Covent Garden.

In *The Blue Carbuncle*, a salesman named Breckinridge sold geese, but it was not typically possible to buy fowl at Covent Garden (it was a fruit and vegetable market after all).

In 1974, Covent Garden Market moved south of the Thames to Battersea and the Covent Garden Piazza is now home to a shopping arcade, bars, restaurants and enthusiastic street performers. The pickpockets have remained though, as has the litter, although today's tourists are more likely to slip on a half-eaten burger than a banana skin.

The plot of *The Blue Carbuncle* centres on the pursuit of a Christmas goose, in which is hidden the Blue Carbuncle, a gem stolen from the Countess of Morcar's hotel room at the Hotel Cosmopolitan. The reward for its return is £1,000 which, according to Sherlock Holmes, is not a twentieth of its market value, adding that there were 'sentimental considerations in the background which would induce the Countess to part with her fortune if she could but recover the gem'. The stone, like many famous gems, had a violent history, including two murders, a vitriol throwing, a suicide and several robberies.

Holmes's investigation leads him to the Alpha Inn in Bloomsbury and then to the freezing and windswept Covent Garden Market, right to the stall of the fowl-dealer Breckenridge. The thief is not Breckenridge, however, but a man named James Ryder whose sister sold the goose to the stallholder not knowing of its precious contents. It being Christmas, the detective proves generous and allows the culprit to escape, declaring to Watson: 'I am not retained by the police to supply their deficiencies.'

The Blue Carbuncle was quite possibly inspired by a true story, as on 25 April 1891, nine months before its publication, an article entitled 'Strange Recoveries of Lost Jewels' appeared in *Cassell's Saturday Journal* (Doyle often sought inspiration from true stories published in the popular magazines of the day). It related the tale of a wealthy landowner who, when hunting, raised his gun to shoot but fell short of pulling the trigger when he noticed that his most precious ring was missing. Despite much frantic searching, there was no sign of the prized piece of jewellery anywhere. The landowner had just about given up when he had the bright idea of checking the barrel of the gun and, of course, 'the diamond had slipped into the muzzle while he was loading it and without his observing it; and, but for that lucky thought, £500 of pure carbon might have been blown into the inside of a bird, and have astonished the cook when she came to prepare it'.

'When I had no money [for a meal],' he wrote, 'I took a turn in Covent Garden and stared at the pineapples.'

The young Charles Dickens was a frequent visitor to the market.

25. Return up the pedestrianised area north as far as Long Acre and turn right. Then take the left into Endell Street, walk the length of this road, crossing High Holborn into Bloomsbury Street, and then turn right into Great Russell Street. Head east, passing the British Museum, and then left into Montague Street, up to the junction with Montague Place.

> When I first came up to London, I had rooms in Montague Street, just round the corner from the British Museum, and there I waited, filling in my too-abundant leisure time by studying all those branches of science which might make me more efficient.
> *The Adventure of the Musgrave Ritual*

Violet Hunter (*The Adventure of the Copper Beeches*) lived in Montague Place, as did Sir Arthur Conan Doyle, who lived at No. 23 in 1891 for several months when he first came to London. The British Museum opened on 15 January 1759, but only for three hours a day, and to visit you had to apply in writing. Visiting the museum involved so much bureaucracy that only a few bothered. But in 1879 unrestricted access to the galleries was at last permitted. Its treasures are far too many to list here but include the Rosetta Stone, Captain James Cook's journals, a gold cup made for the Kings of England and France in 1380, Egyptian mummies, the 7th-century Lindisfarne Gospels, two of the four copies of the Magna Carta, the world's oldest printed document, Shakespeare's first folio and Captain Scott's diary. The famous library, which Holmes would undoubtedly have made extensive use of, has since moved from the circular Reading Room to the British Library at King's Cross, where many papers of Doyle are now held, including the correspondence quoted here.

One of the items in the possession of the British Library is Conan Doyle's 'lost' novel, *The Narrative of John Smith*, written when he was just 23. He sent it to a publisher but the manuscript was lost in the post. He tried to reconstruct it from memory but eventually gave up. He later said 'my shock at its disappearance would be nothing to my horror if it were suddenly to appear again – in print.' That happened in 2012, when the British Library published it.

26. Return to Great Russell Street and turn right. The Museum Tavern is just across a pedestrian crossing, opposite the main entrance to the British Museum.

> In a quarter of an hour we were in Bloomsbury at the Alpha Inn, which is a small public-house at the corner of one of the streets which runs down into Holborn. Holmes pushed open the door of the private bar and ordered two glasses of beer from the landlord.
>
> *The Adventure of the Blue Carbuncle*

The Alpha Inn is fictional but from his description, this might well be the pub that Conan Doyle was thinking of and, anyway, it's a pleasant place to end the tour. Situated opposite the main entrance to the British Museum, the Museum Tavern has played host to many writers and artists since it opened in 1842.

And so here the tour ends. Sherlock Holmes has continued to fascinate through the 19th, 20th and now 21st centuries, and his stories are as popular as they were when they were first published. Sir Arthur Conan Doyle was right when he said: 'Crime may not pay, but it certainly sells.'

WEST

Continued overleaf...

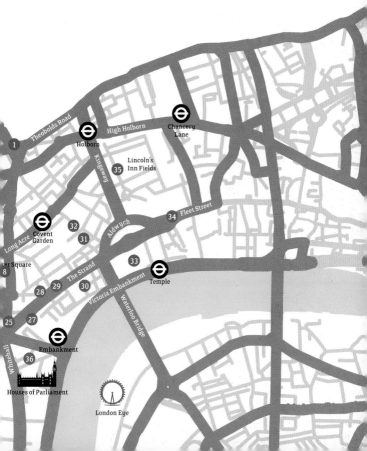

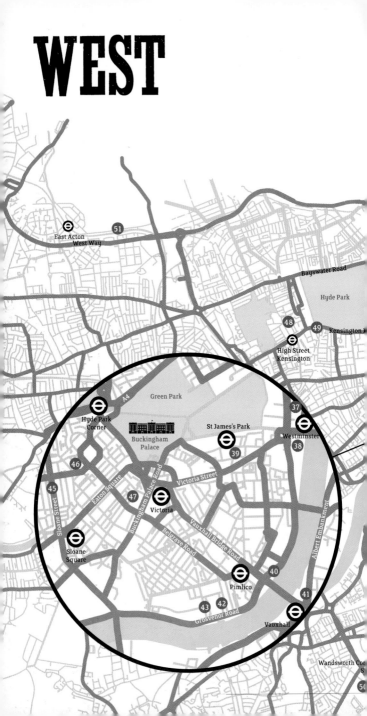

WEST

East Acton
West Way
51

Bayswater Road

Hyde Park

48
49 Kensington
High Street
Kensington

A4 Green Park

Hyde Park
Corner

Buckingham
Palace

St James's Park

37
Westminster

38

39

46

45

47 Victoria

Victoria Street

Sloane Street

Eaton Square

Buckingham Palace Road

Vauxhall Bridge Road

Albert Embankment

Sloane
Square

Belgrave Road

40

Pimlico

41

43 42 Vauxhall

Grosvenor Road

Wandsworth Co
S

50

1. Dr Crippen Meets His Lover

◎ **Albion House and James Smith & Sons Umbrellas**

◯ 55 and 53 New Oxford Street, WC1

☏ 0207 836 4731

Ⓦ www.james-smith.co.uk

🕐 Mon, Wed, Thurs, Fri 9.30am-5pm, Tues and Sat 10am-5pm

⊖ Tottenham Court Road Tube *(Northern and Central Lines)*

Dr Hawley Harvey Crippen was born in Michigan, USA, in 1862. The definition of a mild-mannered man, Crippen had a high, balding forehead, a thick, sandy moustache and prominent eyes that shone behind gold-rimmed glasses. After his first wife died in 1891, he married 17-year-old Cora Turner, who was half-Russian, half-German, in New York.

In 1900 the Crippens moved to London, where Cora found work at Munyon's, a patent medicine company. She had a good singing voice and attempted to build a career as a singer. She became honorary treasurer of the Music Hall Ladies Guild, which hired a room here in Albion House, also the offices of Munyon's, where Dr Crippen became a manager. Albion House has since been rebuilt but No. 53, James Smith & Sons Umbrellas, just next door, looks the same today as it did in 1900. This was also where Crippen met, employed and fell in love with his typist, Ethel le Neve.

In 1909 the Crippens moved to 39 Hilldrop Crescent in North London (a block of flats now stands on the location; the tree in front was there at the time).

In December 1909 Cora found out that her husband was having an affair. She threatened to leave and take their substantial joint savings with her.

In January 1910 Dr Crippen ordered five grains of hyoscine hydrobromide at Lewis and Burrow's shop in New Oxford Street, across the road from Albion House. Crippen then told Cora's friends that his wife had been taken seriously ill in the USA, and that she was not expected to live. This raised their suspicions and they contacted Scotland Yard.

Chief Inspector Walter Dew visited Crippen at Albion House, where the doctor admitted he'd lied about his wife's illness. She was still alive, he explained, and had gone to Chicago with a lover. Dew's interest panicked Crippen, and he fled by ship to Canada, taking Ethel with him. Dew searched Hilldrop Crescent and found Cora's remains buried in lime in the cellar.

As part of Crippen's escape plan, Ethel disguised herself as a boy, but the ship's captain saw through the disguise and radioed London. Dew boarded a faster ship and was waiting to arrest Crippen when he arrived on 31 July 1910.

This was pathologist Sir Bernard Spilsbury's first murder case. He was able to identify the headless body in the cellar thanks to a scar on Cora's abdomen.

At the Old Bailey trial in October 1910, the jury took 27 minutes to find Crippen guilty. Ethel was found not guilty. John Ellis hanged Crippen at Pentonville prison in London on 23 November. Crippen had a photograph of Ethel le Neve in his top pocket.

Ethel le Neve sailed for New York on the morning of Crippen's execution. She changed her name, remarried and died in 1967, aged 84.

2. Little Knocking-Shop of Horrors

◎ **Manor House**

⬆ **21 Soho Square, W1**

⊖ **Tottenham Court Road Tube** *(Central and Northern Lines)*

The site of this austere Grade II listed building hides an extremely fruity past. The original structure at No. 21 was similar in style – on the outside at least. Known as the White House, it was built in 1678 and was owned by various aristocrats until 1776, when it was bought by entrepreneur Thomas Hopper and converted into what he claimed was a 'hotel'. It was in fact a high-class magical brothel with thematically arranged, garishly decorated chambers including Gold, Silver and Bronze, as well as a Painted Chamber, the Grotto, the Coal Hole and, infamously, the Skeleton Room, in which a mechanical skeleton lurked, ready to scare the wealthy patrons. Despite this odd device, the White House remained an extremely popular, if illegal, palace of pleasure for several decades.

Writer and social researcher Henry Mayhew (1812–87) described the White House as a 'notorious place of ill-fame'. He wrote:

> Some of the apartments, it is said, were furnished in a style of costly luxury; while others were fitted up with springs, traps, and other contrivances, so as to present no appearance other than that of an ordinary room, until the machinery was set in motion. In one room, into which some wretched girl might be introduced, on her drawing a curtain as she would be desired, a skeleton, grinning horribly, was precipitated forward, and caught the terrified creature in his, to all appearance, bony arms. In another chamber the lights grew dim, and then seemed gradually to go out. In a little time some candles, apparently self-ignited, revealed to a horror stricken woman, a black coffin, on the lid of which might be seen, in brass letters, ANNE, or whatever name it had been ascertained the poor wretch was known by. A sofa in another part of the mansion was made to descend into some place of utter darkness; or, it was alleged, into a room in which was a store of soot or ashes.

Sex has been for sale in Soho ever since and even today there are still houses of 'ill-fame' in the streets surrounding Soho Square.

The White House's saucy history continued in 1838, when pickle supremos Crosse and Blackwell took over the building for their headquarters.

The strangely appropriate figures in the foreground, in the gardens of Soho Square, are part of an installation by the artist Bruce Denny, entitled *Intrigue*.

3. The London Nail Bomber

◎ **Admiral Duncan Pub**
○ Old Compton Street, W1
☎ 020 7437 5300
◑ Mon-Sat 12-11pm, Sun 12-10.30pm
⊖ Piccadilly Circus Tube *(Bakerloo and Piccadilly Lines)* and Leicester
 Square Tube *(Northern and Piccadilly Lines)*

David Copeland's 13-day bombing campaign began on 17 April 1999 when he left a nail bomb in Brixton Market in Southwest London, the commercial hub of one of London's largest black communities. The explosion injured 39 people. Among the victims was a 23-month-old boy who was left with a 2cm nail in his brain, which was successfully removed by surgeons at Great Ormond Street Children's Hospital.

The next bomb exploded in Brick Lane, Shoreditch, the heart of London's Bangladeshi community, at 6pm on 24 April. It had been left in a red Ford Sierra. The innocent car owner had returned to his vehicle to find the bomb inside. He placed it in the boot and was about to drive it to a police station when it exploded. No one died but 13 people were injured.

Then, in Old Compton Street at 6.37pm on 30 April, a bomb exploded inside the Admiral Duncan pub, the centre of London's gay community. Three people were killed, including a pregnant woman. Altogether, 129 people had been injured by the three bombs, four of whom lost limbs.

Police used a CCTV image of the suspected bomber, which was put on the front pages of the national press, to help track him down. A man then came forward, who said the picture looked like his workmate, David John Copeland. Copeland, 22, was a member of the right-wing groups the British National Party and the National Socialist Movement. When police arrested him on 1 May, they found a shrine to Nazism on his bedroom wall.

During questioning the police asked Copeland why he had targeted ethnic minorities. He answered: 'Because I don't like them, I want them out of this country, I believe in the master race.' Copeland wrote to a journalist after his arrest, stating: 'I bomb the blacks, Pakis, degenerates. I would have bombed the Jews as well if I'd got a chance.'

Copeland was diagnosed with paranoid schizophrenia and personality disorder. He said that he had been having sadistic dreams since he was 12. In one such dream, he said he'd been reincarnated as a Nazi SS officer. Copeland's plea of diminished responsibility was rejected by the prosecution, who were determined not to let him get away with the lesser crime of manslaughter. They won. Copeland was convicted of murder on 30 June 2000 and given six concurrent life sentences.

4. The Scourge of Soho

◎ Golden Lion Pub

⌂ 51 Dean Street, W1

🕐 Mon-Thurs 12-11pm, Fri-Sat 12pm-12am, Sun 12-10.30pm

⊖ Leicester Square Tube *(Northern and Piccadilly Lines)*

Unbeknown to its staff, serial killer Dennis Nilsen liked to drink at this pub; it's where he picked up at least two of his victims and, in November 1981, one man who was lucky enough to escape.

After spending the night together, Nilsen tried to strangle the other man, a student, with a necktie. His intended victim escaped but didn't call the police – they had a poor reputation for dealing with crimes involving gay people. Nilsen went on to kill another three times, bringing his suspected tally of murdered young men to 16.

Born in Scotland in 1945, Dennis Nilsen's parents divorced when he was four. He joined the army in 1961, staying until 1972, when he joined the police for a short time, before leaving for a career as a civil servant. It has been argued that the lonely Nilsen, who was gay, was driven to kill by a warped desire for company, after his live-in roommate, who was younger by ten years, left him in 1977, but, in truth, his motivation remains a matter for speculation.

Nilsen's first murder took place while he was living in Cricklewood, North London, in December 1978 – a young Irishman whom he brought home and strangled with a necktie. He kept the body in the house, masturbating over it before hiding it under the floorboards, eventually cremating it in August 1979 on an outdoor bonfire.

In November 1979, he travelled to Soho in search of 'company' and picked up a Chinese student. The young man escaped and called the police – who accepted the former constable's claim that the student had tried to rob him. Days later, Nilsen strangled a 23-year-old Canadian with electrical cord. He cut up the body, flushing parts away and hiding the rest under his floor.

In May 1980 Nilsen murdered a 16-year-old boy from Birkenhead. 'I can't remember the details,' Nilsen said later. 'It's academic. I put him under the floorboards.' However, he remembered victim 11 – a skinhead with a tattoo of a dotted line around his neck, with the words 'Cut Here'. Nilsen followed this instruction.

In September 1981 Nilsen found a man in his twenties in a doorway near his home in the midst of an epileptic fit. Nilsen helped him, telephoning for an ambulance. When the man recovered he called on Nilsen to thank him – the serial killer murdered the 24-year-old the same night. The following month, Nilsen moved from Cricklewood to Muswell Hill.

The end came when Nilsen murdered a 20-year-old heroin addict on 1 February 1983 and his attempts to dispose of the body parts blocked a drain. The downstairs neighbours called a plumber and the plumber called the police. When his solicitor asked him why he'd killed the men, Nilsen answered: 'I was hoping you could tell me that.' Nilsen is one of about two dozen British prisoners on a 'whole life' tariff, meaning he'll never be released.

5. Albert Pierrepoint's First Hanging

◎ **The Palm Beach Bottle Party**

⌂ **37 Wardour Street, W1**

⊖ **Oxford Circus Tube** *(Central, Bakerloo and Victoria Lines)*
   and Tottenham Court Road Tube *(Central and Northern Lines)*

In the early 1940s the West End had become the subject of a turf war between Jewish and Italian gangs. Antonio 'Babe' Mancini (38) was a member of the Sabini crime gang (see Saffron Hill, page 137) and the manager of Soho dive, the Palm Beach Bottle Party, in the basement of 37 Wardour Street.

On the first floor was the West End Bridge and Billiards Club, of which Mancini was a member. It was here, between 3am and 4am on 1 May 1941, that a fight broke out involving Billy Hill's enforcer 'Italian' Albert Dimes (see page 251) and Harry 'Scarface' Distleman. Mancini was in the Palm when he heard the ruckus and ran upstairs with a knife, plunging it into Distleman's armpit and severing a major artery. Harry's dying words were: 'Babe's done it.'

Two failed appeals later, on 17 October 1941 Mancini found himself on the scaffold at Pentonville, standing before Albert Pierrepoint, who would become the 20th century's most prolific hangman. Pierrepoint would go on to hang 19-year-old Derek Bentley for his part in the murder of a policeman, and then Timothy Evans for the murder of his family. Evans was granted a posthumous pardon in 1966, when it was discovered John Christie was probably the killer. Albert hanged Christie too: 'I hanged the Monster of Rillington Place,' he wrote in his autobiography, 'in less time than it took the ash to fall off a cigar I had left half-smoked in my room at Pentonville.'

Both Pierrepoint's father and an uncle were hangmen. During his career he hanged more than 400 people – his record was 17 in a day. Included in his impressive tally are the convicted staff of the Belsen Concentration Camp, where, on Friday 13 December 1945, he executed 13 people before lunch.

So, how did he fare with his first? Well, Mancini made it easy for him. He bade everyone present a good-humoured 'Cheerio!' as he launched Albert's long career as Chief Executioner.

Although the clubs of this era are long gone, the Star Café and Bar (pictured), established in 1933, looks exactly like it did then. Turn into the short Hollen Street at the Oxford Street end of Wardour Street and this hidden gem is on the right.

6. 'Brilliant' Chang

◎ Chinatown

◉ Gerrard Street, W1

Ⓦ www.chinatownlondon.org

◉ Piccadilly Circus Tube *(Piccadilly and Bakerloo Lines)* and Covent
Garden Tube *(Piccadilly Line)*

Chinatown began not long after World War I when a few Chinese restaurants
– responding to demand from servicemen who'd spent time in the Far East –
opened in Lisle Street, the road that runs parallel to Gerrard Street, and where
'Brilliant' Chang – drug dealer extraordinaire – ran his nightclub.

Not much is known about Chang's early life but it is known that he was a
womaniser who quickly saw profit in a new post-war craze for cocaine. This
'craze' had been created after the licensing laws were tightened in 1915 – for
fear that boozing was harming the war effort.

A drugs scene developed in Soho alongside prostitution, drawing in floods of
soldiers looking to get high, get laid, and forget about the horrors of the war. The
resulting drugs threat was considered so grave that an emergency regulation
was passed, this becoming the Dangerous Drugs Act 1920.

Chang achieved a lifestyle that went far beyond the means provided by the
takings from his Palm Court Club restaurant, which was located opposite No. 43
and was probably the first Chinese business in the area.

Chang had a 'soft spot' for attractive young women and when beautiful
nightclub 'dance instructress' Freda Kempton died from an overdose after
spending an evening with Chang, the news caused a sensation. Chang told the
coroner: 'Freda was a friend of mine but I know nothing about the cocaine. It is
all a mystery to me.'

One newspaper wrote that after Chang was cleared, girls rushed up to him
and 'patted his back, and one, more daring than the rest, fondled the Chinaman's
black, smooth hair'.

Although the coroner said there was no evidence that linked Chang to
Freda's death, the police and press thought otherwise. 'White Girls Hypnotised
by Yellow Men' the *Evening News* blared. The *World Pictorial News* wrote:
'Sometimes one girl alone went with Chang to learn the mysteries of that
intoxicatingly beautiful den of iniquity above the restaurant. At other times
half-a-dozen drug-frenzied women together joined him in wild orgies.'

Chang (the inspiration for fictional criminal genius Fu Manchu) was often
raided and after two failed attempts the cops finally got lucky when they found
a single wrap of cocaine in his house. They claimed they had captured the
man responsible for providing 40 per cent of London's illegal coke. Considering
demand was confined to just a few streets in Soho and Limehouse, this would
have been no more than a tiny fraction of the amount trafficked into London
and sold in the city today.

Chang was sentenced to 14 months, after which he was deported. As his ship
left it was reported that one girl shouted out: 'Come back soon, Chang!'

He never did.

7. The Dope King

◎ **Mrs Fox's Restaurant**

⌂ **9 Little Newport Street, WC2**

⊖ **Covent Garden Tube** *(Piccadilly Line)*

Edgar Manning, a handsome Jamaican jazz drummer in his early thirties, was one of London's earliest known drug dealers. In the 1920s Manning held opium parties and had a dozen prostitutes and others selling for him around the West End. The press dubbed him the 'Dope King' and ran lurid stories about how he was able to control innocent white women with his drugs.

Narcotics had risen in popularity in London thanks in part to World War I, as many injured ex-soldiers became addicted to the opiates that alleviated mental and physical pain. Young people wanted to live fast after the misery of the Great War and cocaine was consumed by the great and good alongside the downright criminal at wild parties.

The basement of 9 Little Newport Street was once the hangout for Soho's underworld drug dealers, including Manning. The restaurant owner, Elizabeth Fox, was by all accounts loved by all and was known as the 'underworld's auntie'.

In July 1920, Mrs Fox had been with friends to the races at Lingfield and had returned £70 richer. She was celebrating with Edgar Manning when a man known as 'Yankee Frank' entered and demanded a slice of their winnings. Manning refused and Frank went on to rage at the other people in the basement bar before punching actress Molly O'Brien in the eye and running out. After checking she was alright, Manning left.

Frank was with his brother and a third man, Robert Davis, on Charing Cross Road when they ran into Manning. As the three men charged, Manning pulled out a pistol and 'kneecapped' all three men. Manning was initially charged with attempted murder but this was later reduced to unlawful wounding. He was tried at the Old Bailey and went down for 16 months.

His time done, Manning partnered up with a Greek woman called Zenovia Iassonides, 'the Cocaine Queen', who ran the Montmartre Café in Soho's Church Street, where girls from all walks of life came to score drugs – up to 20 girls could be found passed out there at any one time.

Manning was eventually caught with 15 tablets of morphine, a bottle of cocaine, a revolver, 13 ounces of opium and a silver-topped walking stick, in which an 18-inch glass tube acted as a drug stash. He fell ill while serving a three-year sentence and died in 1930. By then drugs and sex had become integral parts of Soho life.

8. The First Identikit

◎ **Louis Meier's Bookshop (now Goldsboro Books)**

⌂ **23 Cecil Court, WC2**

☎ **020 7497 9230**

🌐 **www.goldsborobooks.com**

🕐 **Mon-Sat 10am-6pm**

⊖ **Charing Cross Tube** *(Mainline, Northern and Bakerloo Lines)*

Cecil Court, which is today full of antique bookshops, has barely changed since the 1960s. Back then, No. 23 was an antique shop, owned by Louis Meier. It's now part of Goldsboro Books at 23–25, but the original shop frame is still there. On Friday 3 March 1961, Meier arrived at the shop to find his assistant Elsie Batten, the wife of Mark Batten, the President of the Royal Society of British Sculptors, had been stabbed to death with antique daggers for sale in his shop.

One nine-inch blade had been plunged into the victim's neck, right up to the hilt. A dagger with an ivory handle protruded from her chest, its blade sunk eight inches into the body.

Detective Sergeant Raymond Dagg from Bow Street interviewed Louis Meier who, along with a neighbouring shop assistant, told him that they'd seen a suspicious youth of 'Indian appearance' at the shop a few days earlier.

Dagg decided to use a new tool employed by American detectives – the Identikit. It was the invention of legendary lawman and former intelligence officer Hugh C. Macdonald, who would go on to become the Chief of Los Angeles Police Department. Macdonald had developed sets of facial features on transparencies to save time sketching descriptions of criminals. Using a similar technique, Dagg compiled an image of the suspect before circulating it across the police force and publishing it in the newspapers.

A few days later, March Hilton Cole, a policeman from West End Central, spotted 21-year-old Edwin Bush in Old Compton Street and, recognising him from the Identikit pictures, arrested him. Bush had a newspaper clipping with the Identikit picture in his pocket. Examination of his shoe soles revealed they were similar to marks left at the scene. After being picked out at an identification parade by Paul Roberts, another antique dealer to whom he had tried to sell the sword he had stolen, Bush confessed.

He said in his statement, 'I am sorry I done it, I don't know what came over me. Speaking personally the world is better off without me.' He was convicted and hanged on 6 July 1961 in Pentonville, thereby earning the dubious distinction of being the last person to be executed at the prison.

9. The West End Sex Trade

◎ Strip Clubs
⌂ Great Windmill Street, W1
☎ 020 7439 3558
Ⓦ www.windmillinternational.com
🕐 Mon-Sat 8.30pm-5.30am, closed Sunday
💲 £15 per person
⊖ Piccadilly Circus Tube *(Bakerloo and Piccadilly Lines)*

Great Windmill Street has a long association with the sex industry, starting in 1851 when entrepreneur Robert Bignall opened his Assembly Rooms. In little time they had become the haunt of prostitutes but in 1878 (by which time Bignall had become a very rich man) the council refused to renew his licence. He subsequently moved into music halls, but Great Windmill's prostitutes never left.

In the 1930s, Laura Henderson, an elderly, bored widow, bought a run-down cinema on the present site of the Windmill International (pictured). After failed attempts to stage plays, show films and host variety acts, she decided to put on a show featuring nude women. The first performance of Mrs Henderson's Revudeville on 4 February 1932 was a triumph. Six times a day, six days a week, from noon until 10.35pm, non-stop revues lit up the Windmill's glass stage.

While the dancers performed themed 'numbers', a girl posed somewhere on the stage, naked and unmoving — 'If it moves, it's rude,' was the Lord Chamberlain's ruling. A small scarf or piece of scenery hid her pubic hair. The theatre also had to supply the Lord Chamberlain's office with photographs of planned nude poses ahead of the opening of a new show. This may seem tame today but at the time it was a sensation.

The Windmill was most popular during World War II, when they claimed they never closed. Girls, whose average age was just 19, slept at the theatre during bombing raids. One night a café just opposite was hit, killing an electrician working at the Windmill and burying a few of the girls in rubble, all of whom recovered.

The club was subjected to regular inspections but some fans in Whitehall were kind enough to telephone ahead to warn that Mr Titman (this really was his name), the government inspector, was on his way. Mrs Henderson's girls would then tone things down a bit to make sure he left satisfied.

During the war soldiers on leave formed long queues first thing in the morning, desperate to grab one of the 300 seats or, if they were really lucky, a seat in the first six rows. The men would often forget themselves, sometimes charging the stage, vaulting over the rows, in what was dubbed 'the Windmill Steeplechase'.

Henderson had lost her only son in World War I, and the Windmill became her family. When she died in 1944, aged 80, she left the theatre to its manager, Vivian Van Damm. By the late 1950s, Soho was full of strip clubs and the competition was too much for the Windmill. The theatre muddled on into the 1960s, until Van Damm died and his daughter sold it in 1964.

Today there are still naked girls in the Windmill but, apparently, these ones move.

10. The Transvestite Bank Robber

◎ **Marlborough Street Magistrates' Court (now the Courthouse Hotel)**
⚲ **19–21 Great Marlborough Street, W1**
☎ **020 7297 5555**
Ⓦ **www.courthouse-hotel.com**
⊖ **Oxford Circus Tube** *(Central, Bakerloo and Victoria Lines)*

The Grade II listed Great Marlborough Street Magistrates' Court building dates back to the 1800s. Charles Dickens worked as a reporter here for the *Morning Chronicle* in 1835, and in 1847 Louis-Napoleon Bonaparte (Napoleon's nephew, and soon to become Napoleon III as Emperor of France) appeared as a witness in a fraud case.

A century later, in 1963, Christine Keeler attended Marlborough over sex allegations, which led to the infamous Profumo Affair (see page 311) and the resignation of a Cabinet minister, and in 1981 John Miller, kidnapper of Ronnie Biggs (Miller led an attempt to kidnap Biggs from Brazil so the Great Train Robber could be extradited to serve the rest of his sentence in the UK), was brought here after being arrested on arrival from Barbados.

Other luminaries who have passed the court's pillars include John Lennon, Oscar Wilde and Johnny Rotten. Mick Jagger was fined for drugs possession here in 1969 but Keith Richards outdid him in 1973 when he was fined £205 for possession of marijuana, heroin, Mandrax, a revolver *and* an antique shotgun – must have been quite a party.

Although Keith was undoubtedly 'out there', the title of the wildest London criminal to attend Marlborough Court goes to transvestite bank robber David Martin, who robbed the Barclays Bank in Highgate dressed as a woman. He shot a policeman during his escape but was eventually captured in Belsize Park.

On Christmas Eve 1982, Martin, who was also an excellent lock picker, escaped from the cells in Marlborough Magistrates' Court. Martin had once yelled 'You'll never take me alive!' to police officers who were chasing him and was therefore considered armed and extremely dangerous.

When two Flying Squad officers thought they'd spotted the escapee in a Mini they fired without warning. But it wasn't Martin. They had shot Stephen Waldorf, a BBC film editor – seven times in the head and stomach. Miraculously, Waldorf survived.

Martin was caught a few weeks later and hanged himself while awaiting trial. The police officers were tried for the attempted murder of Waldorf but were found not guilty.

Many original courtroom features remain. The bar's private tables are actually inside three of the original prison cells, and the hotel restaurant is in the old Number One court, complete with judge's bench, witness stand and dock.

11. The Greatest Crime Reporter of Our Time

◎ White Slavery

⬡ Kingly Street, W1

⊖ Oxford Circus Tube *(Central, Bakerloo and Victoria Lines)*
   and Piccadilly Circus Tube *(Bakerloo and Piccadilly Lines)*

The Messina brothers, Carmelo, Salvatore, Attilio, Alfredo and Eugenio were born in Malta and Egypt, and, from the 1930s, ran a prostitute ring. Eugenio briefly came to the attention of the police when he sliced off the tops of two fingers of a rival Maltese pimp, but otherwise they went unnoticed.

They imported women from all across Europe to work in brothels in London's Mayfair, their business spreading here, to the edges of Soho at Kingly Street. There is a hairdressers at No.7, which has been in business for a hundred years, that was next door to one of their brothels.

The Messinas bought protection from police officials and at their peak ran 30 brothels. Attilio once said: 'We Messinas are more powerful than the British Government. We do as we like in England.'

It was the Messina brothers – or rather the journalist who hounded them, legendary *Sunday People* reporter Duncan Webb – who brought the private world of the brothel to mass public attention in 1951.

As *Time* magazine wrote:

Webb, 37, is sometimes called the 'greatest crime reporter of our time.' In almost 20 years of covering crime he has been slugged, kicked, lunged at with knives, shot at, knuckle-dusted and was once the target of a speeding automobile that raced onto the sidewalk of a narrow Soho street and tried to smash him against a building. Last week Webb was still wearing a plaster cast on his right wrist, broken two months ago when a London gangster known as 'Jack Spot' objected to one of his stories.

Legend had it that Webb's office was protected by bullet-proof glass and that he had eight locks fitted to his front door at home.

Duncan Webb established links to the brothers by following the women they ran to various addresses and interviewing more than 100 of them. The *People* then risked the libel laws to publish pictures of four of the Messina brothers under the headline 'ARREST THESE FOUR MEN! They are the emperors of a vice empire in the heart of London.'

After this, four of the brothers fled abroad, leaving Alfredo, who had not been named, to get their fortune safely out of the UK. The police were embarrassed into action and when they raided Alfredo's home they found him living with a well-known prostitute – in sumptuous circumstances. Alfredo offered Detective Superintendent Gary Mahon a £200 bribe, which was declined. He was jailed for two years and fined £500 and the Messina empire was quickly swept up by rival gangs of Soho.

THE PEOPLE

SUNDAY, SEPTEMBER 3, 1950 No. 3591—69th Year

RREST THESE FOUR MEN

ey are the emperors of a vice mpire in the heart of London

y 'The People' has found he facts about a vice ring e heart of London that is a national scandal.

• This is an unsavoury story but we believe it is our duty to the public to reveal it so that swift action can be taken.

THE MESSINA GANG EXPOSED

By Duncan Webb

YESTERDAY I made the final entry in a dossier that uncovers the activities of a vice gang operating in the West End of London on a scale that will appal every decent man and woman.

Today I offer Scotland Yard evidence from my dossier that should enable them to arrest four men who are battening on women of the streets and profiting from their shameful trade.

And, to support that demand, I intend to expose in detail the way in which this gang operates—a story so sordid that I am certain public opinion will now demand that this state of affairs should not be tolerated a moment longer.

The four men I am accusing are brothers, members of what is openly known to the police—and even to Parliament—as The Messina Gang.

Let there be no doubt as to whom I am naming as the members of this gang on these grave charges. The four men are:—

EUGENE MESSINA, who normally calls himself Edward Marshall and who lives at 24, Bruton-place, a mews flat off New Bond-st., Mayfair.

ATTILIO MESSINA, who is usually known as Raymond Maynard and who has been living in a block of flats in Kensington Park Gardens, London. W.11.

CARMELO MESSINA, who has changed his name to Charles Maitland and who lives at 3, Lancaster Lodge, a respectable block of flats in North Kensington

SALVATORE MESSINA, who has changed his name to Arthur Evans and who lives at Kings Court, Hammersmith, London.

These four brothers are Maltese, and therefore have British nationality They have been in London for some years and they are now wealthy men.

"Lives of shame"

They are engaged in business as dealers and merchants, and undoubtedly they have made some of their money legitimately.

But, by the most detailed investigation which has taken me and my assistants three months to complete, I have proved that in fact they are controlling a chain of flats used for immoral purposes.

They are emperors of an empire of vice in London's West End.

There are women of the streets who are virtually in their power. Many of these women have come from the Continent to carry on their disgusting business.

And these four men know full well that the wives of some of them are openly taking part in this life of shame.

It is a state of affairs that would disgrace one of the licentious ports of the Middle East. That it should exist in London on this scale is almost incredible.

This newspaper commissioned me to uncover the operations of the Messina Gang as a public duty.

For too long the Messinas have been talked about in high places But, for too long nothing has

FOUR DESPICABLE BROTHERS

HERE are the four Messina brothers we accuse today.

Top left is Eugene Messina, who calls himself Edward Marshall.

Top right is Carmelo Messina, who has changed his name to Charles Maitland.

Below him is Attilio Messina, who is usually known as Raymond Maynard.

Last of the four in this gallery of despicable brothers is Salvatore Messina, who has changed his name to Arthur Evans.

have been in trouble with the police before.

EUGENE MESSINA was born on June 26, 1908, in Alexandria, Egypt.

He was convicted in London in 1947, and sentenced to three years' penal servitude for unlawful wounding.

CARMELO MESSINA has been convicted for bribing a warder while visiting his brother in prison. He got two months.

SALVATORE MESSINA was convicted in Egypt in 1932 for living on immoral earnings, and was sentenced to six months imprisonment.

Let me now put on record some of the facts I have uncovered about the despicable side of these men's business interests I have no intention of affronting public decency by printing in detail the way in which their women conduct their hideous business.

It is enough to say that I have records of what has been observed over long periods to have taken place at flats and other residential premises in the West End of London—places that are owned, rented or leased by one or other of these Messinas.

They are able to flout the law in this way partly because they have operated on the grand scale —strange as that may seem—but also because they have been expert at covering up their tracks.

Take first Eugene Messina. He is a man of many addresses, official and otherwise, and he has built around himself a smoke-screen that is not easy to penetrate.

"I watched"

When he was released from prison some months ago, he gave his official address as 3, Lancaster Lodge, London, W.11, which is also the official address of his brother Carmelo.

But, for rating purposes, he gives to the Westminster City Council the address of 24 Bruton-

RS WAS AN MARRIAGE

E is Jean Gilson, e of the women ted with the Mes-

RED IN IN S

AFTER two a 50-mile Korea ha cisive break-t troops had be foothills rising the Naktong R

This was th and American general pictur pected to be I moment.

"The posit way to being from Genera

In this centra eight to ten mi only have been warfare.

But last nig were weakening ward units were lost touch wi headquarters.

American ta engineers yeste YONGSAN, piv miles north of M out along the nyong. This co turn out to be t of the battle.

Further nort were attacking i WAN, and in t they had pushe battered HAMS to protect Ma town on the ro

Heavy cas

Light Comm within five mi they were forc 25th Division, enemy losses battle as wounded.

The latest 48-ton Patto guns, went i first time.

"We have positions—Ma said a division

On the east the Communis have captured was no evide weight of the likely to be s Later, the Am progress in a

Everywhere suffered heav aircraft knoc tanks.

Jellied petr loosed by 300 the Red troo Naktong rive at points w tempted day

THEY HELD BR WIFE AS 'S

A BRITISH housewife, mother of a seven returned to her home, after spending t the Soviet sector of Germany, and bein Russians, who accused her of being a spy

She is Mrs. Joan Brennan, of Gipsy-lane said last n

"I was in and quite ing in a wo dered into denly I st Russian tr

"I was to run. I to me to through th him raise and aim. a good sho

She was headquarte searched woman, w hair and taken for at a time from her questioned.

Hunge

"They spy and American went on. before I grandmo much m from Eng said I di

"They be punish and I to

After went on lowing d be releas had take would ha recovered

A few

Good Morning People!

IN spite of the rebuff he received last week from President Truman, General MacArthur is still up to his trouble-making tricks. Now he has thought up a new dodge to force the American Government to claim Formosa as a defence bastion in the Far East. He has been trying to convince Washington that Red China was about to intervene in the Korean War. From his headquarters reports were spread that Chinese Communist troops had already crossed the Yalu River, which forms the frontier between China and North Korea.

These reports are untrue. The British Government's latest and most reliable information is that, far from crossing the Yalu, the Chinese are building fortifications on their own side of it! They are simply digging in against a possible backwash of the war.

THIS supports our Foreign Office's confident belief that

12. The Project

◎ Eastcastle Street

⬤ Junction with Newman Street, W1

⊖ Goodge Street Tube *(Northern Line)*

Billy Hill (1911–84) grew up in Seven Dials in Covent Garden and quickly graduated from small-time thefts to smash and grabs before leading his own gang, the Heavy Mob, in the 1930s.

Throughout World War II, Hill took advantage of the police shortage and the demand for black-market goods to rob and sell everything from whisky to sausage skins. In the late 1940s, he began a lifelong affair with the beautiful Gypsy Riley – a female bus conductor from the East End.

Hill's gang, which included 'Mad' Frankie Fraser (see Cabbell Street, page 191), robbed several West End jewellers. Then, in 1952, a job cropped up that made diamond watches look like spare change.

By this time, Hill had conquered Soho and was running brothels as well as illegal drinking and gambling clubs. It was a post office worker, who had run up a debt to Hill in one such club, who offered information about a cash-heavy mail van in return for the cancellation of his dues. Hill agreed.

This cash van was kept under observation for months on its journey from Paddington to the City. It was a sitting duck – it never changed route and was poorly protected by three Royal Mail staff.

Hill recruited a nine-strong gang, including 20-year-old Terry 'Lucky Tel' Hogan, who would go on to become one of the UK's most successful robbers. The gang used two cars to sandwich the postal van. The driver and two attendants were pulled out and the robbers drove off in the vehicle. The cash was then transferred to a fruit lorry. The postal van was later found abandoned in Augustus Street near Regent's Park, with 18 of the 31 mailbags missing.

The haul came to £287,000 – around £6.5m today. It was the first major successful post-war robbery. It was also the birth of the 'project': the carefully organised heist. This method would be repeated continually throughout the 1960s, 70s and 80s, until the vans and the cash they carried were simply too well protected with tracking devices, permanent dyes, smoke bombs and reinforced containers.

After the robbery, Prime Minister Winston Churchill demanded daily updates on the police investigation, and questions were asked in Parliament. Although the Flying Squad were certain Hill was behind the job, they were unable to uncover any evidence and no one was ever prosecuted for the robbery. However, Hill wrote about the heist in his autobiography: *The Boss of Britain's Underworld*.

Billy Hill retired from crime in the 1970s. Both he and Gypsy Riley (who died in 2004) are buried in the City of London cemetery in Wanstead, East London.

13. The British Baader-Meinhof

◎ BT Tower
⌂ Cleveland Street, W1
🕐 Not open to the public
⊖ Goodge Street Tube *(Northern Line)*

At 189 metres high, including mast, the BT Tower (originally known as the Post Office Tower) was the capital's tallest building (overtaking St Paul's) when it opened in 1965. Costing £2m to build, the cylindrical tower is made from 13,000 tonnes of concrete, steel and glass. Its purpose was to take advantage of new wireless transmission technology for broadcasting TV and ferrying phone communications – so central London wouldn't have to be covered in cables.

Two high-speed lifts whisked people up to the revolving restaurant at seven metres per second – 22mph. There was no fire escape – and a special Act of Parliament had to be passed so that in case of fire, people could escape via the lift.

In the small hours of 30 October 1971, a bomb exploded in a toilet on the lowest of the public observation galleries. Luckily, the damage was minimal and the observation gallery was simply patched up with steel mesh and closed to the public. The restaurant soon reopened.

Although an initial anonymous caller to the police claimed the attack was the work of Irish terrorists, the official and provisional wings of the IRA in Dublin denied this.

Then another call was made: 'The bombing of the post office tower was a protest against the government's taking the British people into the Common Market ... It was not the IRA, it was the Angry Brigade.'

West Germany had the Baader-Meinhof gang and here in the UK we had the Angry Brigade, a disparate home-grown anarchist gang who managed to explode 25 bombs between 1968 and 1971 – slightly injuring one person and killing none. Targets included senior policemen and Conservative politicians, as well as a London boutique, which they argued was exploiting child labour. They also bombed Tintagel House (see page 63), aiming to destroy the mighty five-tonne police 'supercomputer' (at the time, it had a memory of 72kb).

The police finally caught up with the Angry Brigade in a Stoke Newington squat, where they found guns and ammunition, along with a polythene bag stuffed with 33 sticks of gelignite. Eight people were arrested and then endured what was at the time the longest criminal trial in English history (30 May to 6 December 1972). The press enjoyed the revelations produced by the court: 'Girl slept with bedside arsenal' and 'Dropouts with brains tried to launch bloody revolution' were just two headlines. The defendants became anti-heroes and thousands of badges with the slogan 'I'm in the Angry Brigade' were sold.

John Barker, Jim Greenfield, Hilary Creek and Anna Mendleson each received sentences of ten years. The others were acquitted, including Angela Mason, who went on to become the director of the Government's Women and Equality Unit and was awarded an OBE in 1999.

Today the Grade II listed tower is used for corporate entertainment and remains fully operational – 90 per cent of what we see on TV passes through it.

14. Witness and Executioner

⦿ Fitzroy Tavern

⌂ Charlotte Street, W1

☎ 020 7580 3714

🕐 Mon-Sat 11am-11pm, Sun 12-10.30pm

⊖ Goodge Street Tube *(Northern Line)*

On 29 April 1947 at about two o'clock in the afternoon, Albert Pierrepoint, London's executioner, was having a quiet drink in his regular pub, the Fitzroy Tavern in Charlotte Street, when, hearing a commotion, he glanced out of the window. He saw three masked men carrying guns running down the street.

The leader was Charles Henry Jenkins, 23, aka the 'King of Borstal'. With him was 21-year-old Christopher James Geraghty and 17-year-old Terence Peter Rolt. They were fleeing the scene of an aborted attempt to rob Jay's Jewellers on Charlotte Street. As they had burst into the shop, one of the raiders jumping over the counter, the firm's director, Alfred Stock, slammed the safe shut.

Alfred was pistol-whipped for his trouble. As he lay bleeding on the floor, the robbers demanded the keys from 70-year-old Bertram Keates. Keates, defiant, threw a wooden stool at them. One of the young robbers fired; the bullet missed. Panicking at this unexpected resistance, the three men turned and ran, only to discover that a lorry had blocked their getaway car. With no other option, they took off down Charlotte Street, past the Fitzroy Tavern (now popular with students due to its legendarily low prices).

Alec De Antiquis, a handsome 30-something Anglo-Italian, was riding his motorbike down Charlotte Street when he saw the robbers and instantly decided to drive at them. As he did so, one of the gang raised a revolver and fired – the bullet hit the have-a-go hero in the head and he died at the scene as the robbers made their getaway.

Superintendent Robert Fabian was put on the case. Nicknamed 'Fabian of the Yard', he was a detective in the truest manner, relying on the systematic investigation of straightforward evidence. In this case, two of the men were seen by a taxi driver entering a building, where Fabian discovered a scarf and raincoat. The raincoat was eventually traced to Jenkins. Fabian quickly tracked down the other two and once 17-year-old Rolt realised how bad the situation was for him, he confessed to save himself.

All three were tried at the Old Bailey. It took the jury no longer than 15 minutes to reach a guilty verdict. Jenkins and Geraghty were sentenced to death. Albert Pierrepoint – who had seen the young men run past him while he was in the Fitzroy Tavern – hanged both of them on 19 September 1947. Rolt, being only 17, was detained at His Majesty's Pleasure and was released in June 1956.

This case inspired *The Blue Lamp*, a crime film released in 1950 by Ealing Studios. Directed by Basil Dearden, it starred Jack Warner as Police Constable George Dixon. Even though Dixon is murdered in the film, his character was brought back to life for the long-running television series *Dixon of Dock Green*.

15. The Tottenham Court Road Mystery of 1884

◎ Fitzroy Square

⌂ 33 Fitzroy Square, W1

⊖ Warren Street Tube *(Northern and Victoria Lines)*
   and Goodge Street Tube *(Northern Line)*

This Grade I listed Georgian townhouse, in one of London's finest squares (used as a film location for *The King's Speech*), was once the setting for a macabre crime scene.

On 28 October 1884, a constable was passing No. 33, which was then a military drill hall and armoury, when he noticed a large brown paper parcel in front of the railings. He pulled it open, revealing a portion of a human torso.

The next day the *Pall Mall Gazette* wrote that the area was 'constantly patrolled by police' and guessed that the parcel was dropped between shifts.

Press interest was already high because a skull and a chunk of flesh from a human thigh had been found in a nearby street on 23 October. Then, a parcel containing a human arm was found in the gardens of Bedford Square. The female arm, which was tattooed, suggested that the victim had been a prostitute. The following day, *The Times* reported: 'Yesterday considerable excitement was caused in the neighbourhood of Tottenham Court Road by the discovery of human remains, supposed to be those of a woman, under circumstances suggesting foul play.'

An inquest was held at St Giles Coroner's Court on 11 November. Doctors stated that the body parts came from the same woman and that, as *The Times* had reported, the parts had been 'divided by someone skilled, but certainly not for the purpose of anatomy'. Proceedings were adjourned for several weeks in the hope that new information would come forward. It did. By the time the inquest reconvened on 9 December a parcel containing bones of the right arm, right and left feet and right forearm had been found in Mornington Crescent, just over ten minutes' walk from Fitzroy Square. Dr Jenkins, a police surgeon, stated that the female bones 'had been skilfully dissected', and were from a different woman.

The remains were stored at St Pancras Mortuary before being buried without the women ever being identified or the mystery solved.

From 1913, No. 33 would become the home of the short-lived Omega Group, a design collective started by Bloomsbury artist Roger Fry which closed after just seven years. Subsequently the building became part of the London Foot Hospital and today it is used to host private events. The two properties next door – worth £6m – are owned by film director Guy Ritchie, and underwent extensive renovation after squatters, calling themselves The Really Free School, were evicted early in 2011 at a hearing held at the City of London Court. The squatters had claimed that the empty house was a waste of a valuable resource and had taken it over to run a daily schedule of public events, including films, workshops and discussions. Squatting was once considered essential after WWII, as it allowed bombed-out families to live temporarily in unoccupied homes. It was outlawed in September 2012.

16. Bent Coppers

⊙ West End Central Police Station

⬤ Savile Row, W1

⊖ Oxford Circus Tube *(Victoria, Bakerloo and Central Lines)*

The six-storey police station that stands at the northern end of Savile Row was built in 1939–40. The Kray twins were brought here after their arrest for the murders of Jack 'the Hat' McVitie and George Cornell in 1968. This station was also at the centre of a scandal Scotland Yard would sooner forget.

One of Soho's most successful pornographers was Jimmy Humphreys, who courted and then ended up becoming best pals with Commander (no less) Kenneth Drury, based at West End Central – the two men even went on holiday together with their wives to Cyprus. When they got back, however, a journalist was waiting: 'Police Chief and the Porn King', said the headline in the *Sunday People*.

The Obscene Publications Act of 1959 was supposed to help the police keep a tight grip on the hardcore pornography being sold in the Soho area. But people walking around Soho in the early 60s would be hard pressed not to spot the dozens upon dozens of sex shops open seven days a week, all selling illegal material inside. It was obvious that bungs were being paid and few people believed Drury when he said he'd gone to Cyprus to look for escaped Great Train Robber Ronnie Biggs.

When a team of honest coppers raided Humphreys' house they were dumbfounded to discover that the porn baron had kept a diary in his wall safe that listed names of all the police officers he'd made payments to – and how much he'd paid them. The list contained the names of 17 senior policemen and payoffs totalling over £100,000 each year. Policemen such as Bill Moody, Head of the Obscene Publications Squad, and his superior, Commander 'Wally' Virgo, were on Humphreys' payroll.

As the corruption investigation progressed, there were many 'discreet' early retirements but George Fenwick, Bill Moody, Wally Virgo and Kenneth Drury did not escape and in 1977 all were given between 10 and 14 years in prison.

A subsequent inquiry – Operation Countryman – lasted six years, during which time over 400 police officers lost their jobs. Even though the report recommended 300 of them should be prosecuted, no one was ever charged.

17. The Pink Panther Gang

◎ Graff's Jewellers
🏠 8 New Bond Street, W1
☎ 020 7584 8571
🌐 www.graffdiamonds.com
🕐 Mon-Fri 9am-6pm, Sat 10am-5.15pm, closed Sunday
⊖ Green Park Tube *(Jubilee, Piccadilly and Victoria Lines)*

Many of the world's top jewellers, including Chopard and Harry Winston, have showrooms containing tens of millions of pounds' worth of gems in this small section of New Bond Street.

The Graff's raid, which took place in May 2003, was just the latest in a series of gem-shop hold-ups the 'Pink Panther Gang' had pulled off across the globe, netting them over £50m. The Graff's haul, at £23m, was the UK's biggest ever.

They'd previously struck at the Cannes Carlton Hotel in August 1994. Firing blanks from machine guns, they made off with £30m in jewels. In another daring raid, in June 2000, four men on high-performance motorcycles roared up to a Paris jeweller, smashed glass displays and used a battery-operated vacuum cleaner to suck up the gems in seconds.

The Graff's heist involved three Serbian men: Nebojsa Denic, 33, Milan Jovetic, 24, and mysterious mastermind 'Marco from Montenegro'. The staff tried not to stare at the ridiculously large black wig Denic decided to wear as a disguise on the day of the robbery. 'I thought he was a rock star or had a disease,' said one. During the robbery, Denic reached inside his jacket and produced a gun. But as the gang shoved 47 items into a black drawstring bag, a security guard grabbed Denic in a bear-hug. Denic's gun went off in the struggle – the bullet ricocheted off a building and grazed the nose of a woman passer-by.

Marco fled in a panic, telling Jovetic he had 'lost a man'. The police soon tracked down the latter and found a single blue diamond worth £500,000 in a tub of baby cream – it was Jovetic's share from the robbery. This led the press to dub the gang the Pink Panthers after the Peter Sellers film, which uses the same ruse.

Denic, who was captured at the scene, got 15 years. Jovetic was sentenced to five. 'Marco' – in fact Pedja Vujosevic, 29, a Serbian, based in Paris – escaped. Some stones were recovered but gems worth £20m are still missing. The London robbery has been followed by dozens of other Pink Panther heists, in Europe and in Asia; the total take from which is estimated at a quarter of a billion dollars.

The Pink Panthers seem to be made up of an ever-changing gang of middle-Europeans, many of whom are now in jail; but it doesn't look like the robberies are going to stop any time soon – the lure of the bounty is simply too great.

PICCADILLY W1

THIS SIDE
← 230–167   166–157 →

OTHER SIDE
← 1–56   57–149 →

CITY OF WESTMINSTER

18. From Russia, with Polonium

◎ ITSU

⌂ 167 Piccadilly, W1

☎ 020 7495 4048

ⓦ www.itsu.com

🕐 Mon-Fri 11am-9pm, Sat 12pm-7pm, Sun 12-5pm

⊖ Green Park Tube *(Jubilee, Piccadilly and Victoria Lines)*

Early in November 2006, in a Scotland Yard briefing room, a detective inspector told his assembled murder squad that an extraordinary and most urgent murder investigation, codenamed Operation Whimbrel, was under way. It was so extraordinary, he said, because the victim was still alive: he was the key witness to his own murder.

The victim was the Russian dissident Alexander Litvinenko, a former officer of the FSB, the Russian State Security Service. Litvinenko had been granted political asylum in the UK in 1998, after accusing his former paymasters of ordering him to carry out an assassination. He'd since become one of then President Vladimir Putin's most famous critics, accusing him of a variety of unproven crimes. He had also written a book, *Blowing up Russia: The Return of the KGB*, in which he blamed the Russian State for a series of apartment bombings in Russia.

On 23 November 2006, Alexander Litvinenko's heart stopped twice. His death was just three hours away when scientists from the Atomic Weapons Establishment in Aldermaston concluded that he had been poisoned with polonium-210, a highly radioactive isotope. At 9.21pm that evening, Alexander passed away with his father at his bedside, after saying goodbye to his wife Marina and eight-year-old son Tolik.

Meanwhile, 60 police officers from several departments in SO15, the Metropolitan Police's Counter Terrorism Unit, followed the very noisy radioactive trail left by the assassins all over the West End, from a Moroccan restaurant on Rupert Street in Soho to a boutique hotel near Harrods, from a lap-dancing club in Jermyn Street to the Millennium Hotel in Mayfair, and Litvinenko's family home in Muswell Hill, North London. The highest readings were recorded in the ITSU Sushi Bar in Piccadilly, where Litvinenko had gone to eat and to meet a friend after leaving the Millennium Hotel in Grosvenor Square. The radioactive traces that remained were too weak to cause any harm.

SO15's prime suspect is Andrey Lugovoy, a former KGB officer who has since become a Russian MP as well as the successful owner of his own private security firm. Lugovoy had tea with Litvinenko at the Millennium Hotel on 1 November, the day he fell ill. They had met to discuss a business opportunity. A cup, a teapot, the bar and bar staff at the hotel all tested positive for polonium-210. Although efforts were made to extradite Lugovoy (who denies involvement in the death of Litvinenko) from Russia to the United Kingdom, they proved fruitless.

Scotland Yard remain confident that they will one day bring Alexander Litvinenko's assassin to justice.

19. A Cat Burglar's Comeuppance

◎ Lefevre Gallery
⚫ 31 Bruton Street, Mayfair, W1
☎ 020 7493 2107
🌐 www.lefevrefineart.com
🕐 Mon-Fri 10am-5pm (by appointment only)
⊖ Oxford Circus Tube *(Central, Bakerloo and Victoria Lines)*
   and Bond Street Tube *(Central and Jubilee Lines)*

In the 1960s Peter Scott was London's most celebrated cat burglar. His career spanned three decades, most of which seemed to be spent creeping across the rooftops of Mayfair – from Bond Street to Park Lane and Oxford Street to Piccadilly. Known as the 'Human Fly', Scott was the ultimate 'catch me if you can' villain, poking fun at Scotland Yard detectives with his daring.

Belfast-born Scott arrived in London aged 22 and served an apprenticeship with master-thief George 'Taters' Chatham. Scott was a fast learner and was soon scaling roofs and picking locks on his own. Amongst his many victims were celluloid stars Lauren Bacall, Shirley MacLaine, Vivien Leigh and Zsa Zsa Gabor. However, he drew a blank at the homes of Bette Davis, Elizabeth Taylor, Anne Bancroft, Shirley Bassey, Maria Callas, Alexander Korda and Ginger Rogers, where Scott said he failed 'to find anything worth stealing'.

Scott, who at one time drove a Bentley (probably bought from the Bentley showroom on the corner of Bruton Street and Berkeley Square, right under the noses of his victims), stole – with the help of an accomplice – Sophia Loren's jewels whilst she was in London making *The Millionairess*. He ended up with £19,000 and watched her list the stolen items in a press conference: A big ruby necklace, a sapphire necklace with earrings, diamonds, an emerald necklace with earrings, a diamond ring, three stripped pearls – and on the list went – half-a-million pounds' worth, all uninsured. Loren offered a reward of $56,000 for its return.

After doing a lot of porridge in London's prisons Scott eventually renounced his life of crime to become a 'celebrity tennis coach'. However, in 1998, aged 67, he was arrested leaving the Sherlock Holmes Hotel in Baker Street with a plastic bag full of cash after delivering a Picasso painting – *Tête de Femme* – stolen at gunpoint from the Lefevre Gallery a few weeks earlier. The painting was said to be worth £650,000.

Scott claimed he'd been an innocent go-between in a private deal arranged by a business accomplice and someone else who'd robbed the Gallery. This someone, he said, was a 'surrogate son'. Scott was sentenced to three-and-a-half years and has, by all accounts, since retired from crime.

20. The Inside Man

⊙ Bank of America Robbery

⌂ Davies Street, W1

⊖ Bond Street Tube *(Central and Jubilee Lines)*

As with most 'big jobs', the gang of thieves behind this infamous 1975 heist relied on an inside man: 27-year-old Stuart Buckley, who worked at the bank as an electrician.

There'll always be someone on the inside 'opening doors' (often literally). It might start with a poorly paid security guard working in a bank or cash depot who begins fantasising with his mates down the pub about what it would be like to take all that money. Then, before he knows it, he's being approached – and made an offer he can't refuse for fear of what might happen to him if he does.

Buckley had first helped the gang get inside the bank to drill through the vault's lock. When that failed, the robbers came up with a plan whereby Buckley hid in the roof space above the vault door and watched as bank officials typed in the combination.

At the time, the Bank of America raid was the world's biggest: at least £8m was stolen. The total haul may well have been more as safety-deposit boxes were in the vault and, for legal reasons, not every owner came forward.

Chief Superintendent Jack Slipper, the cop who'd gone after the Great Train Robbers, quickly realised the gang must have had inside help, and made sure his officers put pressure on the bank's staff. Buckley quickly cracked and turned informant. By that time, some of the ringleaders had fled to Morocco – which had no extradition treaty with the UK.

The Old Bailey trial lasted 93 days and cost £500,000 – the same amount of money the police managed to recover.

Judge Alan King-Hamilton was adamant that the thieves would never get to enjoy their spoils. 'What has been concealed will remain salted away so far as you are concerned for a great many years … Whatever has happened to it, it will not be used for your benefit.'

He passed the longest sentences on those considered to be the ringleaders: safe-cracker Leonard Wilde, who described himself as a grocer, was sent to jail for 23 years while Peter Colson, 32, a company director and used car dealer, was jailed for 21 years. In all the judge handed out a century's worth of jail time.

Others in the ten-strong gang were sentenced to periods ranging from 18 years for robbery to three years for receiving stolen goods. Buckley was jailed for seven years. Frank Maple, the supposed mastermind – along with three others – escaped justice. He made it to Morocco and was never heard of again.

21. Gamblers' Paradise

◎ **The Clermont Club**
⬠ **44 Berkeley Square, W1**
☎ **020 7493 5587**
ⓦ **www.theclermontclub.com**
🕐 **Members only**
⊖ **Green Park Tube** *(Jubilee, Piccadilly and Victoria Lines)*

This smart address in an 18th-century mansion in London's Berkeley Square, today home to one of London's most respectable private members' clubs, has a murky past. In the 1950s and 60s, this elegant townhouse was an illegal gambling den for the gentry, run by gambling supremo and zoo owner John Aspinall (1926–2000).

At this time gambling outside a racetrack was forbidden in Britain but in the 1950s Aspinall set up illegal dens in Mayfair and Belgravia to feed the desire of the rich to bet their fortunes at cards.

Aspinall was once the subject of a police raid. After the cops crashed into his Mayfair flat they told him he was charged with 'keeping a common gambling house'.

'Young man,' Aspinall's mother replied, 'there was nothing common in this house until you entered it.'

Members of the Clermont included Lord Lucan, who would later murder his children's nanny in 1974 (see page 320) and was rumoured initially to have fled here after the crime. Lucan and Aspinall were great friends. Other members included Lord Boothby (who had an affair with Ronnie Kray), James Bond creator Ian Fleming and billionaire Jimmy Goldsmith.

What the Clermont's clientele never found out was that they were being conned out of their cash. London's biggest underworld boss Billy Hill (see page 251) had approached Aspinall with an ingenious scheme.

Using a method devised by the Marseilles Mafia, a small, mangle-like machine bent the Clermont's customised playing cards just a fraction, one way or the other, to denote their value. The cards would then be repacked in cellophane wrapping, sealed as new and opened in front of the trusting guests' eyes. A trained 'reader' then joined the game and won big for the house. On the first night the winnings for the house were about £14,000 – £280,000 in modern money – and over the course of another, in 1958, landowner Lord Derby lost in excess of £300,000 – £7m today. Together, Hill and Aspinall took millions.

When he died in 2000 Aspinall was most proud of his private zoo, which had seen the birth of eight elephants, 70 gorillas and 14 black rhinos.

22. The Hanging Tree

◉ Tyburn and Marble Arch

⬥ Marble Arch, W1

⊖ Marble Arch Tube *(Central Line)*

This was a place of execution from 1388 until 1783, when hangings started to take place at Newgate (see page 125).

Hanging days were so popular they were often declared public holidays, and the crowds could be huge – 200,000 people (one third of London's population) turned up for the hanging of Jack Sheppard in 1714. The 22-year-old robber had achieved fame for his relentless pursuit of crime, his love of the good life and for his numerous escapes from prison, including Newgate (see Spitalfields, page 150). The artist Hogarth depicted a hanging day in his series titled *Industry and Idleness*, featuring vendors selling gingerbread and gin, ballad and orange sellers – and of course the pickpockets and ladies of the town. Also visible are the spectators' seats for those wealthy enough to afford tickets for a grandstand view.

The modern scaffold was named after Thomas Derrick, the Elizabethan executioner who perfected a method that relied upon a hoist and pulley instead of the old rope-tossed-over-a-beam method. Using the Derrick method, scaffolds were built that could hang more than 20 people at a time. Estimates of the total number of people hanged at Tyburn vary, with the figure being somewhere between 40,000 and 60,000.

Derrick was hired by the Earl of Essex. Derrick had been sentenced to death for rape but, thanks to a shortage of executioners and no willing applicants, the Earl offered it to Derrick.

The two men met again when Derrick executed the Earl of Essex for treason in 1601 (the Earl had tried to overthrow the government). Distantly related to Elizabeth I, and having once been a royal favourite, the Earl was beheaded on Tower Green, at the Tower of London. It took Derrick three swings of the axe before the job was done.

The approximate site of the gallows is marked by a stone in the traffic island at the junction of Edgware Road and Bayswater Road, just a few metres northwest from the oddly placed Marble Arch (pictured), designed by John Nash. Work started on Marble Arch – originally an entrance gate to Buckingham Palace – in 1827. It was moved to the northeast corner of Hyde Park in 1851 and turned into a traffic island in 1907. From 1907 to 1950 it was used as a police station (there are rooms inside). Samuel Parkes, who won the Victoria Cross at the Charge of the Light Brigade, worked as an inspector in this strange little station.

23. The Kray Twins Meet the Mafia

◉ **Hilton Hotel**
◒ **Park Lane, W1**
⊖ **Hyde Park Corner Tube** *(Piccadilly Line)*

This 28-storey hotel, which opened in 1963, has been the unwitting host of much bad behaviour and many remarkable criminal moments. In 1975 it was the target of an IRA bombing. Left in the lobby, the device detonated as police were clearing the building, killing two and injuring 63.

More recently a visit from the Beastie Boys resulted in the rappers smashing through the floor of their room into the suite below – leading to a lifetime ban. Also banned from the Hilton was The Who's drummer Keith Moon, who liked to flush explosives down the toilet – one flush could cause as much as £250,000-worth of damage. In 1978, Moon died from a drugs overdose at a friend's flat at 9 Curzon Square, about 100 yards from the Hilton.

The hotel is also a magnet for practitioners of extreme sports: more than one base-jumper has ended up in court after leaping from its roof, 328 feet up. The 25-year-old thrill-seeker, Darren Newton, lost his life this way in 1992.

Back in 1968 the Park Lane Hilton was the location of an extraordinary meeting. Ronnie and Reggie Kray had been trying to get in with the New York Mafia. A trip to the US confirmed that there was money and power to be had by organising the Firm along Mafia lines – notably through moving into unions, docks, taxis and construction.

The twins met with Angelo Bruno, head of the Philadelphia Mafia, who was in London ostensibly to check whether there were fortunes to be made in West End casinos.

Ronnie decided to impress his guest by assassinating a West End club owner with a car bomb. Luckily, the police foiled the attempt, but the Firm and the Mafia did end up striking a fifty-fifty deal to launder millions of dollars in stolen bearer bonds. The bonds came via Joseph Pagano, a senior member of the Genovese crime group, one of the five Mafia families that ran organised crime in New York. The twins disposed of the bonds via their banker Alan Cooper, who had previously asked them for help to get rid of a couple of gangsters from South London who'd been strong-arming him for money. Their names were Charlie and Eddie Richardson.

The twins had first heard of Charlie when they were all in Shepton Mallet military prison together in the 1950s; compulsory national service hadn't agreed with any of them. As the Kray and Richardson gangs grew, it was perhaps inevitable that they would end up warring, but it was Cooper who was the catalyst for a bloody headline-grabbing feud that would eventually destroy both families (see page 43).

No. 100, PALL MALL,
or the National Gallery of England.

To The Right Honᵇˡᵉ Charles Earl Grey,
FIRST LORD OF THE TREASURY &c. &c. &c

This Print is most respectfully dedicated,
by his obedient Servant,
THE PUBLISHER.

Published by J. Hogarth, New Road, opposite Sᵗ Pancras Church.
Printed by C. Hullmandel.

24. Lord Byron Kills His Neighbour

◉ Star and Garter
◯ 100 Pall Mall, SW1
⊖ Piccadilly Circus Tube *(Piccadilly and Bakerloo Lines)* and
   Charing Cross station *(Mainline, Northern and Bakerloo Lines)*

Pall Mall takes its name from a croquet-like game involving balls and mallets, introduced in England and made popular in London by Charles II, which was played here during the 17th century. By the start of the 18th century, Pall Mall was known for its expensive boutiques, along with many grand houses. In the 19th century, it was home to many famous gentlemen's clubs, including Brooks's, Boodles, the Carlton, the Athenaeum, the Reform and the Royal Automobile Club.

The Star and Garter pub was a four-storey building made of two houses, the east house including a shop at ground level. In 1759 the licensee was James Fynmore, the landlord present when the famous duel between William Byron, 5th Baron Byron (1722–98), great-uncle of the famous poet, and his Nottinghamshire neighbour and cousin William Chaworth took place in 1765.

Byron had become a lieutenant in the Royal Navy at the age of 16. At 17 he represented his family as a founding Governor of the Foundling Hospital, a charity that looked after abandoned babies.

The two men had been drinking wine (the pub was famous for its claret) and got into an argument about — well, it's not too clear what the argument was about; either who had the biggest estate, or had the most game on their estate. They retired to a back room to settle their differences and Byron ended up spearing his opponent through the stomach with his sword.

Chaworth survived until the next day, bemoaning the fact that the location had been a pretty poor choice for a fight right up until he died. Byron was tried for murder but was instead found guilty of manslaughter, for which he paid a token fine. He mounted the murder weapon on his bedroom wall. From this time on he was known as 'The Wicked Lord', a reputation that was reinforced when he shot his coachman during an argument and took over the reins himself, leaving the poor man in the back with the Lord's long-suffering wife.

When Byron died aged 75, his estate passed to his great-nephew, George Gordon Byron, the famous poet.

The Star and Garter survived until 1800, when the Light and Heat Company took over the premises, followed soon after by a shoe-blacking firm, before the building became the original home of the National Gallery, until 1838, when it was demolished. Today 100 Pall Mall is home to a huge block of serviced offices, but the nearby Red Lion, one of London's oldest pubs, was around in Byron's day. Situated in Crown Passage (gas lit to this day), which runs off Pall Mall and is a short walk west of No. 100, it is easy to imagine Byron and Chaworth duelling in one of the back rooms.

25. The One-Man Police Box

◎ Trafalgar Square

⌂ Southeast Corner, WC2

⊖ Charing Cross station *(Mainline, Northern and Bakerloo Lines)*

The southeast corner of Trafalgar Square, opposite South Africa House, is home to a rarely spotted oddity. Most people overlook it precisely because it's designed to blend in.

At the end of World War I, a police box was placed at the entrance to Charing Cross station. In 1926 the box was removed while the station was being renovated and it was suggested that it would be more usefully placed in Trafalgar Square, so that an officer could keep an eye on protesters and alert Scotland Yard to any trouble.

This idea of putting a police station, no matter how small, in Trafalgar Square, met with some resistance, until the head of the Office of Works, Sir Lionel Edwards, came up with a subtle solution. He suggested that a 'station' could be built into the granite base of the lamp plinth on the southeast corner of the square. The idea met with agreement and the 'station' opened in 1927.

With slits to give the officer a 360-degree view and a direct line to the Yard, this was a front-line posting for a brave officer in times of trouble. It was also designed to hold two prisoners until such time as they could be carted off to Charing Cross Police Station. When the receiver was lifted or if it rang, the light on top (connected in 1936) flashed to draw the attention of nearby officers. Legend has it that the ornamental light is originally from Nelson's HMS *Victory*, but there is no evidence to support this.

The station is now used to store cleaning and building materials for the council, used in the upkeep of the square. The police today rely on 10,500 crime-fighting cameras across Greater London to keep an eye out for troublesome Londoners.

Trafalgar Square has several laws peculiar to it which include: no placing of canoes or inflatable objects in any fountain; no barbecuing; no feeding the birds; no erecting tents for the purpose of sleeping; and no riding on any animal in the Square. You have been warned.

26. The Battle for Trafalgar

◎ Trafalgar Square, WC2
⊖ Charing Cross station *(Mainline, Northern and Bakerloo Lines)*

In 1812 the architect John Nash had a vision of creating an open cultural and public space in what were once royal stable yards. In 1830, it was officially named Trafalgar Square. Nelson's Column was erected in 1843. The fountains followed two years later and the bronze lions that guard Nelson arrived in 1867.

This public space, a short distance from No. 10 Downing Street and the Houses of Parliament, has been seen as the ideal space for protests and demonstrations – not all of which have finished peacefully.

On 31 March 1990, 100,000 demonstrators marched from Kennington to Trafalgar Square to protest at the Prime Minister Margaret Thatcher's flagship policy: the Community Charge, or Poll Tax. The tax would see the abolition of rates based on a property's value, replaced by a fixed charge per adult resident. In practice, critics argued, a millionaire living alone in a mansion would pay less than the average family.

It was an unusually warm spring day; people who had never been on a demo before came out. There was a carnival atmosphere, with drummers, bands and jugglers. The 70,000-capacity square filled up very quickly. Thatcher was incredibly unpopular at this time – polls put her public support at 15 per cent. As one protester said, 'There were so many people, it felt like we were going to overthrow the State.'

At around 4pm, the demonstrators refused to move from outside Downing Street, the location of the Prime Minister's official London residence, and started to pelt the police with missiles. When the Met officers charged up Whitehall, the angry crowd, having nowhere else to go, and outnumbering the police by some margin, charged back. At which point the cops understandably broke ranks and ran for their lives – it was clear that this was going to be a long day for the police.

Rioting spread quickly to the square. Protesters lit fires on the southeast corner, as a police commander, standing in the shadow of Nelson, directed charges from the empty plinth in front of the National Gallery.

The police blocked exits from the square, causing panic among the peaceful protesters – many of whom had brought their children – who were now trying to flee through the smoke. Tube stations were closed and streets cordoned off as cars were set alight, shops looted and fire-fighters attacked. By the time order was restored at 3am there was at least £400,000-worth of damage, 400 arrests had been made and 113 people (45 of whom were police officers) and 20 police horses were injured.

The riots, it is argued, contributed to Margaret Thatcher's downfall. An estimated 17 million people in England refused to pay the tax when it took effect in April, leaving councils £2 billion in arrears. Thatcher resigned and left Downing Street in tears seven months later. The tax was abolished in 1993 by her successor, John Major.

27. That Bloody Trunk

◎ Charing Cross Left Luggage

⬆ Charing Cross Station, WC2

⊜ Charing Cross station *(Mainline, Northern and Bakerloo Lines)*

On 10 May 1927, the police received a report from staff at the Charing Cross left luggage office that they had forced open a trunk that had started to smell and discovered the body of a dismembered woman.

Chief Detective Inspector George Cornish took charge of the case. The murdered woman was Minnie Alice Bonati, a 30-something former cook to a large family in West London. Unemployed, she'd turned to prostitution to make ends meet.

Cornish's team quickly tracked down the trunk, which had been bought second-hand from a shop on the Brixton Road six days earlier. Then, the taxi driver who had dropped off the trunk told them he'd picked up his client from Rochester Row in Victoria, just opposite the police station.

The police canvassed Rochester Row and found that John Robinson, a 36-year-old failed estate agent, who'd just vacated his office in a hurry, had kept a large empty trunk in the hallway. Cornish tracked Robinson down but the suspect was released after none of the witnesses identified him.

Cornish searched Robinson's former office again and turned up a bloodstain that was matched to Bonati. Robinson was brought back to Scotland Yard on 23 May. This time he confessed. He said he'd fallen in with a 'strange woman' at Victoria station. Back at his office in Rochester Row she told him she was hard up and asked for a pound. When Robinson said no, she flew into a rage and slapped him.

He said: 'She bent down as though to pick up something from the fireplace and came towards me. I hit her on the face with my right hand … She fell backwards; she struck a chair in falling and it fell over. As she fell she sort of sat down and rolled with her head in the fireplace.' Robinson said he left her there and went home. The next day, he said he was amazed to find her still there, dead. In a 'hopeless position', he detailed buying the trunk and a knife.

Some of the detectives who worked on the case thought that Robinson might have been telling the truth. Bonati's husband testified that she was an alcoholic and sometimes very violent. So, was it murder or manslaughter? Pathologist Bernard Spilsbury asserted it was murder, stating that the woman may have been suffocated after she'd been knocked out. Spilsbury was – perhaps mistakenly – regarded as infallible and his evidence helped convince the jury that Robinson was guilty of murder. He was hanged at Pentonville prison on 12 August 1927 by John Ellis (see Pentonville, page 180).

28. The Birth of Forensic Ballistics

◎ Charing Cross Police Station
⊙ Agar Street, WC2
Ⓦ www.content.met.police.uk/PoliceStation/charingcross
⊜ Charing Cross station *(Mainline, Northern and Bakerloo Lines)*

Originally the Charing Cross Hospital, this building opened for business in 1834 with 60 beds. One famous medical student was missionary and explorer Dr David Livingstone.

The building was converted into a police station in 1994 and, thanks to its West End location, has often been used to keep unruly pop starlets, footballers and tycoons under lock and key.

At the beginning of the 20th century, Agar Street was home to Edwin John Churchill, a remarkable gunsmith and champion pigeon shot – the only man ever to have shot dead two elephants on British soil. Both times (1900 and 1902), the unhappy animals had fled a circus procession – the first in Crystal Palace, while the second rampaged from the Agricultural Hall in Westminster to Trafalgar Square, where Edwin met him with his .500 Express. Churchill's gun shop was at No. 8. The original building is no longer there but No. 12 on the corner with Chandos Place looks just as it was then.

Churchill's nephew Robert, the world's first forensic ballistics expert, took over the family business in 1910. He was frequently consulted by Scotland Yard. One of the most famous cases Robert Churchill assisted on occurred in 1903 when a body was discovered in a ditch at Moat Farm, Clavering, Essex. They were the remains of Camille Cecille Holland, who had been murdered some four years before by Samuel Herbert Dougal. He was a womaniser and had swept the 56-year-old, wealthy spinster off her feet, only to murder her three weeks later and hide her body in a drainage ditch. He then set about forging her signature and, until his arrest, obtained large sums of money from her bank account.

The body was in a poor state and Miss Holland was only identified by the shoes she was wearing (these are now in the Essex Police Museum). A postmortem revealed she had been shot in the head. Churchill conducted experiments with a sheep's head bought from the butcher's next door to his shop. From comparing powder marks, penetration and destruction of tissue, he was able to determine whether a bullet wound in a victim was self-inflicted or otherwise. In this case, he was able to produce the same fracture in the head as the bullet found in Miss Holland's skull.

From this Churchill concluded that an expanding bullet had been fired from a revolver (recovered from Moat Farm), at a distance of six to twelve inches. As a result of this finding, Dougal was prosecuted and convicted for the murder of Miss Holland, and was hanged at Chelmsford prison on 14 July 1904.

29. The Murder of an Actor

◎ Adelphi Theatre
◐ The Strand, WC2
☎ 0844 412 4651
Ⓦ www.adelphitheatrelondon.com
⊖ Charing Cross station *(Mainline, Northern and Bakerloo Lines)* and Covent Garden Tube *(Piccadilly Line)*

In the later 19th century pleasure-seekers flocked to the Strand to sample its many restaurants, jolly public houses and smoking rooms. The title of a popular song of the time, 'Let's All Go Down the Strand', became an expression of having fun. In 1890, the Strand had more theatres than any other street in London but today only three remain: the Savoy, the Vaudeville and the Adelphi.

On 16 December 1897, the most popular and much-loved actor of the day, 49-year-old William Terriss, known for both his action (particularly Robin Hood) and Shakespearean roles, arrived at the Adelphi, where he was starring in a play called *Secret Service* written by the American actor William Gillette (who was famous for playing Sherlock Holmes, see page 217).

As Terriss started to open the theatre's side door in Maiden Lane, a young man ran up to him and stabbed him twice in the back. The wounds weren't deep and Terriss turned to face and fend off his attacker, but as he did so the knife came down again and this time with so much force that it pierced Terriss's heart. He bled to death in the arms of his leading lady and lover, Jessie Millward, who had run out to see what the commotion was.

The attacker was quickly captured and taken to Bow Street Police Station. Richard Prince was insanely jealous of Terriss's success. Terriss had supported Prince for many years but the young actor had become increasingly deranged in recent months.

The murder brought the capital to a halt – literally. The funeral procession was over 100 carriages long and fifty thousand people gathered at Brompton cemetery. Among the guests were Sir Henry Irving and Lillie Langtry.

The Prince of Wales sent a magnificent wreath of white lilies and orchids with a card of condolence. It was reported that the tributes were so numerous that it seemed as if 'all London must have been stripped of flowers'.

Prince was sent to Broadmoor, where he was finally able to take on the role of the leading man. He put on plays, with other inmates as actors, until he died there 39 years later.

30. The Merry Widow

◎ The Savoy Hotel

⌂ Strand, WC2

☎ 020 7836 4343

ⓦ www.fairmont.com/savoy

⊖ Temple Tube *(District and Circle Lines)* and Charing Cross station
(Mainline, Northern and Bakerloo Lines)

The Savoy Hotel, which reopened in 2010 after a £200m refurbishment, took its first paying guests in 1889. The pots and pans of its first chef – Auguste Escoffier – are still in the kitchen, despite the redevelopment.

The Savoy has been no stranger to scandal – Oscar Wilde entertained rent-boys in room 361 – but in spite (or perhaps because) of this it has remained a centre of glamour. In 1923 alone, Fred and Adele Astaire (they danced on the roof), golfing supremo Walter Hagen and the opera singer Luisa Tetrazzini were just a few of its more famous paying guests.

On the morning of Sunday 1 July that same year a limousine delivered Prince and Princess Fahmy to the hotel. The 22-year-old Ali Fahmy had met Marguerite, who was ten years older than he, in Paris the year before. They had married in Egypt two months earlier but wedded bliss did not last long. The couple's fights sometimes turned physical, and Marguerite was often forced to cover her bruises with make-up. During their stay at the Savoy, Marguerite called for the hotel doctor. She had external haemorrhoids and claimed that Ali had 'torn her by unnatural intercourse' and was 'always pestering her' for anal sex.

On 9 July the couple went to Daly's Theatre on Cranbourne Street and decided to see a film called *The Merry Widow*. After the movie, the couple returned to the Savoy for a late supper, during which they fell into a terrible argument. At around 2am Marguerite shot her husband in the head and, as he lay dying, she said: *'Qu'est-ce que j'ai fait, mon cher?'* ('What have I done, my dear?')

She was defended at the Old Bailey by legendary barrister Marshall Hall. He was 65, six foot three, handsome and known in the press as 'The Great Defender'. Marshall Hall portrayed Marguerite's husband as a monster of Eastern amoral bisexual depravity, accusing both Prince Fahmy and his private secretary of being homosexuals.

Fahmy, said Hall, 'developed abnormal tendencies and he never treated Madame normally'. His wife, he said, was to him no more than a belonging. And after Marguerite related the arguments, the beatings and, God forbid, the anal sex, the judge was unable to contain himself: 'These things are horrible; they are disgusting … We in this country put our women on a pedestal: in Egypt they have not the same views …' Perhaps unsurprisingly, the jury returned 'not guilty' to both murder and manslaughter. Madame Fahmy – as the press now called her – was released.

Sadly for Marguerite – who had been a prostitute with an illegitimate daughter back in France – her husband had left no will so she could claim none of his fortune. She tried faking a 'son' so that he could inherit but this was quickly exposed and she returned to France a recluse, dying in January 1971.

31. Murder at the Opera

◎ Royal Opera House
○ Bow Street, WC2
☎ 020 7240 1200
ⓦ www.roh.org.uk
🕐 A range of tours are available throughout the year. See website for details.
⊖ Covent Garden Tube *(Piccadilly Line)*

When it opened in 1732, the Royal Opera House was the most luxurious theatre in London – to mark the occasion the famous artist Hogarth produced an engraving of the triumphant entry of its owner, John Rich. The entrance pictured opposite is the Floral Hall in Bow Street, constructed as part of a major redevelopment in the 1990s.

Martha Ray (1742–79) was a well-known singer here but was perhaps more famous for being the beautiful mistress of John Montagu, 4th Earl of Sandwich; they lived as man and mistress from when Ray was 17 (the earl's wife had succumbed to mental illness). Together they produced five children.

James Hackman, a soldier, became infatuated with Ray and asked for her hand in marriage several times. At some point in 1778, Ray and Hackman had a brief fling, after which time Ray left him.

On 7 April 1779 Hackman, who'd become increasingly obsessed with Ray, collected two pistols from his house and waited near the Opera House, at the Bedford Coffee House. At 11.15pm Martha Ray left the Opera House with a friend. The street was crowded, and as Ray had one foot on the step of a waiting carriage, Hackman came up behind and pulled her down.

Horace Walpole, the politician and historian, reported later: '... on her turning round, [he] clapped the pistol to her forehead and shot her through the head. With another pistol he then attempted to shoot himself, but the ball grazing his brow, he tried to dash out his own brains with the pistol, and is more wounded by those blows than by the ball.' Hackman was arrested as Martha Ray's body was carried to the Shakespeare Tavern.

At Hackman's Old Bailey trial on 16 April 1779, seats in the public gallery sold for a guinea. Lawyer and diarist James Boswell was present and described the murder as 'one of the most remarkable that has ever occurred in the history of human nature'. Hackman pleaded not guilty on the grounds of temporary insanity, claiming that he had only meant to commit suicide – not kill Martha Ray. He was found guilty of murder, sentenced to death and was hanged at Tyburn three days later. His body was removed to Surgeons' Hall for public dissection.

In 1808 the Opera House went the way of most London theatres and burned to the ground (theatres were candle-lit and therefore highly combustible). Sadly the composer Handel's organ went up in smoke with it, along with many of his manuscripts. The new opera house opened in 1809 and in 1855 it was sublet to theatre manager John Anderson, who had lost two previous theatres to fire. He made it three in a row when the Opera House burned down again in 1856, one day before his lease was due to expire.

32. The Bow Street Runners

◎ Bow Street Magistrates' Court
🜚 Bow Street, WC2
⊖ Covent Garden Tube *(Piccadilly Line)*

Bow Street is so called because of its shape. It grew between 1633 and 1677 and was known as a place for respectable gentlemen to have their lodgings. No. 1 was home to Will's Coffee House between 1671 and 1749, where Pepys, Dryden, Gay, Pope and Swift were just some of the local literary stars who made it their regular place of refreshment. By the early 19th century the street had grown notorious for its brothels; whether this was the result of so many well-to-do gentlemen in the near vicinity is unclear.

The famous writer Henry Fielding took over the nearby Haymarket Theatre in 1735. Unfortunately his plays were not a success and he left the theatre – making a very unusual career change – for law enforcement in 1737. Fielding was a better justice of the peace than playwright and from Bow Street Magistrates' Court (the present building dates back to 1879), he managed to establish the building blocks of modern crime-fighting.

Fielding created the Bow Street Runners, originally six elite detectives who wore no uniform and took private commissions from the great and the good as well as the bad and the ugly. The only thing that mattered was that the client should be wealthy enough to afford their services. They did not consider themselves liable 'to interfere in any criminal case, unless they were expressly called upon to do so', i.e. unless they were paid.

One runner, James Townsend, was a bit of a dandy and on friendly terms with George III. Another, George Ruthven, spent a great part of his time travelling in Russia and Germany in the service of the Empress and the Prussian government. Runner John Sayer conducted negotiations between the bank robber James MacKoull and the Paisley Bank in Glasgow for the return of £20,000 on condition that the charges against MacKoull were dropped. When Sayer died, he left behind an incredible £30,000 in cash – and some of the notes were those stolen from the Paisley Bank. Henry Fielding's blind brother, John, took over after Henry's death in 1754 and it was said that he was instantly able to identify over 3,000 robbers by the sound of their voice alone. The Bow Street Runners were disbanded in 1839 once the newly formed and publicly funded Met Police had established itself.

Famous appearances at Bow Street Magistrates' include: Giacomo Casanova, Roger Casement, Dr Crippen, Abu Hamza al-Masri, the Kray twins, General Pinochet, Oscar Wilde and James Earl Ray, who fled to London after assassinating Martin Luther King. The five red telephone boxes just around the corner were put there for the benefit of the dozens of reporters who attended infamous trials here on a weekly basis.

The court was closed in 1992, when it moved to a new location in Westminster. Sold to a hotel chain, the building is currently awaiting redevelopment.

33. The Jackal Passport Scam

◎ **The Register of Births, Marriages and Deaths**

⊙ Somerset House, Strand WC2

☎ 020 7845 4600

ⓦ www.somersethouse.org.uk

🕐 Galleries open daily 10am-6pm. The courtyard is open 7.30am-11pm.

ⓕ Galleries £6-£8 for adults. Discounts available, see website for details.
  Access to the Courtyard is free.

⊖ Temple Tube *(District and Circle Lines)*

The best thriller writers turn to the real world to give their books the authenticity that readers crave. Arguably, the master of the genre is Frederick Forsyth, author of *The Day of the Jackal*, published in 1971.

In this book, about an English hit man (the Jackal) employed to assassinate French president Charles de Gaulle, the nameless anti-hero acquires a genuine UK passport, but in a false name. He then travels through Europe, where he commits several murders and evades the police – thanks to the passport, which the police are left trying to trace. The amazing thing was that Forsyth had exposed a genuine loophole, one that has long been used by criminals and terrorists.

It was shockingly simple. The Jackal searches through three village graveyards to find the headstone of a baby boy who would have been about the same age as he is. Taking the details to the Central Registry of Births, Marriages and Deaths (based here in Somerset House from 1836), the Jackal buys a copy of the deceased's birth certificate – all the proof he needs to apply for a passport, which is issued four days later.

It has been estimated that 1,500 passports were acquired in this way in the UK each year. And a range of international ne'er-do-wells, from Soviet spies to IRA terrorists, have strolled into Somerset House to collect their fraudulent birth certificates.

It's a method that has since been used by identity fraudsters who know that nothing counts more in terms of ID than an official British passport. ID fraud costs Britain £1.3 billion a year and UK courts have recently heard many cases involving illegal immigrants buying passports based on the identities of dead babies.

'When the book was published, I assumed this loophole would have been closed by officialdom within weeks,' Forsyth told the BBC, almost 35 years after the novel first came out. But as recently as November 2006, a man calling himself the Earl of Buckingham was jailed after he stole the identity of a child who had died in the 1960s. Even when faced with jail he refused to reveal his true identity.

It wasn't until 2007 that the Identity and Passport Service set up a system to try and close the loophole. They quickly uncovered 1,200 cases, leading to 290 arrests, 100 convictions and 38 deportations, showing just how popular the scam had become.

The records office has since moved (most of its duties are now performed by the Family Records Office in Myddelton Street, EC1) and Somerset House has been turned over to public use with an art gallery, skating rink (formerly a car park for civil servants employed by the register), bar and café.

34. Appeals, Inquests and Rock Stars

◎ Royal Courts of Justice

⬆ Strand, WC2

☎ 020 7947 6000

ⓦ www.justice.gov.uk/courts/rcj-rolls-building

🕐 Public opening hours are 9am-4.30pm. Courts sit between 10am and 4.30pm.

🅕 Free but come prepared to be searched. No photography.

⊖ Temple Tube *(District and Circle Lines)*

Opened by Queen Victoria in 1892, the Royal Courts of Justice (known popularly as the Law Courts) were built using 35 million bricks faced with Portland stone. Inside, 3.5 miles of corridors link 1,000 rooms.

Over the main entrance (shown here) are statues of Christ (centre), King Solomon (west) and King Alfred (east), while Moses watches over the back door. The magnificent, overwhelming hall is 75 metres long and 24 metres high. Gothic arches lead off to cramped courts on either side of the corridor. Although many have been converted for other uses, such as offices and video rooms where interested parties can watch proceedings, there are still 60 functioning courtrooms spread throughout the building, where criminals come in the hope – often forlorn – of successfully appealing their sentences in front of three Court of Appeal judges, who preside above one and all at the far end of each court.

Some of the famous appeals heard here include, James Hanratty, hanged on 4 April 1962 in Bedford prison for the murder of Michael Gregston, as well as for raping and shooting Gregston's mistress Valerie Storie. Campaigners claimed the evidence was too weak to justify guilt, let alone the death sentence, but a posthumous appeal in 2002 still failed as newly completed DNA testing proved, according to the judges' ruling, that Hanratty's guilt was 'beyond doubt'.

The Dome Diamond Robbers (see Millennium Dome, page 72) were more successful and had their sentences reduced by two to three years after the judges accepted they had not intended any harm or violence.

The Law Courts also hear inquests, such as that into the death of Princess Diana, and inquiries (at the time of writing, the Leveson inquiry into 'phone hacking' has taken over Court 73).

Then there are the civil cases which feature many rock and pop stars, including Bruce Springsteen (who successfully won an action against firms pirating his early material), former Take That member Robbie Williams (arguing over royalty payments) and 1980s pop combo Spandau Ballet (ditto).

In February 2008 Court 34 played host to one of the most famous divorce hearings in recent years when Heather Mills, ex-wife of former Beatle Paul McCartney, asked for £125m of his reputed £450m wealth. Mills was eventually awarded a lump sum of £16.5m and assets of £7.8m, plus yearly payments of £35,000 to cover nanny and school costs for their daughter.

35. The Assassination of a Prime Minister

◎ Lindsey House

⌂ 59–60 Lincoln's Inn Fields, WC2

⊖ Holborn Tube *(Central and Piccadilly Lines)*

The square's only surviving original property, Lindsey House dates back to 1638. Divided into two addresses, it was rejoined in 1802 by architect Sir John Soane (whose former home, No. 13 Lincoln's Inn Fields, is now London's most eclectic museum) for the British Prime Minister Spencer Perceval (1762–1812), who took office in 1809.

Perceval entered Parliament as an MP on 9 May 1796 and in 1807 became Chancellor of the Exchequer and Leader of the House of Commons. He succeeded the elderly Duke of Portland as Prime Minister in 1809.

Perceval took charge at a difficult time – a severe economic depression had stalled the Industrial Revolution, the Napoleonic Wars were still being fought and George III was slipping into madness.

Just as things started to look up, on 11 May 1812, John Bellingham, a merchant who had amassed business debts in Russia, stormed into the lobby of the House of Commons with a pistol. Bellingham had sought compensation from the government for his losses, but was refused. He'd therefore decided on vengeance and shot Perceval, whose last words were, accurately, 'Oh, I have been murdered.'

Someone shouted, 'Where's the murderer?' and Bellingham, still holding the pistol, answered, 'I am the unfortunate man.' When asked for his reason, the assassin answered: 'Want of redress, and denial of justice.' He also pointed out that he bore Perceval no personal grudge but simply wanted to strike out at the office he represented.

One week later John Bellingham was executed in front of the Debtors' Door at Newgate prison. The executioner was William Brunskill, one of London's most prolific hangmen (as principal hangman he put to death 537 people outside Newgate, plus a further 68 at Horsemonger Lane gaol).

Bellingham remained calm on the scaffold, in front of a large mob, some of whom shouted, 'God bless you!' and 'God save you!' as the hood was placed over his head. He was praying when the support was struck away. His body was taken to St Bartholomew's Hospital, where it was dissected for study.

Previously, in 1683, Lord William Russell – a friend of Lindsey House's then resident Lord Winchester – was beheaded in Lincoln's Inn Fields after being convicted of treason for his part in a plot to assassinate Charles II in order to prevent a Catholic accession. Afterwards, Russell's body was brought into the house and his head sewn back on before being carried off for burial.

36. The Met's First Home

◉ Old Scotland Yard

⬤ Great Scotland Yard, SW1

⊖ Charing Cross station *(Mainline, Northern and Bakerloo Lines)*

Scotland Yard was originally used as residences for the Kings of Scotland before the newly created Metropolitan Police took over in 1829 under the supervision of Sir Robert Peel. Their first job was to get control of the criminal gangs that had overrun London.

An empty house at No. 4 Whitehall Place was turned into the commissioner's offices. There were two commissioners to start with: Sir Charles Rowan and Sir Richard Mayne. Rowan (a military man, injured at the Battle of Waterloo) was the senior of the two, so he was entitled to use the bachelor quarters at the top of the building.

Rowan would remain senior commissioner for 21 years. Mayne, a barrister, remained for 39 years — a record to this day. Rowan handled the logistics and man-management while Mayne dealt with the legal aspects of policing.

The servants' rooms at the back of the station were converted into a police station for 'A' division and a recruiting office, pictured here, and this became the front and public entrance. It wasn't long before those who came through the arch dropped the term Metropolitan Police Force and started to refer to the police as Scotland Yard.

Rowan and Mayne managed to recruit and train a force of nearly a thousand men in just three months. On 16 September 1829, the two commissioners swore in their new constables at the Foundling Hospital in Brunswick Square, WC1, and these pioneer lawmen first took to the streets at 6pm on 29 September.

As the force expanded to match the crime rate, it outgrew the 'dingy collection of mean buildings'. In 1887 the Police HQ spread throughout Whitehall Place, taking over Nos. 3, 4, 5, 21 and 22 and Nos. 8 and 9 Great Scotland Yard (pictured). Nos. 1, 2 and 3 Palace Place were also taken, including a freestanding building in the centre of the Yard that has been used for storage, and to house the Public Carriage Office (responsible for taxi licensing) and the offices of the Criminal Investigation Department (CID).

The offices were hopelessly muddled. *The Times* wrote: 'Innumerable books are piled up on staircases, so that they are almost impassable, piles of clothing, saddles and horse furniture, blankets and all manner of things are heaped up [in] little garrets in a state of what outside Scotland Yard would be called hopeless confusion.'

The police HQ would eventually move in 1890 (see page 300) but the Met took the name 'Scotland Yard' with them.

37. Old New Scotland Yard

◎ **Norman Shaw Building**

⬤ Victoria Embankment, SW1

⊖ **Westminster Tube** *(Jubilee, District and Circle Lines)*

This Grade I listed building, the headquarters of Scotland Yard from 1890 to 1967, was built to the designs of architect Norman Shaw (1831–1912). It was constructed between 1888 and 1889, the year of the Jack the Ripper murders.

This 'very constabulary type of castle' ended up taking about 20 years to build – it even took Scotland Yard eight years to negotiate the sale of the land, during which time its price increased from £25,000 to £125,000. It was built, appropriately enough, from granite quarried by convicts on Dartmoor. The police moved in during 1890 and it was named New Scotland Yard, but the building was almost immediately discovered to be too small and so work started again so extensions could be built.

It was along this stretch of the Thames, as the foundations of the building were being built upon, that the body of one of the Thames Torso murder victims was found in 1888 (see page 64).

The last commissioner to occupy this building was Sir Joseph Simpson (1909–68). 'Joe', as he liked to be called, was the first commissioner who began his police career as an ordinary constable. He believed in a more equal police force, where senior officers and lower ranks had a closer relationship. He led the force from1958 to 1968 and did a great deal to improve police–public relations. He also encouraged the public to 'have a go' against crime, although he did issue a warning against tackling armed criminals.

Simpson established the Obscene Publications Squad, Drugs Squad (1963), Special Patrol Group (1961), Art Squad (1967), and Antiques and Philately Squad (1967), laid the foundations for the Scenes of Crime Branch established shortly after his death, and greatly expanded the Flying Squad. He was expected by some to retire in 1964, but stayed in post until the move to Broadway was complete. He died suddenly at his home in Roehampton four years later at the age of 58, his early death probably brought on by stress caused by overwork.

The building is now used as offices for Members of Parliament and is said to have a secret tunnel connecting it with Westminster Palace. It is also rumoured to have its own secret entrance to the District Line section of Westminster Underground station.

38. The Right Criminal Member

◎ The Palace of Westminster

⌂ Westminster

☎ 0844 847 1672

ⓦ www.parliament.uk

🕐 Open for pre-booked tours on Saturdays from 9.15am-4.30pm (except during the Christmas recess). Tours are also available on other days during the summer. See website for details.

🔓 Adults £15, Child (5-15 years) £6, under 5's free

⊖ Westminster Tube *(Jubilee, District and Circle Lines)*

Not including the seven Members of Parliament recently sent to prison for fiddling their expenses, a surprising number of MPs have finished up behind bars over the last hundred years or so.

Jonathan Aitken, one-time Chief Secretary to the Treasury and potential candidate for the Tory leadership, was jailed for 18 months in 1999 for perjury and perverting the course of justice after he lied under oath and tried to persuade others to do so. Aitken was followed by Jeffrey Archer, former MP and deputy chairman of the Conservative Party, in 2001 (see Peninsula Heights, page 60). Archer had fabricated an alibi during a 1987 libel trial.

Poll tax rebel Terry Fields, Labour MP from 1983 to 1992, was imprisoned for his principled refusal to pay the unpopular new Community Charge levy introduced by Margaret Thatcher's Conservative government in 1990 (see Trafalgar Square, page 279).

Somewhat less admirably, John Stonehouse was found in Australia a few weeks after faking his own death while still an MP in November 1974. He'd left behind a wife, a daughter, a mistress and a mountain of debts – and a pile of clothes on a Miami beach during a holiday. The former Labour MP, Minister for Technology and Postmaster General, was later sentenced to seven years on 18 counts of theft, fraud and deception.

Peter Baker, Conservative MP for South Norfolk, and at 28 once the youngest MP in the House, was sent down for seven years for forgery, including writing false signatures, and fraud in December 1954.

Horatio Bottomley, the independent MP for South Hackney, was hugely popular until he was expelled from the House in August 1922 after being convicted of the fraudulent conversion of others' property. He was sentenced to seven years. He was so corpulent – at 17 stone – that no regulation uniform would fit him. He fell into obscurity after his release but briefly reappeared at the Windmill Theatre (see Great Windmill Street, page 244) after his release, delivering anecdotes about his public life shortly before his death in 1933.

Occasionally, like the assassination of Spencer Perceval (see Lincoln's Inn Fields, page 296), criminal acts have been carried out in Parliament itself. Shadow Northern Ireland Secretary Airey Neave was killed by an Irish National Liberation Army car bomb as he left the House of Commons car park in 1974.

39. New Scotland Yard

◎ Metropolitan Police Headquarters
⬠ 10 Broadway, SW1
Ⓦ www.content.met.police.uk
⊖ St James's Park Tube *(District and Circle Lines)*

In 1967, in a move spread over 23 days, Scotland Yard relocated to a high-rise block on the corner of Broadway and Victoria Street, between Westminster Abbey and Victoria station, where it remains today.

With 20 storeys and 700 officers spread over 11 acres of floor space, it provides everything a modern crime-fighting police force could ask for, from major incident control centres to the HOLMES computer database (the Home Office Large Major Enquiry System, deliberately named to echo the fictional detective).

Patrolled by armed officers from the Diplomatic Protection Group, the Yard is protected by concrete walls, with concrete slabs placed in front of ground-floor windows. It is home to the Commissioner of the Metropolitan Police, arguably, as the head of Britain's largest police force of 30,000 officers, the most powerful lawperson in the country.

Commissioners have always faced controversy, and no less so in recent years. In 2008, Ian Blair was the first commissioner to hand in his resignation in 120 years. His decision came after London Mayor Boris Johnson said he no longer had confidence in him.

Then, Blair's successor, Paul Stephenson, resigned in July 2011 at the height of the *News of the World* phone-hacking scandal, when the relationship between police and the media was placed under intense scrutiny.

The only other commissioner to resign was Sir Charles Warren (1840–1927), who had the top job during the hunt for Jack the Ripper in 1888 (see page 160). The press pilloried Warren for a number of failings – none of which were his fault. In particular, he was criticised for not using bloodhounds, but when he did bring dogs into the hunt he was attacked for being obsessed with them (it didn't help when some of them went missing).

The night after Warren finally threw in the towel, Jack the Ripper murdered Mary Jane Kelly. Detectives on the scene, not knowing Warren had resigned, waited three hours for him to arrive before entering the crime scene – as per his instructions. This cost the investigation precious time.

In November 2012, the Metropolitan Police announced plans to sell New Scotland Yard, part of a dramatic government-ordered cost-cutting drive. The plan is to move to a smaller building on the Embankment, which would save the Yard £6.5 million a year. It is not known whether they will be taking the name with them.

40. A Grim Penitentiary

◎ Morpeth Arms
⌂ 58 Millbank, SW1
☎ 020 7834 6442
🕐 Mon-Sat 11am-11pm, Sun 12pm-10.30pm
⊖ Vauxhall station (*Mainline and Victoria Line*)

The idea for a circular Millbank prison was originally based on the ideas of social reformer Jeremy Bentham, according to whom prisoners should be kept in the circumference of a jail with their guards in the centre, giving a feeling of perpetual surveillance. He also believed convicts should be encouraged to work and even enjoy what their shared labour produced.

Although Bentham purchased this site on behalf of the Crown, plans for his 'Panopticon' fell through and in 1813 the government took over the project, building a modified star-shaped version, which opened its gates in 1816. Covering seven acres, this damp and gloomy prison was London's largest and even experienced warders got lost in the three miles of maze-like passages. In accordance with Bentham's original idea, prisoners were put to work making shoes or mailbags but, against his wishes, they were forbidden to communicate with each other for the first half of their sentence.

Conditions in the prison were horrendous. Scurvy and cholera swept through Millbank in 1822–23, not long after it reached capacity; 30 inmates died. The tragedy led to some improvements – women were pardoned while the prison was cleaned and repaired and when the men returned they found teachers and games waiting for them – along with better lighting.

The prison, never a success, was closed in 1890 – the Tate Gallery now sits on the original site. Opposite the Tate, just by the Thames, a bollard commemorates the penitentiary. The inscription reads: 'Near this site stood Millbank Prison which was opened in 1816 and closed in 1890. This buttress stood at the head of the river steps from which, until 1867, prisoners sentenced to transportation embarked on their journey to Australia.'

Amazingly, some underground prison cells survive. To see them, you have to pay a visit to the Morpeth Arms (just east of Vauxhall Bridge on Millbank), originally built for prison warders in 1845. When it opened, tunnels were built connecting the pub and prison and if you go into the cellar it's possible to access a handful of truly appalling-looking cells where unlucky deportees were held before boarding. Photography is now forbidden (thanks to a misbehaving film crew) but if you go in at a quiet time and ask nicely, the staff will take you down for a look.

41. A Most Unusual Murder

◉ **MI6 Headquarters**
⬠ **Vauxhall Cross, SW8**
Ⓦ **www.sis.gov.uk**
⊖ **Vauxhall station** *(Mainline and Victoria Line)*

Although this is not a book about spying, more than a few spies have earned a place in these pages thanks to their criminal dalliances and indiscretions, and they have occasionally – as in this case – become victims.

On 23 August 2010, at 6.30pm a police officer arrived at the top-floor flat of a Georgian townhouse on Alderney Street – a quiet residential area a short distance from where this photo – of MI6 HQ – was taken. The officer noted the flat was 'spotless'. Phones, sim cards and an Apple laptop had been left on a table. And in the bath he found a holdall, surrounded by red liquid. Upon opening the bag he discovered the body of 31-year-old MI6 and GCHQ employee Gareth Williams. The body was so twisted that the officer thought the man's 'legs and arms had been cut off'. The flat, used by the Secret Intelligence Service as a safe house, was soon full of MI5 agents, Counter Terrorism and Murder Squad detectives.

The body had been there for two weeks and the heating had been left on, aiding decomposition, meaning it was in an 'advanced state of decay'. Consequently a postmortem proved inconclusive. Williams had not been stabbed or shot. Toxicology studies turned up no poisons. There was no weapon, no sign of forced entry, or a struggle – but Williams could not have got into or closed the bag himself and the door was locked from the outside.

Police investigated theories of suicide or a sadistic or masochistic sexual act gone wrong but could find no evidence that Williams had paid for escorts, S&M equipment or porn and found no drugs of any kind. Williams didn't even drink.

Williams worked for Government Communication Headquarters (GCHQ), the top-secret listening station that gathers intelligence from across the world, and he had been seconded to MI6 where he'd investigated a handful of high-profile spying cases. Sir John Sawers, the head of MI6, went to Williams' funeral, where he said: 'I wanted to be here today as the only public face of the Secret Intelligence Service. My deepest sympathies go to the family. Gareth was a hugely talented person, and he was very modest and generous as well. He did really valuable work with us in the cause of national security.' By all accounts he worked well and loved his job. Although the case is not closed, the police admit they've got very few leads.

42. Governmental Trouble

◉ The Apartments
⌂ Dolphin Square, SW1
⊜ Pimlico Tube *(Victoria Line)*

This huge block of 1,250 flats covering 7½ acres was in 1937 – the year it was built – the largest apartment complex in Europe. Dolphin Square has since been connected with politics, espionage and, in two particular cases, sex.

It is home to a large number of MPs. In 1994 there were 59 MPs living here: 23 Tories, 27 Labour, and 9 Lib-Dems. Plenty of MI5 and MI6 employees, needing to stay close to their desks, lived here, too.

One resident, William Joyce, was better known during World War II as Lord Haw-Haw. He fled Dolphin Square for Germany in 1939 and spent the next six years broadcasting Nazi German propaganda to the UK. He was hanged by Albert Pierrepoint on 3 January 1946 at Wandsworth prison, just across the Thames. The last words Joyce heard were Pierrepoint's: 'I think we'd better have this on, you know' (referring to the hood).

Another resident associated with the Far Right was Sir Oswald Mosley, head of the British Union of Fascists, who left the Square with Lady Diana Mosley for internment in May 1940 (Oswald in Brixton prison, Diana in Holloway). In 1936, Oswald caused a riot when he tried to march his 'Blackshirts' through a Jewish section of the East End. The riots led to the Public Order Act 1936, and political marches have required police consent ever since.

Another notorious resident was William John Christopher Vassall, who lived in Hood House. Vassall, who was gay, was on the staff of the naval attaché to Moscow. In 1954 he was invited to a party (arranged by the KGB), where he was plied with drink and photographed in a compromising position with several men. Confronted with the photos (homosexuality was illegal in the UK and the USSR), Vassall sent the Soviets several thousand classified documents concerning British radar, torpedoes and anti-submarine equipment. He was caught and sentenced to 18 years in 1962.

Christine Keeler, the prostitute at the heart of the Profumo Affair, also had a flat here. On 14 December 1962 journalists picked up on the story that War Secretary John Profumo had slept with a prostitute. At first, Profumo publicly denied any close relationship but was eventually forced to admit he'd been lying and resigned from the government the following year. The scandal nearly crippled Harold Macmillan's Conservative government and contributed to their defeat in the general election of October 1964.

Keeler's pimp, Stephen Ward, was charged with living off immoral earnings and was being tried at the Old Bailey when he committed suicide – although some conspiracy theorists have speculated that MI5 silenced him so he wouldn't reveal any more ministerial dalliances. Ward was found guilty while still in a coma – he died three days later.

43. The Pimlico Poisoning Mystery

◎ 85 Claverton Street, SW1

⊕ Pimlico Tube *(Victoria Line)*

Born in Orleans, France, in 1855, Adelaide Bartlett née de Tremoille – the illegitimate daughter of a French count – was sent to the UK when she was 16, to live with her maternal uncle and aunt.

Edwin Bartlett, a wealthy owner of six grocery shops, 11 years Miss Bartlett's senior, fell for the beautiful French 'countess' and they eventually married in 1875. Their relationship remained almost completely platonic – Adelaide later claimed that they only had sex once and that this led to a stillborn child.

Strangely, in 1885 (after they'd moved into Claverton Street) Edwin encouraged his young wife to enjoy – and deepen – her relationship with George Dyson, a young Methodist minister. Edwin even told George – who'd been retained to teach Adelaide Latin and maths – that he should marry Adelaide if he died. A maid later testified that she often 'discovered' George and Adelaide in 'positions unusual for tutor and pupil'.

Edwin was a hypochondriac, convinced he had syphilis (he didn't). He went as far as to take mercury poison as a treatment. When 40-year-old Edwin complained of illness, Adelaide said to a doctor, 'if Mr Bartlett does not get better soon his friends and relations will accuse me of poisoning him'.

At 4.10am on 1 January 1886, Adelaide woke their landlord, Mr Doggett, saying, 'Come down, I think Mr Bartlett is dead.' The landlord, along with Dr Leach, the first doctor on the scene, was suspicious. A postmortem revealed that Edwin's stomach contained chloroform and concluded that it was this that had killed him. Adelaide and George were arrested. Adelaide was accused of murder while George was accused of helping her when it was revealed he had bought chloroform for Adelaide – to 'treat' Edwin. This was enough to set up a sensational Old Bailey trial that gripped London: did the young illegitimate French beauty and her lover, the handsome parson, poison the wealthy grocer?

The prosecution dropped the charges against George for lack of evidence. Adelaide was defended by the leading barrister of the day, Sir Edward Clarke, whose brilliant defence relied on common-sense expert testimony. Various medical men stated that liquid chloroform was not necessarily fatal and that there was no chloroform in Edwin's windpipe or lungs, which there would have been, had it been poured into his mouth as he slept.

The jury concluded: 'Although we think grave suspicion is attached to the prisoner, we do not think there is sufficient evidence to show how or by whom the chloroform was administered.' So, Adelaide was acquitted – and the mystery of her husband's death was never solved. What happened after the trial is not known, although some researchers have claimed Adelaide left for a new life abroad – and found work as a nurse.

44. Young Scarface

◎ Knightsbridge Security Deposit

⌂ Knightsbridge, SW3

⊖ Knightsbridge Tube *(Piccadilly Line)*

Knightsbridge, July 1987. It was a job straight out of the movies. Security guard uniforms, metal-cutting equipment, walkie-talkies and an inside man – the managing director of the centre who was heavily in debt – enabled the gang to clear 114 boxes in under two hours.

The victims were royalty, celebrities, millionaires and criminals. No shots were fired and no one was injured. The loot: £60m plus all those valuable knick-knacks and secrets that the publicity-shy customers of the safety-deposit boxes didn't want anyone to know about (30 of the 120 owners never came forward).

The mastermind was 32-year-old Valerio Viccei, a playboy and serial seducer, who had arrived in London looking for 'weapons, beautiful women and fast cars'.

He was caught after returning to London – after having spent some time in South America. He was at the wheel of his Ferrari when police blocked the road, smashed the window and dragged Viccei out and into the street. He'd been traced thanks to a fingerprint left at the scene. Suave, with a knowing smile and endless jokes, the handsome young man wowed the press, who dubbed him the 'Italian Stallion' (when not describing him as the 'Wolf', or 'gentleman thief').

Viccei was in fact a vain thug with Nazi sympathies. While studying philosophy at the University in Rome, 16-year-old Viccei fell in with the neo-fascist terrorist leader Gianni Nardi. He daubed swastikas on public buildings, took part in bombings and pulled off about 54 robberies.

Sentenced to 22 years, he started prison life in Parkhurst on the Isle of Wight. Then in November 1992, he was extradited to Italy. Within three years, he was strolling the beachside cafés on his way to work at a publisher's office, visiting his flat and returning to jail every night.

Nevertheless, he planned another robbery in 2000, but as he and an accomplice were staking out a property on a lonely road, a policeman approached and Viccei decided to pull his revolver. Big mistake. The policeman had a machine gun and moments later, Viccei was dead.

Viccei, who modelled himself on Al Pacino's Scarface, had told the Old Bailey Judge: 'Maybe I am a romantic lunatic but money was the last thing on my mind.' It seems so, as he was unable (or unwilling) to tell detectives where any of the Knightsbridge loot was hidden. Only £10m was ever recovered.

45. The Arrest of Oscar Wilde

◎ Room 188, The Cadogan Hotel

⌂ 75 Sloane Street, SW1

☎ 020 7235 7141

ⓦ www.cadogan.com

⊖ Knightsbridge Tube *(Piccadilly Line)* and Sloane Square Tube
  (District and Circle Lines)

On 6 April 1895 Oscar Wilde was arrested at the Cadogan after losing a libel case he'd brought against the 9th Marquess of Queensberry, aka John Sholto Douglas.

The marquess, angered by Wilde's apparent homosexual relationship with his son, Lord Alfred Douglas, had accused Wilde of 'posing as a sodomite'. Homosexuality was a criminal offence in the UK (until 1967), so Wilde was able to sue for libel, but dropped the case when Queensberry's lawyers told him they had a long list of male prostitutes who would be called to give evidence against him.

Wilde was arrested, found guilty of 'gross indecency' and 'sodomy', and was sentenced to two years' hard labour. The trial of the Irish Oxford graduate, the author of brilliant and popular plays, including *The Importance of Being Earnest* (1895), as well as the novel *The Picture of Dorian Gray* (1890), shocked Victorian society – especially as Wilde was married with two children, for whom he wrote many fairy tales, including *The Selfish Giant*.

Between January and March 1897 Wilde wrote his extraordinary masterwork *De Profundis*, a 50,000-word letter to Lord Alfred Douglas. His jailers refused him permission to send it but he took it with him after he was released. Wilde wrote that he forgave Douglas and accepted responsibility for his own fall: 'I am here for having tried to put your father in prison.'

Released in 1897, Wilde departed the UK for Paris. He started writing again, producing *The Ballad of Reading Gaol*, based on his experiences in prison. But, an outcast to the end, most of his friends and all of his good fortune deserted him. He spent the days wandering the streets before returning to the glum hotel where he lived.

'My wallpaper and I are fighting a duel to the death. One of us has got to go,' he wrote. The wallpaper won. Wilde died of cerebral meningitis on 30 November 1900.

The 65-room Cadogan Hotel, built in 1887, has named one of its suites after Wilde.

46. A Hang-out for Classy Criminals

◎ The Star Tavern

⌂ 6 Belgrave Mews West, SW1

☎ 020 7235 3019

🕐 Mon-Fri 11am-11pm, Sat 12pm-11pm, Sun 12pm-10.30pm

⊖ Hyde Park Corner Tube *(Piccadilly Line)* and Knightsbridge Tube
    (Piccadilly Line)

Throughout the 1950s and 60s, the Star welcomed many celebrities to its bar, including Diana Dors, Peter O'Toole, Albert Finney and film director Alexander Korda.

Also among its patrons, often quaffing champagne alongside the movie stars, were a certain class of London criminal including Peter Scott, the Mayfair cat burglar, who raided Korda's nearby home but found nothing worth taking (see page 264). After Scott had burgled Sophia Loren he turned up at the Star and said, 'I hear poor Sophia has been robbed,' as he wet his fingers and started to flick through a huge bankroll.

Another notable Star regular was robber Bruce Reynolds, who'd been brought there by Terry 'Lucky Tel' Hogan. Hogan was involved in the record-breaking Eastcastle Street postal robbery in 1952 (see Eastcastle Street, page 251). Even though 1,000 police were put on the case, no one was caught. However, despite his success as a robber, Hogan struggled to find happiness and committed suicide in 1995 at the age of 64.

It was at the Star that Reynolds met with the known train robber 'Buster' Edwards (see Greet Street, page 52) when they began planning what would become known as the Great Train Robbery. Many more meetings were held – the golden rule being that no more than four members of the gang would assemble in public at any one time, in case the police were watching.

The 18-man gang, which also included Charlie Wilson and Ronnie Biggs, successfully robbed the train and escaped with £2.6m – about £40m in today's money. But the robbery didn't go smoothly – train driver Jack Mills was struck on the head and never worked again.

Reynolds fled to Mexico where he blew his £150,000 share, before returning to the United Kingdom and serving 10 years of a 25-year sentence for the robbery. After his release, he retired from crime and wrote his autobiography. He no longer drinks at the Star.

47. **Lord on the Run**

◎ The Lucan Family Home and The Plumbers Arms

◐ Lower Belgrave Street, SW1

☎ Plumbers Arms: 020 7730 4067

◑ Plumbers Arms open Mon-Fri 12pm-11pm, closed Sat and Sun

⊖ Victoria station *(Mainline, Victoria, Circle and District Lines)*

Early on the evening of 7 November 1974, 39-year-old Richard Bingham, the 7th Earl of Lucan, popularly known as Lord or 'Lucky' Lucan, telephoned the Clermont Club (see page 268) to reserve a restaurant table. His wife, Veronica Mary Duncan, Countess of Lucan, was at home in Lower Belgrave Street, as was the nanny to their three children, Sandra Rivett. The countess had separated from her husband and had recently won custody of the children after a difficult legal battle.

Countess Lucan and Rivett were the same height, five foot two, although Rivett, a 29-year-old redhead, had a slightly larger build. It was Thursday, which was normally Sandra's night off, but she'd changed the night to Wednesday.

Lord Lucan, an aristocrat and former member of the Coldstream Guards, lived from the gaming tables but his luck had finally run out and, with family, household expenses and legal bills, he was living on overdrafts. He stopped by the Clermont at about 8.45pm and asked the doorman if any of his gambling friends were there. He said he would return later.

At 8.40pm Rivett went downstairs to make some tea – something the countess normally did. After Rivett had been gone an unusually long time, Lady Lucan went to find her at 9.15pm. As she did so, Lord Lucan attacked her, hitting her several times before trying to strangle her. The countess reached between her husband's legs and squeezed as hard as she could. Lord Lucan released her and suddenly gave up on the idea of killing his wife. He said they should talk and attend to her injuries. As they went upstairs he confessed to killing the nanny. She was dead in the basement, battered to death with a blunt instrument.

While Lord Lucan was in the bathroom, Lady Lucan fled to the Plumbers Arms, where she cried: 'Help me, help me, help me, I've just escaped being murdered. He's in the house. He's murdered my nanny.' Some investigators have argued that Lucan had attacked in the dark, mistaking the nanny for his wife.

At 11pm, disturbed and unkempt, Lord Lucan arrived at the house of some friends in Uckfield. He left at 1am. Three days later his car was found abandoned in the coastal town of Newhaven. After that we simply don't know what happened – although theories abound, from suicide to starting a new life abroad with the help of powerful friends.

On 19 June 1975, an inquest jury took just 30 minutes to pronounce Lord Lucan as Rivett's murderer. Lucan was the last person ever to be declared a murderer this way, as the law was changed with the introduction of the Criminal Law Act 1977.

48. Jack the Stripper

◎ The Pavement

⌂ Hornton Street, W8

⊖ High Street Kensington Tube *(District and Circle Lines)*

On 26 November 1964, the naked body of a young woman was found at the bottom of this Kensington side street. She'd been half-hidden under a pile of leaves, weighed down by the metal lid of a rubbish bin.

Thanks to a distinctive 'Mum and Dad' tattoo, police identified her as 21-year-old Margaret McGowan, a prostitute. Margaret had testified for the defence, under the name Frances Brown, in the case against Stephen Ward (see the Profumo Affair, page 311). She denied that other prostitutes had whipped men in Ward's flat but confessed that she'd been there for 'foursomes'.

McGowan was the seventh in a series of eight related prostitute murders between 1959 and 1965. The victims were Elizabeth Figg, 21, found floating in the Thames, 17 June 1959, strangled; Gwyneth Rees, 22, skeleton unearthed during clearance of riverside rubbish dump on 8 November 1963; Hannah Tailford, 30, naked corpse discovered in the Thames by boatman, 2 February 1964; Irene Lockwood, 20, four months pregnant, found naked in the Thames, floating 300 yards from the spot where Tailford was discovered, 9 April 1964; Helen Barthelmy, 20, naked body found in Brentwood sports field, four front teeth missing, 24 April 1964 – traces of multicoloured spray paint on the body suggested that she had been kept in a paint shop; Mary Fleming, 30, left naked on a dead-end London street, 14 July 1964, suffocated or choked to death – dentures missing; Margaret McGowan, who had the same traces of paint on her skin as Barthelmy; and Bridget O'Hara, 27, body found in bushes on the Heron Trading Estate in Acton, 16 February 1965. Her front teeth were missing. Pathologists said she died on her knees.

All the victims were prostitutes working from squalid flats and bedsits in North Kensington, Bayswater and Soho – addresses that are worth millions today. All were small in stature and all were found naked. They were all picked up between 11pm and 1am and driven by car to the killing spot where they were attacked from behind. After death their bodies were stripped and stored before being dumped – between 5am and 6am.

Some of the victims were known to have been engaged in an underground party and pornographic movie scene; it was possible the victims knew each other and that the killer may have been connected to this scene as well.

Despite the biggest and costliest manhunt in British criminal history, no one was ever arrested or charged with the killings. Like Jack the Ripper, the Stripper suddenly stopped killing. The officer leading the hunt, Detective Assistant Commissioner John du Rose, later announced that Jack the Stripper had been identified but, as he had committed suicide, his identity would never be revealed.

Like Jack the Ripper, various candidates have since been put forward by several amateur sleuths, but it seems as though we will never know the Stripper's identity.

49. The Vampire of Kensington

◎ The Goat Tavern

⊘ 3A Kensington High Street, W8

☎ 020 7937 1213

🕐 Mon-Thurs 11am-11.30pm, Fri and Sat 11am-12.30pm, Sun 12pm-10.30pm

⊜ High Street Kensington Tube *(District and Circle Lines)*

On 9 September 1944, 35-year-old John Haigh, a divorcee, failed businessman and former mechanic with a conviction for forging documents, entered the Goat Tavern and bumped into William Donald McSwann. Haigh had worked as chauffeur to the McSwann family but he'd lost the position after another swindle cost him four years in prison. After another short stint inside for theft, Haigh was released in 1943 and found work as a salesman for a firm in Crawley.

The two men shared a drink at the Goat before going to 79 Gloucester Road, in South Kensington (just around the corner), where Haigh had a workshop and where he smashed McSwann's skull and stuffed his body in a barrel full of sulphuric acid.

Haigh then saw McSwann's parents and told them that their son had gone on the run to avoid being called up for the war. In July the following year he murdered the rest of the McSwanns, dissolving their bodies in the same way. Haigh passed himself off as William McSwann and sold the family's possessions for £4,000 – a considerable sum in 1945.

Haigh employed the same method with Dr Archibald and Rosalie Henderson in 1948. They thought they were investing in a property when the killer shot them dead in his new workshop in Crawley. Again, he dissolved their bodies before stealing everything of value the Hendersons owned.

By February 1949 Haigh was living in the Onslow Court Hotel in Brompton Road (not far from the Goat Tavern, but the building is no longer there). While there, Haigh murdered Olive Henrietta Olivia Robarts Durand-Deacon, a 69-year-old widow and fellow resident.

Haigh told Durand-Deacon that he was an engineer and inventor. She said she'd designed some false fingernails and asked Haigh if he could improve upon the idea. Haigh agreed and they drove to Haigh's ramshackle workshop in Crawley where Haigh shot Durand-Deacon in the back of the head. He left her dissolving in sulphuric acid while he returned to the Onslow Court Hotel for a three-course dinner.

When the hotel reported Durand-Deacon missing, suspicion fell on Haigh. After several interviews, Haigh confessed to Detective Inspector Albert Webb: 'I've destroyed her with acid,' he said. 'Every trace has gone. How can you prove murder if there's no body?' He added that he'd killed his victims so that he could drink their blood.

When Home Office pathologist Dr Keith Simpson examined the Crawley workshop, he found a hatpin, three gallstones, 28 pounds of animal fat, part of a foot and a full set of dentures – identified by Durand-Deacon's dentist. It took the jury 17 minutes to find Haigh guilty. Albert Pierrepoint hanged him at Wandsworth prison on 10 August 1949.

50. The Great Escape

⊙ Wandsworth Prison
⌂ Heathfield Road, SW18
☎ 020 8874 4377
⊖ Wandsworth Common station *(Mainline)*

Originally known as the Surrey House of Correction, Wandsworth was designed in the radial style with five wings and could hold a total of 1,000 prisoners in individual cells.

The hard-labour prison opened in 1851 when male prisoners were admitted, followed by women in 1852. In 1870 the toilets were removed from the cells to make room for extra prisoners and 'slopping out' was introduced – a practice that lasted until 1996.

Oscar Wilde (see page 316) spent the first six months of his sentence here. Lord Haw-Haw (see page 311), Patrick Mahon (see page 48) and George Chapman were hanged here, as was Derek Bentley, later granted a posthumous pardon in 1998. Although hanging for murder was abolished in 1965, the gallows stayed at Wandsworth until 1992 as technically, one could still be hanged for treason, piracy with violence and mutiny in the armed forces.

Ronnie Biggs broke out of Wandsworth in 1965, when he was 35, just two years after the Great Train Robbery. He escaped by using a rope ladder (thrown over the wall during exercise) to scale a 30-foot climb with three other prisoners. Biggs was the second Great Train Robber to escape from prison after Charlie Wilson broke out from Winson Green in Birmingham the year before. Biggs was free for nearly 40 years before he returned voluntarily to Britain from Brazil in 2001 aged 71, impoverished and weakened by a series of strokes, to receive free medical treatment. He was immediately taken to a top-security prison to serve the remaining 28 years of his sentence but was granted release on 'compassionate grounds' in August 2009, after developing a severe case of pneumonia.

Charlie Wilson was recaptured in Canada in 1968. He was released from prison in 1978 (after serving about one-third of his sentence). He was shot dead in his Spanish villa in April 1990. The killing was thought to be payback for his cheating drug dealers out of their money.

More recent guests include former Libertines front-man Pete Doherty and Julian Assange, the Internet entrepreneur behind Wikileaks who was there on remand in December 2010.

In 2011 the prison, which has a capacity of 1,371, making it London's largest, was heavily criticised by the Chief Inspector of Prisons for the high levels of self-harm and suicide among the inmates as well as the amount of time prisoners were restricted to their cells – between 16½ and 22 hours a day.

51. The Massacre of Braybrook Street

◎ Wormwood Scrubs

⬢ Du Cane Road, W12

☎ 020 8753 4103

⊜ East Acton Tube *(Central Line)*

'The Scrubs' was built by prison labour between 1874 and 1890, with more prisoners being added to the workforce as each cell-block was completed. The buildings were arranged in parallel blocks so every cell would benefit from natural light. The building was given a Grade II listing in 2009.

Despite refurbishments a 1999 report said the conditions at Wormwood were 'terrible', but they have since improved for the 1,160 prisoners currently incarcerated there.

Notable inmates have included Soviet spy George Blake who, sentenced to 42 years, escaped from here in 1966 and made it all the way to Moscow. Keith Richards and Pete Doherty were also reluctant residents (in fact both have spent time in more than one London institution, see pages 247, 327). Lord Alfred Douglas, once the lover of Oscar Wilde (page 316), ended up here after being arrested for attacking Winston Churchill in a pamphlet published in 1923. John Stonehouse, the MP who faked his own death, was also held at the Scrubs (page 303). It is also where the 'lifers' are sent.

One of the UK's most infamous crimes, the Massacre of Braybrook Street, took place just outside the prison grounds on 16 August 1966. Detective Sergeant Chris Head (30) and DC David Wombwell (25), members of the Criminal Investigation Department, were in plain clothes when at around 3pm they approached a blue Standard Vanguard Estate parked outside the prison; the vehicle contained notorious criminal Harry Roberts and his friends John Witney and John Duddy.

The detectives were concerned that the van might be part of an escape attempt. As they checked the vehicle registration, the man in the passenger seat, Harry Roberts, shot DC Wombwell through the eye, killing him. As DS Head ran back to the police car Roberts also shot him in the head. Meanwhile, Duddy grabbed a revolver from the bag next to him and ran towards the police car, shooting driver PC Fox three times, killing him as he tried to reverse towards the criminals.

The murders sparked outrage and led to demands for the return of the death penalty. Instead the three men were jailed for life. Roberts remains in jail while Duddy died in Parkhurst Prison on the Isle of Wight in 1981. Witney was released early in 1991 but was beaten to death in 1999 by a heroin addict.

The murders are remembered every year on their anniversary, when police officers and family members lay flowers at a memorial in Braybrook Street and observe a minute's silence.

52. The Escapee Who Needn't Have Bothered

◎ Brixton Prison
◐ Jebb Avenue, SW9
☎ 020 8588 6000
◉ Brixton Tube *(Victoria Line)*

In 1819, during Brixton prison's construction and just after the wall and gatehouse were completed, 25 prisoners were sent to help finish the project. Three escaped, the governor was sacked and the experiment was not repeated until work started on Wormwood Scrubs in 1874 (see page 328).

Soon after it opened in 1820, the crescent-shaped, hard-labour prison passed its capacity of 175, eventually reaching 400. As a result it was one of London's most disease-ridden jails. Alterations were eventually made so that the prison could hold 700 inmates and from 1853 Brixton was used to keep female convicts who were awaiting transportation. It then became a military prison in 1882 and after some more rebuilding it reopened its cells to male civilian prisoners in 1902.

Today it holds 798 offenders whose sentences do not exceed two years. A large part of the population is made up of asylum seekers awaiting deportation and, in 2004, 20 per cent were Muslim. Like Wandsworth, Brixton has been criticised in recent years for its poor conditions and for its poor treatment of prisoners.

Notable inmates have included 89-year-old philosopher Lord Bertrand Russell, who spent a week here in 1961. He was one of 36 members of the Campaign for Nuclear Disarmament sentenced to two months after demonstrating outside the Russian Embassy.

Oswald Mosley (see page 311) spent some time here after being interned in World War II. Mick Jagger spent a single night in Brixton jail when he was sent down as 'an example' after being convicted of a drugs charge (see page 247). Jagger said his cell was no worse than some hotel rooms he'd stayed in.

On 16 December 1980, IRA bomb maker Gerard Tuite, suspected armed robber Stanley Thompson and legendary security-van robber James Moody escaped from Brixton using tools smuggled in by visiting relatives. Thompson needn't have bothered – he escaped while the jury was out on his trial. When they returned they found him not guilty.

Moody knew the Krays and worked for the Richardsons and at the time of his escape he was on remand for three armed robberies totalling £930,000. Built like the brick proverbial, Moody's speciality was robbing armoured trucks using a chainsaw to cut through the side of vehicles to get at the cash. He was shot dead by a mystery hit man in the Royal Hotel, his local pub in Hackney, East London, in 1993.

In 2011, Brixton, which has a capacity of 500, was the subject of a critical report by the Chief Inspector of Prisons who said the jail was 250 prisoners over normal capacity, with many sharing small cells described as 'dirty and in a poor state of repair ... [and many] spending 21 hours a day locked up'. At the end of 2011, the number of prisoners held here had risen to 800 – a result of arrests arising from the London riots that summer.

INDEX